THE END OF AMERICA

The Role of Islam in the End Times
and
Biblical Warnings to Flee America

Christian House Publishers, Inc.
Indianapolis, IN 46240

THE END OF AMERICA
The Role of Islam in the End Times and
Biblical Warnings to Flee America

Copyright © 2009 by John Price

www.endofamericabook.com

www.christianhousepublishing.com

Unless otherwise indicated, Scripture quotations are from *The Holy Bible,* New International Version (NIV), © 1973, 1984 by International Bible Society. Scriptural quotations may also be from the King James Version (KJV), The Message, New American Standard Bible, © The Lockman Foundation.

Library of Congress Control Number – 2009905165

Price, John
THE END OF AMERICA
The Role of Islam in the End Times
and Biblical Warnings to Flee America

ISBN-13: 978-0-9840771-1-3
ISBN-10: 0-9840771-1-1

First Edition published in 2009
Printed in the United States of America

GOD BLESS!

"Declare what is to be, present it—
let them take counsel together.
Who foretold this long ago,
who declared it from the distant past?
Was it not I, the LORD ?
And there is no God apart from me,
a righteous God and a Savior;
there is none but me."

Isaiah 45:21

"See, I have told you ahead of time."

Jesus in Matthew 24:15

TABLE OF CONTENTS

FOREWORD

I have known John Price since he was a young Attorney. Over the past 30 years plus, I have observed him build a successful corporate law practice and have witnessed him as he fought many Constitutional legal battles. John has fought for Hoosier parents' right to home educate their children; for high school graduating seniors' right to pray at commencement ceremonies; and for the State's pro life organizations right to have a booth at the Indiana State Fair. He represented a school corporation sued by the Indiana branch of the ACLU for allowing Gideon Bibles to be distributed and defended a Mayor and County Commissioners who were sued in two Indiana communities for allowing the Ten Commandments to be viewed in public buildings. He has taught two Bible Studies a week for business persons, one for 25 years. John Price is a serious student of the Bible, and not prone to jump to wild conclusions.

I was delighted to be one of those who proofread *"America at the Crossroads"*, which was then published in 1979 by Tyndale House, and with three printings achieving success for such a book at that time. The major theme of the book was that America could either repent, turn to God and be healed, as He promised in II Chronicles 7:14, or it could continue upon the same road it was traveling and face ultimate destruction. Unfortunately, America did not repent and has turned from God.

When John asked me to proofread this literary endeavor, I readily agreed, because it constituted a natural sequel to *"America at the Crossroads"*. What John Price has written is worthy of our immediate and most serious consideration, as Americans, regardless of one's religious or political persuasion.

John has approached the issue of Biblical revelation of America's future as he would a court trial. He makes a prima facie case for his argument and presents his evidence, based upon Biblical prophecy and the geopolitical and religious facts available to us today. He has established his case not merely by a preponderance of the evidence, but beyond a reasonable doubt. As a many years Bible teacher and over forty years student of scripture, I find this book to be compelling, persuasive and chilling in its conclusions. So, buckle up your seat belts my dear reader, you're in for a potentially life-changing experience. May you profit from this study of the "mystery" of what the Lord has revealed about a rich and powerful end times nation, and the clues He provided us in His Word as to her identity.

Jack C. Brown
United States District Attorney –
Southern District of Indiana
(1947-53)
Three Times Chairman –
Christian Businessmen's
Committee of Indianapolis
and Director of Christian
Businessmens Committee
International

INTRODUCTION

It was 1976. Though I had been a Christian just a few years, I knew that something was seriously wrong in America. Only three years before, in 1973, the nation's highest Court had authorized the aborting of infants in the womb, even though almost every State then prohibited abortion as a criminal act. By 1976 there had been very little public debate and there were but few books published about the issue. I decided to see what the Bible said. I'll not soon forget weeping as I read in God's Word His view of fetal murder, and I'm not normally given to tears.

I then outlined and penned a book, which we originally published as Christian House Publishers entitled *"America at the Crossroads: Repentance or Repression"*. The book included a brief history of America's four great spiritual awakenings (1725-1760; 1787-1805; 1857-1865 and 1900-1910) to hopefully give a vision for a fifth great awakening, if America's Christians complied with II Chronicles 7:14. *("If my people, which are called by my name, shall humble themselves, and pray, and seek my face, and turn from their wicked ways; then will I hear from heaven, and will forgive their sin, and will heal their land.")* . The subtitle of the Tyndale House 1979 edition was *"Can America Escape National Decline, Economic Collapse and Devastating Conflict?"* This book will address that question asked thirty years ago.

In *"America at the Crossroads"* we looked at some key societal issues:

The Economy: *"Given the unbridled right to create money, government will do so and eventually cause the destruction of the entire system."*

Banks: *"We should anticipate that at any point in time our U.S. banking system could suffer a blow from which it could not bounce back and which would result in government takeover…In whatever way it may start, if it starts, a series of major bank failures would totally alter the nation as we now know it."*

Politics/Government: *"We must not confuse cause with effect. God will heal; that's the effect. But the cause, the reason He will heal, is our repentance. Just electing Christians to office won't change the nation and heal its wounds. Instead, we'll repent and God will then allow godly men and women to be elected to office and He will use them in the healing process. Some well-meaning Christians want to heal the nation by organizing the 'Christian vote' and voting our problems away."*

Don't be too impressed by the last statement, as within a few years of writing it, I ignored my own words, and declared my candidacy for Congress, hoping to heal America from Capitol Hill, though without first witnessing a spiritual awakening. My electoral efforts thereafter were not successful, though not the fault, certainly, of friends and supporters who worked long hours, from a heart conviction to see God heal our land.

Sadly, for almost a hundred years, America has not experienced national repentance, nor a spiritual awakening, and no healing of our nation. After *"America at the Crossroads"* was published I began to look with some intensity at the role of the United States of America in Biblical prophecy. In studying the possible role of America in Bible prophecy, I soon learned that there were very few authors who had concluded that America was portrayed, or even alluded to, in the Bible, except in the most general sense. Best-selling Christian authors Dr. Tim LaHaye and Dr. Lester Sumrall represent that view:

"Does the United States have a place in end times prophecy? My first response is no, there is nothing about the U.S. in prophecy. At least nothing that is specific...The question is why? Why would the God of prophecy not refer to the supreme superpower nation in the end times in preparation for the one-world government of the Antichrist?" (Tim LaHaye's Perspective, August, 1999)

"The absence of any mention (in the end times) of a nation we could say is the United States, therefore, is a cause

for great distress among those of us who live in and love this nation. Where will America be at that time? The conclusion we must draw is very sad and sobering, and it should serve as a loud warning to our beloved United States. Simply put, the United States will no longer be a world power in the end times. It will not be a significant enough nation to play a major role in the events of those days – that is the obvious answer." (*Jerusalem: Where Empires Die,* Lester Sumrall, Sumrall Publishing).

The only published writer at the time who had concluded that America is set forth in the Bible was C. Franklin Logsdon, who in 1968 wrote *"Is the U.S.A. in Prophecy?"* (Zondervan, 1968). Logsdon's little book was an eye-opener, because the author focused on a subject in the Bible not much mentioned by Bible expositors, the *"Daughter of Babylon."* (Throughout the book, the name the *"Daughter of Babylon"* will be used in reference to the end times nation that the Bible also labels as *"Babylon the Great"* (Revelation 17-18). It's obvious from the text and context that both titles refer to the same end times nation.)

I pursued studying what the Bible said about the Daughter of Babylon, wrote some limited pages on the subject, spoke in a few churches on the topic, and then, ultimately, concluded that though the verses describing the end times Daughter of Babylon certainly appeared to apply to our nation, there were several pieces that just did not, *at that time,* seem to fit properly together.

Prophetic interpretative questions at the time included:

a.) America was a world superpower, but not the *only "hammer of the whole earth"* that Jeremiah said the Daughter of Babylon would be. The Soviet Union was then seen by most as equal to America in military power;

b.) The nations of Europe were not yet united in any meaningful way;

c.) Several Arab nations mentioned in prophecy were without any power or influence; and d.) Prophetically, the Daughter of Babylon will bring judgment on itself from God for doing things that America had not itself done a third of a century ago.

After some study of the subject, I filed away what I had learned, and moved on to other matters. Along with my wife, we raised four God-loving children (for whom we are eternally grateful) and watched America change over the last three plus decades.

That changed in the summer of 2007 as I began to pray and ponder the prophetic issues of what would become the contents of this book. I gradually realized that what I had researched and studied almost a third of a century ago, was now, with changed circumstances in the world, beginning to make perfect sense. So, what had happened over those thirty plus years? Many things, obviously, which are covered herein. But by far, the two most important changes since the mid 1970's were:

1.) America has changed. It has taken actions that have brought it closer to fulfillment of prophetic end times verses. It is, therefore, now in a position to do other things it never would have done in the past (more on this later); and

2.) The rise to world prominence, and to public attention, of radical Islamic Jihadists who are able, and more than willing, to conquer the world for Allah.

Islam had not been seen by Bible students or commentators in the last century as having any part in end times Bible prophecy. But now the several pieces that didn't seem to fit in the late 1970's, quickly began to slip into place. Is it of any importance that Christians, and Jews, understand what Muslims believe? Well, actually, it's critical that we know what Muslims believe about the end times, because there is an astounding overlap between what the Bible and the Quran say will happen in the end of this last phase of human history.

We are now closer to end times events than in the last century, so we can now discern much more about *how* these prophecies will be, and are being, fulfilled. We can now, gradually, begin to understand how those formerly somewhat unclear prophecies are now becoming clearer every day. It's like approaching a light in the night through a fog, the closer one gets, the clearer one can see. As we get closer to the end, we can begin to see that only one group of inhabitants of the earth can fulfill these prophecies in our day.

In this regard, the biggest shock to this writer, in beginning to re-study what the Bible calls the *"mystery"* of the identity of the Daughter of Babylon, was that, contrary to the formerly prevailing general belief that America is not in Biblical prophecy, America, as it turns out, is a *major player* on the prophetic end times world stage. A major player, that is, *until a prophesied point in time.* This, then, is a significant conclusion of *The End of America.* The Bible contains numerous prophetic verses that, we now increasingly see and understand, can *only* apply, and *do apply*, to the United States of America, and to no other nation of the past or present. Those verses have always been there, but it is only now, as we approach their fulfillment, that we can perceive them as such.

What must be emphasized is that this is not just another book about the well known and often studied end times topics, such as Armageddon, the Antichrist, the Rapture, the Tribulation and other final days world events. Unlike most books on prophecy, we will study in depth those end times prophecies that *come before* these events that we normally think of when we think of end times prophecies. As it turns out, the Bible contains over 220 verses (and thirty identity clues) that describe a particular end times nation (it's not Israel) which will be fulfilled *before* the final days events with which students of the Bible are well acquainted.

So, grab your Bible, and grab your newspaper. As you do, keep in mind that there are 1,239 prophecies in the Old Testament, and 578 prophecies in the New Testament. Those 1,817 prophecies include 8,352 verses. And because there are 31,124 verses in the Bible, those 8,352 verses are about *27 percent of the total*, meaning that *over one-fourth of the Bible is prophecy.* (*Encyclopedia of Biblical Prophecy*, by J. Barton Payne). Some of those 1,817 prophecies have already been fulfilled, many are *not yet fulfilled*, but *all* will be fulfilled by the end of the end times. Thankfully, God has given us in His Word what will happen *before* it all happens. Let's study those prophecies together to learn what God wants us to know, and more importantly, to *act* on what He has *told us to do* in the beginning days of the end times. Our very lives will depend upon it.

Chapter One

BEFORE OUR VERY EYES

"The Pharisees and Sadducees came to Jesus and tested him by asking him to show them a sign from heaven. He replied, "When evening comes, you say, 'It will be fair weather, for the sky is red,' and in the morning, 'Today it will be stormy, for the sky is red and overcast.' You know how to interpret the appearance of the sky, but you cannot interpret the signs of the times." (Matthew 16:1-3)

"People sense something slipping away, a world receding, not only an economic one but a world of old structures, old ways and assumptions...There is a 'perverse sense of anxiety, as though everyone feels they are on thin ice...maybe it's a sense that we've had it too easy in the years since 9/11 and that the bad guys are about to appear on the horizon'...Something is happening. Yesterday a friend sent the warning of the Evangelical pastor David Wilkerson, of Times Square Church, that a new catastrophe is imminent...One friend looks for small farms in distressed rural areas. Another logs on late at night looking for a house to buy in a small town out West, or down South, or in the Deep South." (Peggy Noonan, Columnist – *Wall Street Journal,* March 14, 2009)

Something is indeed happening. We sense it. We feel it. We know things in our world are changing, and not for the better. Since the September 11, 2001 attacks on America and the financial tsunami that became public on September 17, 2008, our personal anxiety levels have increased significantly.

Our bookstores reflect these perceptions. *The End of Prosperity* (Laffer, Moore & Tanous, Threshold Editions, 2008), *The End of Wall Street (As We Know It)* (Dave Kansas/Wall Street Journal, Collins Business, 2009), and *The End of Food* (Paul Roberts, Mariner Books, 2009) all are views of a new and different world in which we will likely live. What these and other similar books, columns and commentaries are describing pale in significance, though, to what Biblical prophecies tell us will happen to cause *The End of America*.

Biblical prophecies? Some may question if what is happening in the world today was actually foretold in ancient scripture. But the Bible's primary claim to authenticity is fulfilled prophecy, i.e., the ability to know the future with precision. *"I make known the end from the beginning, from ancient times, what is still to come...What I have said, that I will bring about; what I have planned, that will I do."* (Isaiah 46:10a-11b). This claim is somewhat astounding, since we, as mere mortals, can only guess about the future. God shares with us what will happen before it happens. *"Surely the Sovereign LORD does nothing without revealing his plan to his servants the prophets."* (Amos 3:7). Jesus affirmed this in Matthew 24:15: *"See, I have told you ahead of time."*

A fair number of people believe not only that the Bible contains reliable and accurate prophecies, but also that we are today living in the days described in the Bible as the "end times." Ten percent of all Americans believe that we are living in the end times prophesied in the Bible (Pew Forum on Religion and Public Life). That would be about thirty million of us. Though that's a large number, it conversely means that most Americans don't share such a belief. The stark reality, though, is that the *early days* of the final end times prophesied in the Bible have already begun. Most of us don't have a clue that we are now living in the beginning of the last days, which will be completed by a final world war that will end human history. If you would like more background on the history of Biblical prophecy, visit www.endofamericabook.com and click on *PROPHECY 101 – A Brief History of Prophetic Interpretation*.

THE END TIMES

How can we know from prophecy that we are actually in those end times? It's a question of considerable urgency, as Jesus demonstrated by weeping when He came into Jerusalem to present Himself, unsuccessfully, as her Messiah. He wept because Israel ignored the prophecies that should have led to His acceptance:

"As he approached Jerusalem and saw the city, he wept over it and said, "If you, even you, had only known on this day what would bring you peace—but now it is hidden from your eyes. The days will come upon you when your enemies will build an embankment against you and encircle you and hem you in on every side. They will dash you to the ground, you and the children within your walls. They will not leave one stone on another, because you did not recognize the time of God's coming to you." (Luke 19:41-44)

Likewise, for centuries, scriptures prophesying that the sovereign nation of Israel would some day be re-born were generally not believed. That is, until May 14, 1948 when Israel was re-born, to the astonishment of disbelievers. God's Word was, again, proven to be correct. In our day, the re-birth of Israel back in the land is an element of fulfilled prophecy that: a.) can't be overlooked or ignored; b.) is clearly a fulfillment of Old Testament prophecies; and c.) should cause us to watch, as Jesus said, for the end of time, and all that will happen as part of the climax of human history.

Jesus gave us in Matthew 24:32-34, a clear prophecy for our guidance:

"Now learn this lesson from the fig tree: As soon as its twigs get tender and its leaves come out, you know that summer is near. Even so, when you see all these things, you know that it is near, right at the door. I tell you the truth, this generation will certainly not pass away until all these things have happened."

3

These words answered His disciples' initial question as to *"when shall these things be?"* The *"until all these things"* referenced by the Lord at the end of this prophecy was to those events that He had just told His disciples would happen in the end times, including prophecies about the Antichrist, the tribulation, the Lord's return to earth, etc. So, what did He mean when He said the generation that sees the fig tree bloom would not pass away until all those things have happened? Hosea described Israel in this way: *"When I found Israel...it was like seeing the early fruit on the fig tree."* (Hosea 9:10). Over time the clear consensus has been that the reference to the fig tree is an allegorical identification of Israel, and its re-birth in the land, as prophesied, in both the Old and New Testaments (Deuteronomy 30; Matthew 24). Mike Evans has written: *"The fig tree has always been a symbol of the nation of Israel. The leaves of the fig tree are common ornaments on government buildings in Israel."* (*The Return,* Nelson, 1986). Hal Lindsey located a writer as far back as 1611 AD who wrote that Israel would, as the Bible prophesied, return to the land. In 1819 former President John Adams wrote *"I really wish the Jews again in Judea an independent nation."* Many wrote in the 1800's that Israel would some day return to its original location, as unlikely as that must have seemed at the time. See Attachment C (*End Times Time Line*) for details of end times events.

THE BUDDING FIG TREE OF ISRAEL

Before we examine the issue of timing, it's important to note that when Jesus told His disciples about the re-birth of Israel, and illustrated it by describing a future budding of the fig tree, His words were a meaningful symbolic prophecy to His Disciples, because of what they saw and heard from Jesus in about the same time frame. Mark tells us in 11:13 that as Jesus was on His way to Jerusalem in the days before He was to be crucified, he left Bethany, just east of Jerusalem. On the way, He saw a fig tree. Alas, the fig tree, though covered with leaves, had no figs on its branches. Jesus spoke to the tree and admonished it for not bearing fruit. He then pronounced on the fig tree that this particular fig tree would never bear fruit, a malediction which was confirmed the next day, as Jesus and His disciples passed by the same fig tree, now *"withered away"* and *"dried up from the roots."* (Mark 11:20, 21).

Obviously, this was about more than talking to a tree. One of the stated signs of God's blessings on the Israelites was that *"every man will sit under his own vine and under his own fig tree."* (I Kings 4:25; Isaiah 36:16; Micah 4:4) Fig trees bear fruit and are a blessing to their owners. This particular fig tree was no blessing, as it had literally no figs, and symbolically, no spiritual fruit. So, as Jesus ended His earthly ministry, He gave a symbolic assessment of Israel's rejection of Him, by finding no fruit on that fig tree, representing Israel, and by saying that this early fig tree, Israel at the time of Christ, would not bear fruit. His statement, of course, was accurate, as early Israel didn't bear spiritual fruit, itself withering away and going into dispersion within a few short years after the rejection of its Messiah.

Moving forward then to Jesus' prophecy that another, a second, fig tree would bloom signaling the end times, there has been some significant level of dispute as to what Jesus meant by telling us *the generation* that would see the fig tree rebud/Israel return, would not pass away/die until "all these things (the end times prophecies He gave us) have all *"happened."* What is a Biblical generation? Some argue forty years, some one hundred years, but that's not really a relevant question. Jesus didn't invite us to guess how long a generation was considered to be. Instead, He said *the generation* that was in existence or that witnessed the budding of the fig tree would not pass away, or all die out, *before* all of the prophesied events would happen. That's not a terribly difficult concept. How long will that be? One should be careful in this regard, as Jesus warned that no man knows *the day* or *the hour*, except for God the Father.

(Matthew 24:36). But Jesus does invite us to "*watch*" and be aware of a rebudded Fig Tree/Israel.

One writer in 1973 wrote that a generation was forty years, added forty to 1948, and then concluded "...*we should expect the Second Coming by 1987 at the outside*". Another writer, coming closer to the point nevertheless, wrote in 1986 that "the generation of people that saw the blossoming (of Israel), was born between 1925 and 1935. Their lifespan will be roughly seventy years...," thus, pointing to a 1995 to 2005 time of the Second Coming. The first problem with this analysis is that people born as late as the first five months of 1948 "saw" the rebirth of the fig tree/Israel on May 14, 1948. That's 13 years after the author's start date for a Biblical 'generation.' Secondly, seventy years is not today's average length of life because of the medical and healthcare advances we have enjoyed.

So, how much time *should* we expect to pass after May 14, 1948, before all of these things Jesus prophesied actually happen? Well, the last living American World War I (1914-1918) veteran, Frank Buckles, died on March 19, 2008. Once 16 million strong, U.S. veterans of World War II are dying at a rate of more than 1,000 a day, and now number about 2.5 million, the Department of Veterans Affairs estimates. Martin Morgan, historian for the World War II Museum in New Orleans predicts that *all* World War II veterans will be gone by 2020.

Obviously, Jesus gave us enough flexibility and time-spread in His prophecy that no one, just as He said, can know *the day and hour*. Only general parameters are safe: a.) as noted, the end won't come *after* those who saw Israel's re-birth have died off, but instead *before* we who witnessed the rebirth of Israel in 1948 have all passed away; and b.) many critical prophesied world events must occur *before* the end, some lasting as long as seven years, some happening before those specifically prophesied periods of years. This means that the *early events* in the end times, such as the Russian-Arab invasion of Israel (see Chapter 5) and the fall of the Daughter of Babylon (see Chapter 9) could happen at *any time*, but not too much later, because those who witnessed Israel's rebirth won't live that long. People who "saw" Israel re-born in 1948 will be around for several more years. Whatever the specifics of the timing, Jesus just *did not give us the option* of timing the end times for any longer than a few decades after Israel's rebudding. About sixty of those years since 1948 have now passed, so fasten your seat belt.

TWO MAJOR GLOBAL CHANGES

Two major world events have occurred in the last 60 years that should give any person cause to seriously ponder Biblical end times prophecies. The first, which we have already examined, is the re-birth of the nation of Israel back in its original land in 1948. In spite of the good intentions of a lot of good people, to find the end times in *their* times, it was just not going to happen until the Fig Tree of Israel re-budded, which it miraculously did in the middle of the last century. The second event arises from Daniel's prophecy (Daniel 2) that the fourth great world empire would spring from the third, the Roman Empire. Virtually all Bible scholars are in agreement that, when Daniel saw legs of iron, with feet mixed with clay, he was foreseeing a revived Roman Empire, again uniting the majority of the land mass of Europe, as it had been united under the rule of Rome from 2,000 to 1,600 years ago. Until the uniting of Europe in 1993 with the Treaty of Maastricht, a revived Roman Empire fulfillment of Daniel's prophecy didn't appear it would ever happen.

Are these two events, Israel's re-budding and Europe's uniting, important matters, apart from prophecy? Even if we had no Biblical indication that they would take place, their occurrence would constitute two of the more critical geopolitical events in our lifetimes. Israel is in almost every daily newspaper, and very few days pass without articles about the European Union. The EU represents 30% of the entire world's gross domestic product. Israel and the EU are on the world's center stage.

Angel Second Class Clarence Odbody, in Frank Capra's *"It's a Wonderful Life,"* tried to convince George Bailey that suicide wasn't the answer to his problems: *"You see, George, you really had a wonderful life. Don't you see what a mistake it would be to throw it away?"* How does Angel Clarence Odbody relate to a reborn Israel and a united Europe? For those of us who are alive in the world as God has restored Israel and united the continent of the former Roman Empire, we also have had a wonderful life of *observing God at work* without parallel in human history, thus far. It would also be a mistake for us to figuratively throw it away by ignoring God's mighty hand at work.

He said over 2,000 years ago He would bring Israel back–after its forced dispersion around the world. He said a little over 2,600 years ago that He would create the Fourth World Empire, and then much later, in the end times, reform that Empire. Both of these prophesied events have happened *before our very eyes.* We are eyewitnesses to God fulfilling these two major prophecies. Both had to occur *before* the Day of the Lord. We've been privileged to be alive to see both– but if we overlook their significance we will have thrown away the great privilege God has given us to be witnesses of the mystery and miracle of prophetic fulfillment.

As the days after the rebirth of Israel (1948) and the unification of Europe (1993) continue to mount, we are increasingly seeing the curtain pulled further back, revealing to us more of the details of the last days. Since 9/11 what we have seen, and now increasingly understand in more depth than Christians in past generations, is that the final enemies of Jesus and of His people are not who we thought they would be. It may be surprising to learn that the future prophesied destroyers of the United States, and the purported conquerors of the world, pray regularly each day, prohibit abortion, denounce homosexuality, and forbid alcohol. Who are these people? Christian fundamentalists? Well, not quite.

As indicated by the book's sub-title, it is now increasingly obvious that those who would seek to be conquerors of the world in the end times, are radical Islamic Jihadists, who will do exactly what they have been doing in the world for the last 1,400 years (kill for Allah). What they are today telling us they will do in the future includes: a.) destroy America, b.) seek to destroy Israel, and c.) conquer the world for Allah. It will, undoubtedly, be a shocking realization to read how familiar end times prophecies will be fulfilled in a very unfamiliar and surprising way by people whom, a few years ago, were dismissed as mere nomads, living as if they were in the middle ages, with many still dwelling in tents. It is only as radical Islamic Jihadist teachings are understood by us that we can answer questions many of us used to have about end times prophecies. To understand the threat to America, we need to know more about the agenda of Jihadists who regularly fill Muslim city streets chanting, *"Death to America"*.

Chapter Two

THE RELIGION OF PEACE

"Activists identifying themselves as jihadists, although a small percentage of Muslims, are increasing both in number and geographic dispersion...If this trend continues, threats to U.S. interests at home and abroad will become more diverse, leading to increasing attacks worldwide." (National Intelligence Estimate on Trends in Global Terrorism, April, 2006)

"To us they are not accusations. To us they are a badge of honor, which we carry with honor. We are terrorists to the bone. So, many thanks to God. Therefore, killing you and fighting you and terrorizing you, responding back to your attacks, are all considered to be great legitimate duty in our religion. These actions are our offerings to God." (*"The Islamic Response to the Government's Nine Accusations."* Written by five detainees at Guantanamo Bay prison camp, including 9/11 mastermind Khalid Sheikh Mohammed, released in military commission proceedings).

In order to understand what is actually happening, and what is about to happen, in the world today, it is critical to review the history of Islam and its adherents. Many who have written about Islam in the world have glossed over or whitewashed the facts of the history of Islam's expansion. Facts that help us see where Jihadists are heading. But, initially, we need to know, where did the 1.6 billion Muslim population of the world come from? The answer? *"Go in unto my maid."* With these five simple words in Genesis 16:2 Sarai changed the world, including our world today. As with many problems in the life of a person of God, the problems we face today from radical Islamic jihadists started with a lack of faith in God's word. God revealed to Abram and Sarai that he would give them children and descendants as

11

numerous as the stars of the sky. Abram believed God and it was counted unto him as righteousness (Genesis 15:5). Abram and Sarai believed God...for awhile, that is.

After some time, and considering their infertility for so many years, they took the matter of God's promise of children *into their own hands*. Sarai decided what God meant, when He promised they would have children, was that *someone else, not Sarai,* would have Abram's child. So, Sarai suggested Abram have relations with Sarai's handmaiden, Hagar. Scripture records no objection by Abram, who promptly impregnated Hagar, an Egyptian. The future of the world significantly changed with Abram's and Sarai's decision not to trust God for a child. After Ishmael was born to Hagar, the Lord again appeared, now to a renamed Abraham and a renamed Sarah, and again promised them they would have a child. Sarah thought the promise laughable, after which the revealing Angel of the Lord asked her *"Is anything too hard for the LORD?"* (Genesis18:14) Sarah then denied that she had laughed, though the Angel said, "No, you did laugh".

But, Ishmael and his millions of descendants were no laughing matter. Like Jacob, Ishmael had twelve sons. They settled in the areas east of Israel, in Ammon, Moab, Edom, and what we today call the Saudi Arabian peninsula. These descendents of Ishmael became, and remain, a constant thorn in the side of Israel. After many centuries of procreation and growth of their tribes, a descendant of Hagar, Muhammad ibn Abdallah ibn Abd al-Muttalib, also known as Muhammad, was born in Mecca in 570 AD. In 610 AD Muhammad said he received revelations from the Angel Gabriel in a cave. A Christian or a Jew today can read Muhammad's claims in his book, the Quran, concerning the Angel Gabriel, and decide if these words are consistent with what is revealed about the Angel Gabriel in the Bible (Daniel 8:16, 21 and Luke 1:19, 26). Gabriel announced to Mary the coming birth of the Christ, which may explain the choice of Gabriel by Muhammad.

Pre-dating Muhammad, Arab descendants of Ishmael worshipped various 'gods', numbering at least one for each day of the year. *"One of these was the moon god, the male counterpart to the female sun god. The moon god was called by various names, one of which was Allah, and it was the favorite god of Muhammad's family. ...The literal Arabic name of Muhammad's father was Abd-Allah...As Muhammad began to promote his new religion, it was only natural that he would choose to elevate the moon god, Allah, and declare him to be the one true god...in establishing and spreading his religion of Islam, Muhammad slaughtered thousands of people who resisted conversion."* (*What in the World is Going On?* David Jeremiah, Thomas Nelson)

BECOMING A WARRIOR

Muhammad claimed he heard words from Allah for the next twenty two years, many of which he recorded in the Quran. Along with the Quran are the books of Hadith, which record what Muhammad said and did during his life. Muslim scholars have noted that Muhammad's writings can be divided into two distinct categories, those words written when he was in Mecca, which were largely about prayer and meditation, and those words written after he faced opposition in Mecca, and fled in 622, at 52 years of age. He had ten years left to live, mostly in Medina, before he would die in 632.

Before fleeing Mecca, Muhammad faced rejection by his Quraysh brethren, including his uncle, Abu Lahab. He recorded a curse in the Quran against his uncle, that he and his wife would be hanged and burnt to death (Quran 111:1-5). After leaving Mecca because of lack of receptivity to his message, he traveled to Medina. There Muhammad became a warrior, invader and military leader. A band of tribal warriors accepted him as a prophet, and pledged their loyalty to him. Muhammad led his followers in raids and battles, some against his brethren, the Quraysh. A seminal victory was won at Badr by Muhammad's force of three hundred warriors against a thousand in the Quraysh caravan. He made much of this victory and wrote about it in the Quran, even down to discussing how to split up the booty. Muhammad ordered that his enemies/brethren at Badr were to be beheaded. One leader (Uqba bin Abi Mu'ait) begged him for mercy and asked who would look after his children. Muhammad replied that Hell would look after them, and had him beheaded.

Thus began a quite bloody and violent ten-year period, in which Muhammad developed his principles of warfare to be waged against those who rejected his role as Allah's prophet. He stepped up his raiding operations and began to harass the Jewish tribes of the region, who rejected him as a prophet of God. Soon Muhammad ordered his followers to *"Kill any Jew that falls into your power."* Muhammad eventually united various conflicting tribes, and after eight years of fighting with Meccan tribes, his followers, who had grown to ten thousand warriors, conquered Mecca. In 632, a few months after returning to Medina, Muhammad fell ill and died. By the time of his death, most of the Arabian Peninsula had converted to Muhammad's new religion, Islam, with the Quran as its version of the "Bible."

Dr. Mark A. Gabriel, Ph.D., a former professor of Islamic history at Al-Azhar University in Cairo, Egypt has described the contents of the Quran:

"In Medina, Muhammad became a military leader and invader, so the revelations in Medina talk about military power and invasion in the name of Islam (Jihad). Sixty percent of the Quranic verses talk about jihad, which stands to reason because Muhammad received most of the Quran after he left Mecca. Jihad became the basic power and driving force of Islam". (Islam and Terrorism, Charisma House, 2002).

What, then, is Jihad? Dr. Gabriel was an Imam of a mosque in Gaza, Egypt, and a respected professor at Al-Azhar University in Cairo, before he became a follower of Jesus Christ, and changed his name for his personal security. He writes that a major motivator for him to leave Islam was its emphasis on Jihad. Dr. Gabriel was troubled by Muhammad's command, labeled as the *"verse of the sword,"* known to be the final development of Jihad in Islam, found in Surah 9:5:

"Fight and slay the pagans wherever you find them, and seize them, beleaguer them, and lie in wait for them in every stratagem (of war)..."

Politicians often say Islam is 'a religion of peace.' There are peaceful verses in the Quran. There are many, possibly a majority of Muslims, who are peaceful. That, of course, is cold comfort if the significant minority of Muslims who adhere to Jihad are committed to destroy those who are not Muslims. In October, 2008, radical Muslims drove 3,000 Christians out of their homes in Mosul, Iraq, in what the media described as a *"killing campaign."* Nevertheless, one displaced Christian cleric was quoted by the Associated Press as saying, *"We are at a loss to understand the violence. We respect the Islamic religion and the Muslim clerics."* *Respecting* people who are sworn to kill you, because they think your death at their hand is a *favor* to Allah, may not be the wisest conclusion. *"In fact, a time is coming when anyone who kills you will think he is offering a service to God."* (John 16:2)

Even peaceful, 'moderate' Muslims may not turn out to be peaceful or moderate. Case in point, Muzzammill Hassan and his wife, Aasiya, were moderate Muslims living in a wealthy suburb of Buffalo, N.Y. They decided they needed to start a television network in 2004 to *"counter Muslim stereotypes"*, which they named "Bridges TV." The network was available in both the U.S. and Canada, and was believed to be the first English-language cable station aimed at the rapidly growing Muslim population in both countries. Neighbors described the Hassans as peaceful, with one law enforcement officer who knew Muzzammil, saying about him, "I've never heard him raise his voice."

But, after the initial broadcasting success, Mrs. Hassan served divorce papers on her husband. Six days later her body, minus her severed head, was found by police at the television studios of Bridges TV. Muzzammill had gone to the police to tell them about her death, after which he was charged with beheading his wife. In news reports about the slaying of Nadia Shahram, a regular panelist on a Bridges TV law show, and a professor of family law and Islam at Buffalo Law School, told reporters that *"Honor killing is a practice still accepted"* among Muslim men *"who feel betrayed by their wives. If a woman breaks the law which the husband or father has placed for the wife or daughter, honor killing has been justified. It happens all the time."* (Associated Press, February 18, 2009).

HOW DID ISLAM GROW?

"In a major encyclopedia one reads phrases such as: 'Islam expanded in the eighth or ninth centuries...'; 'This or that country passed into Muslim hands...' But care is taken not to say how Islam expanded, how countries 'passed into (Muslim) hands.' Indeed, it would seem as if events happened by themselves, through a miraculous or amicable operation...Regarding this expansion, little is said about Jihad. And yet it all happened through war!" (The Legacy of Jihad, Prometheus Books, 2005).

Muhammad's violent end years and final violent words were quickly followed by those who succeeded him in power, after his death in 632 AD.

"Within thirty years after Muhammad's death Islam achieved the most spectacular expansion in its history. During the caliphate of Muhammad's immediate successors from 632 to 661, Islam conquered the whole Arabian peninsula and invaded territories which had been in Greco-Roman hands since the reign of Alexander the Great....Damascus fell in 635. Jerusalem was captured in 638. In the same year Antioch fell, and the other great Hellenistic capital, Alexandria, became a permanent Arab possession in 646. Coastal cities in Syria, Palestine and Egypt, as well as the island of Cyprus were successively occupied by Arabs in a short period of time...The rapid advance of Islam spread panic and consternation among the Christians in the Greek Near East...The Arabic

wars against the Greeks were not only political and economic wars, but holy wars of Islam against Christianity." ("Greek Christian and Other Accounts of the Muslim Conquests of the Near East," Demetrios Constantelos, article in *The Legacy of Jihad,* Prometheus Books, 2005, Edited by Andrew Bostom, MD).

THE ROOTS OF JIHAD

For anyone who seeks to understand the current Jihadist threat against the nations of the world, they must become acquainted with the branch of Islam known as Wahabism. Wahabism was founded by Muhammad ibn 'Abd al Wahab (1703-1792), who strongly advocated that Islam return to the practices of its first three generations, a time of violence and strict adherence to Muhammad's teachings.

Today's Saudi Arabia was founded on the 18th-century alliance between the Wahhabi religious movement and the House of Saud. In 1745 Muhammad ibn 'Abd al-Wahab made an alliance with the Emir of a small town in central Arabia (Dariya), named Muhammad bin Saud. Over the next seventy years, a Jihad was waged across Arabia, but was driven back in 1818 by the Ottoman Turks. In 1901 a descendant of Muhammad bin Saud, Ibin Saud, with an army of only twenty, assassinated a local governor, and conquered a large area of Arabia, only to be thrown back again by the Ottoman Empire.

Everything changed when the British, during World War I, decided to protect their interests in the Arabian Peninsula by allying with Ibn Saud. Saud used his new alliance with the British, and their financial support, to turn his Wahabi Bedouin tribesmen into a violent and bloodthirsty army. They burned and beheaded thousands, as Ibn Saud consolidated control of the Arabian peninsula. In 1932 Ibn Saud named himself King of a new nation he modestly named Saudi Arabia. Saud's Wahabi Ikhwan followers had no tolerance for 20th century advancements, or for non-Muslims living in Arabia. Forcing their Wahabist principles on others, they killed as many as half a million people. Saud had children with women from thirty tribes, greatly spreading the Saud family influence.

Saudi Arabia went from a backward desert kingdom to a world power, beginning in 1933, with the discovery of vast oil fields in the eastern flat lands of the peninsula. Standard Oil of California briefly owned the oil concession, assigning it to a venture that eventually was named ARAMCO (Arabian American Oil Company). When Ibn Saud died in 1953, at the age of 77, with one hundred wives, 42 sons, and 1500 princes, Arabia had no significant infrastructure, and was populated by a largely poor and uneducated people. Saud has been succeeded by several descendants over time (with some in-family assassinations), who invested their growing treasure of billions of petrodollars in palaces, Rolls Royces, Boeing 747s and lavish trips abroad, sharing generously with their own family members, but sparingly with the citizens of Saudi Arabia. The House of Saud also used its billions to arm itself against its own citizens, and to pay for military ventures by fellow Muslim nations against Israel.

Strict Wahabists have objected to the presence of American military units on Saudi soil, but the House of Saud assuaged them by paying for madrassas, which are schools that indoctrinate students with radical Wahabist doctrines, teaching their students that Jews, Christians and Americans are to be hated and killed. One of Osama bin Laden's objections to America is its presence on the Saudi Arabian peninsula. Wahabism is the dominant form of Islam found in Saudi Arabia and Qatar and is also popular in Egypt, Kuwait, United Arab Emirates and Bahrain. Wahabists control the two holy cities of Mecca and Medina, giving Wahabists great influence in the Muslim world. More important are the extensive oil fields of Saudi Arabia which have been used to fund the promotion of Islam's most radical sect across the world. Saudi oil funds have built most of the Muslim Mosques in the western world since 1975. More than 1,500 mosques across the globe were built from Saudi petro funds over the last 50 years. Wahabism has been referred to as "petro-Islam."

The House of Saud has funded an estimated *"90% of the expenses of the entire faith,"* throughout the Muslim world, according to journalist Dawood al-Shirian. The Saud family lavished funds on journalists and academics who followed Wahabism and built satellite campuses around Egypt for Al Azhar, the most influential Islamic university. The financial power of Saudi Wahhabism has overwhelmed less strict interpretations of Islam. As a result, Wahabism is viewed by Muslims worldwide as the "gold standard" of Islam.

All of this is more than just historically interesting. It explains why the 9/11 terrorists came from the Wahabist nation of Saudi Arabia; it explains why Osama bin Laden came from Saudi Arabia; and it explains how radical Muslim Jihadists have been successful in the spread of their radical philosophy to other Muslims, using the petrodollars we spend at our local gas stations. So, what do the Wahabists say their intentions are for the world?

WHAT DO WAHABISTS BELIEVE?

According to Dr. Gabriel, there are two predominant Wahabist beliefs:

Phase I – The absolute destruction of the heathen world.
Phase II – Muslims will inherit the earth and everything in it.

Upon what, in the Quran, is this plan for world conquest based?

"Those who reject Islam must be killed. If they turn back (from Islam), take (hold of) them and kill them wherever you find them..." *(Surah 4:89)*

"So, when you meet those who disbelieve, smite (their) necks till when you have killed and wounded many of them, then bind a bond firmly (on them, as captives)." Surah 47:4

How do Muslims view Christians and Jews, who the Quran calls *"People of the Book"*? At first, the early Quaranic verses encouraged Muslims to live peacefully with Christians, though verses about Jews were never favorable. However, after Muhammad moved to Medina, his revelations became very hostile to Christians. Dr. Gabriel writes:

"The following verse is considered to be the final revelation from Allah regarding Christians and Jews; therefore, it is understood to override all other revelations: It states:

"And fight them until there is no more Fitnah (disbelief and polytheism, i.e., worshipping others besides Allah) and the religion (worship) will be for Allah Alone (in the whole of the world)...." (Surah 8:39

This fact is also emphasized in Surah 5:52-57 and Surah 4:89. When fighting Christians, the Quran commands severe punishment, so they will leave their homes and be dispersed. (Surah 8:57).

It is not really possible to understand the threat posed not only to the survival of America, but to all free nations in the world, without perceiving that Islam has a simple and single goal . . . *To conquer the world.*

Yes, that may sound like something from Hitler's *Mein Kampf,* or the script of a space invaders movie, but conquering the world for the radical Jihadist movement is their overriding commitment and unshakeable life goal. Again, Dr. Gabriel warns us:

"Jihad is carried out in order to achieve the ultimate goal of Islam – to establish Islamic authority over the whole world. Islam is not just a religion; it is a government, too. That is why it always gets down to politics. Islam teaches that

Allah is the only authority; therefore, political systems must be based on Allah's teaching and nothing else...(Jihadists) consider themselves to have succeeded when a nation declares Islam as both their religion and their form of government."

JIHADISTS IN ACTION IN OUR TIME

After former Egyptian President Anwar Sadat led Egypt to become the first Arab nation to recognize Israel in 1979, and after he said there would be *"no politics in Islam and no Islam in politics,"* a fatwa to assassinate Sadat was approved by Sheikh Omar Abdel Rahman, the leader of al-Jihad terrorists in Egypt. He declared that Sadat was an infidel renegade who must be killed. Sheikh Rahman was later convicted in the U.S. for his role in the bombing of the World Trade Center in 1993. Following Islamic law, al-Jihad carried out its leader's order and Sadat was assassinated on October 6, 1981, at an Egyptian Army Victory Parade. Sadat was heavily protected by security, thus, he should have been safe at the armed parade, due to rules prohibiting ammunition in weapons carried by participants in the parade. However, the officers in charge of that procedure were in Mecca on October 6, 1981.

In the intervening thirty years since Sadat's death at the hands of Jihadists, thousands of terror attacks have occurred in nations across the globe. Two years after Sadat's death the U.S. Embassy in Beirut, Lebanon was bombed, killing 63. Six were killed in the bombing of the World Trade Center in New York City on February 26, 1993. The next month, 250 civilians died in the attacks on Bombay, India. A year later, three members of the Armed Islamic Group hijacked Air France flight 8969 in Algiers, killing seven. In 1996 the Khobar Towers in Saudi Arabia were bombed, killing 19 U.S. Air Force airmen living in the towers. Later, the Pentagon indicated that the relatively new terrorist group named al Qaeda, formed eight years before, was responsible for the Khobar Towers attack on U. S. military personnel. In

21

1998 U.S. Embassies in Tanzania and Kenya were bombed, killing 224, and wounding over 4,000. On October 12, 2000, the *USS Cole* was attacked, killing 56. On September 11, 2001, al Qaeda terrorists hijacked four U.S. commercial aircraft, bringing down both World Trade Center Towers, and crashing into the Pentagon, with the fourth assumed to be headed for either the U.S. Capitol or the White House, brought down by passengers in Pennsylvania; 3,000 died. America's innocence regarding Jihadists' plan to conquer the world for Allah also died at the same time.

Since 9/11, the level of terror attacks has only increased. In late 2001, terrorists launched a suicide attack on the Parliament in India, intended to cause anarchy. In 2002, a Passover Seder in a hotel in Netanya, Israel, was bombed, killing 29 and injuring 133. In the same year, a café was suicide- bombed in Jerusalem, a Hindu Temple in Ahmedabad, India, was attacked, and a Bali nightclub was bombed, killing 202. In 2004, four simultaneous attacks took place in Casablanca, killing 33. On March 11, 2004, multiple bombings took place on trains in Madrid, Spain, killing 191 and injuring 1,460. Al Qaeda claimed credit, particularly so after the near-term Spanish elections turned out of office an administration working with the U.S. in Iraq. In 2005, 36 Christians in Demsa, Nigeria, were killed by Muslim militants; al Qaeda bombed London's Underground, killing 53, and injuring 700; 64 died at the Egyptian resort of Sharm el-Sheikh; 60 died in bombings in Delhi; and 60 died in a series of coordinated attacks on hotels in Amman, Jordan.

In 2006-2008, there were several terror attacks in India, including a coordinated blast of 16 bombs in the industrial city of Ahmedabad in July 2008, and a November 2008, attack on Mumbai, India's financial center. These terrorist killings were clearly meant to provoke confrontation with Pakistan, with the intention to destabilize or depose the Pakistani government to allow the Jihadists to secure the nation's approximate 100 nuclear weapons. And these were only the terrorist attacks that made headlines in the west. In addition, in the years since 9/11 there have been thousands of less spectacular, but still deadly, terrorism incidents, most at the hands of Jihadists. For further details go to: www.thereligionofpeace.com and click on List of Islamic Terror Attacks.

This website, the full name (apparently tongue in cheek) of which is *"Islam – the Religion of Peace (and a big stack of dead bodies)"* lists and documents, by the year, the thousands of terror *attacks* of Jihadists, *since* 9/11. The count at this writing was 13,776 deadly terror attacks since 9/11. Jihadists are following their agenda, doing what they believe Allah has told them to do – kill unbelievers (kafir) and conquer the world, including every nation, for Allah. Much of what motivates Jihadists may be found in examining Muslim prophecies of the Last Day. It is likely, few of us knew that Muslim even had "prophecies", or that they also believed in a "Last Day," but they certainly do.

Chapter Three

MUSLIM END TIMES PROPHECIES

"Is the call for jihad against a particular people a religious right by those calling for it, or is it a human rights violation against the people on which jihad is declared and waged?" (Dr. John Garang, United Nations, Geneva, March 22, 1999)

"In a speech to Turkey's Parliament, the president said, 'The United States is not, and will never be at war with Islam.' It was a noble sentiment. Such a unilateral declaration may soothe many in the West, but there is a central question that comes from Mr. Obama's declaration of conscientious objection: What if Islamic extremism is at war with America, Europe and Israel and everyone who stands in the way of its attempt at supremacy in religion and politics?" (Cal Thomas, Syndicated Columnist for Tribune Media Services, 2009).

"Every single day, Muslims are killing Muslims. You do not see a single Muslim leader get up and say, 'Enough is enough'. It's nearly as if we live in a world where if Christians kill Muslims, it's a crusade. If Jews kill Muslims, it's a massacre. And when Muslims kill Muslims, it's the Weather Channel. Nobody cares." Israeli Ambassador to the U.S. Dan Gillerman, *New York Times*, July 20, 2008

BIBLICAL PROPHECIES TIE DIRECTLY TO MUSLIM PROPHECIES AND PRACTICES

Students of Biblical prophecies describing the future military and governmental leader the Bible labels as the Antichrist, have most likely asked several questions. How will the future Antichrist, based in Europe, the head of many European nations, seize power over other nations, and what will motivate him to do so? Why will he try to change the set times and the laws?

"He will speak against the Most High and oppress his saints and try to change the set times and the laws." (Daniel 7:25)

What times and what laws will he seek to change? Why will he want to alter the calendar? What religion will the Antichrist demand that the people of the world follow and will who they be forced to worship? Why will the Antichrist decapitate Christians and Jews? Until these times we didn't have a clue what those two prophecies meant as we could only guess. Now, however, they make perfect sense. Jihadists' words and their current day deeds fit into these Biblical prophecies like fingers in a glove. Later, in this Chapter we'll examine, why a Muslim Antichrist will want to change the laws and the times.

The Bible also affirms that, in the end times, God's people will be martyred by beheading.

"And I saw the souls of those who had been beheaded because of their testimony for Jesus and because of the word of God. They had not worshiped the beast or his image and had not received his mark on their foreheads or their hands." (Revelation 20:4)

In the past, writers on this subject have conjectured that the Antichrist may possibly bring back the French guillotine in town squares across the globe to kill those who refuse to worship him. That was an educated guess, but as today's events unfold, and as we see the true identity of the Antichrist, as a dedicated Muslim, fulfilling not only Biblical, but also Muslim prophecies, the method of martyring God's people by *beheading* them makes perfect sense. Who kills people in the world today by severing their heads from their bodies? The French? Of course not. The guillotine is a museum exhibit....Any western nation? No, much too barbaric....Any third world nations? Yes, actually, depending upon the nation. CBS News reported in 2004 that Saudi Arabia recently beheaded 52 men and one woman for various crimes, including murder, homosexuality, armed robbery, and drug trafficking. The CBS Report claimed that *"A condemned convict is brought into the courtyard, hands tied, and forced to bow before an executioner, who swings a huge sword amid cries from onlookers of 'Allahu Akbar!' Arabic for 'God is Great."*

RADICAL MUSLIM LEADERS BELIEVE THEY HAVE AN OBLIGATION TO RESTORE THE CALIPHATE AND THUS BRING ABOUT THE END OF WORLD HISTORY

Some may be surprised to learn that Muslims have a deep-seated belief in *"The Last Day,"* as one of the five basic tenets of their faith. The Quran spells out those five tenets:

"It is not righteousness that ye turn your faces to the East and the West; but righteous is he who believes in Allah and the Last Day and the angels and the Scripture and the prophets..." (Surah 2:177)

Note that two of these five basic tenets deal with prophecy (The Last Day and the prophets). The reference in this verse from the Quran, to "scripture", is not to the Bible, incidentally, but to other Islamic writings. What exactly do Muslims believe about The Last Day? Do they believe what we believe? Is learning what Muslims believe about The Last Day important? Since America is target one for Jihadists, her citizens should be aware of the source of what Muslims believe about the end times.

Surah 2:177 of the Quran requires a Muslim to subscribe to the five tenets, the second of which is *"belief in the Last Day,"* and the fifth of which is *"belief in the prophets."* It may surprise the average Christian to learn that Muslims have "prophets," and that they have their own *"prophecies,"* all centered on *"The Last Day."* The Bible proclaims that *"All scripture is given by inspiration of God, and is profitable for doctrine, for reproof, for correction, for instruction in righteousness"* (II Timothy 3:16). That being the case, what is the *source* of Muslim predictions? What do

27

Muslims believe about The Last Day? One can decide that for oneself, and it won't be very hard to arrive at a conclusion.

The predominant Muslim Last Day belief is that a man will come to the earth known as *"the Mahdi,"* which in Arabic means *"the Guided One."* Muslims teach that the *Mahdi* will be a great Muslim political and military world leader. They also teach that there will be an Antichrist (the *"Dajjal"*) and that he will have an enforcer who will kill those who don't worship the *Mahdi*. The *Mahdi* is also referred to in Arabic as *"The Lord of the Age"* and *"The Awaited One"*. Muslims believe in Major and Minor Signs of the Last Day, with the Major Signs centered on the coming of the *Mahdi*, and the Minor Signs, similar to what the Bible would call "birth pangs" which precede the coming of the *Mahdi*.

The *Mahdi* has also been described as Islam's Messiah, equivalent for Muslims to Jesus Christ, the Messiah of scripture:

"Thus it is fair to say that the 'rising' of the Mahdi is to the majority of Muslims what the return of Jesus is to Christians. While Christians await the return of Jesus the Messiah to fulfill all of God's prophetic promises to the people of God, Muslims await the appearance of the Mahdi, to fulfill those purposes. Sheikh Kabbani likewise identifies the Mahdi as Islam's primary messiah figure:
'Jews are waiting for the messiah, Christians are waiting for Jesus and Muslims are waiting for both the Mahdi and Jesus. All (three) describe them as men coming to save the world'" (Antichrist: Islam's Awaited Messiah, Joel Richardson, Winepress Publishing,

Muhammad said the Mahdi, who would some day come, would be a descendant of one of his wives (Fatimah), and would bear his name, ruling over Arabs. Across the Muslim world today, there is a call for the Islamic Caliphate to be restored, which has been vacant since Turkey abolished the Caliphate in 1924. The Caliph is the preeminent political and religious leader of all Muslims, high above all Muslims, even over Imams. Shi'a believe that the Imams are chosen by Allah to be perfect examples for the faithful and that all Imams chosen, chosen by God, are free from committing any sin, and have the same status as a prophet.

Iran's President Ahmadinejad frequently called publically for the Caliphate to be restored, and to rule over the world. The Iranian president, in a speech in 2006, emphasized his theme that "*the return of the Shiite messiah, the Mahdi, is not far away, and Muslims must prepare for it.*" Ahmadinejad has also said, "*We must prepare ourselves to rule the world and the only way to do that is to put forth views on the basis of the Expectation of the Return [of] the Mahdi.*" Efforts to convince Jihadists that America has the best of intentions toward Islam, or that the nation "*isn't at war against Islam*", are wasted words and irrelevant to Jihadists who are preparing to "*rule the world*".

According to Shiites, there were twelve Imams who lived through the seventh and eighth centuries AD. The 12th Imam, Muhammad ibn al-Hassan, is said by Muslims to have disappeared as a child in the year 941, and has been hiding alive in a well since that time. When he returns, *as the Imam Mahdi, The Savior of Times,* they believe he will reign on earth for seven years, before bringing about a final judgment and the end of the world.

BIBLICAL AND MUSLIM PROPHECIES OVERLAP

Biblical prophecies of the coming *Antichrist* and the Muslim predictions of the coming *Mahdi* have an eerie overlap:

a.) *Both* the Biblically-prophesied Antichrist and the Muslim-predicted Mahdi are to be religious *and* governmental leaders, who lead military campaigns, in an attempt to conquer the nations of the earth, and commence a new world order;

b.) *Both* will lead the world to worship themselves in a *universal world religion*. For those who don't worship the new world religious leader, they will be decapitated;

c.) *Both* the Biblically-prophesied *Antichrist* and the Muslim predicted *Mahdi* will seek to kill *as many Jews and Christians* as possible;

d.) *Both* the Biblically-prophesied *Antichrist* and the Muslim-predicted *Mahdi* will *change the laws and the times* (calendars);

e.) *Both* the Biblically-prophesied *Antichrist* and the Muslim-predicted *Mahdi* will make *a peace treaty* with Israel for precisely seven years; and

f.) The Biblically-prophesied *Antichrist* will go to *Jerusalem* and rule from Israel's Temple, just as the Muslim-predicted *Mahdi* will establish the Islamic Caliphate from the Temple Mount in *Jerusalem*.

The Biblical prophecy and the Muslim prediction each forecasting that the final end times leader will change the laws and the times, is telling. Muslims have their Hijra calendar, based on the career of Muhammad, which has twelve purely lunar months and Friday being its sacred day of prayer and a day for sermons at the mosque. Muslims believe that the Hijra calendar is mandatory for all to observe. Jews and Hindus have their own calendar, but have never shown any inclination to impose their calendar on others. A Muslim Antichrist will demand that each nation, coming under Islam, must adopt the Hijra calendar. Thus, the Muslim *Mahdi* will have a reason to do what the Bible says the Antichrist will do—change the times.

As for changing the laws, Muslims, even moderates, are today pushing for Sharia law in nations where they are a growing portion of the population. A poll, by the *Guardian* newspaper in London, found that about two-thirds of British Muslims want to be governed by Sharia law, which has been implemented in Muslim-dominated areas of Great Britain. The Archbishop of Canterbury even endorsed the idea. Melanie Phillips, author of *Londonistan*, (Encounter Books, 2006) writes that *"Instead of acknowledging that Muslim values must give way wherever they conflict with the majority culture, they believe that the majority should instead defer to Islamic values and allow Muslims effectively autonomous development."* Sharia law allows up to four wives, cutting off the hand of a thief, beheading a woman caught in adultery, non-interest bearing 'Sharia compliant' mortgages, required clothing for females, etc. It's a far cry from the English common law, which was developed on Biblical principles.

This prophetic overlay gives, therefore, a clear distinction from what was believed in the last half of the 20th century. It was known that the Antichrist would someday change the laws and the times, but we had then no clue as to why, or what changing the laws and the times would actually mean. Why would a future strong European military governmental leader, who will demand worship, also want to change the laws and the calendar? The answer is now quite obvious. Who but a Muslim Antichrist would make such demands?

THE ANTICHRIST AND THE FALSE PROPHET IN BOTH THE BIBLE AND IN THE QURAN

In the end times, God will allow a rebellion against Himself led by Satan's man, the *Antichrist*, a/k/a the *Mahdi.* In His infinite wisdom, planning, and perfect timing, God will allow mankind to bring an end to the present age, which will lead to the millennium, a thousand years in which Jesus Christ will rule and reign from the Temple in Jerusalem. For further interest in this subject, refer to *Antichrist: Islam's Awaited Messiah* (Joel Richardson, Winepress Publishing, 2007). Joel Richardson is a pseudonym, taken due to numerous death threats from members of the Muslim community with whom he discussed his book as it was being written. His is a unique book in Christian publishing in which, by going back to Muslim writings in the Quran, the Sunna and Hadith literature, he has developed startling parallels between what the Bible tells us about *"the Beast,"* *"the man of sin," "the man of lawlessness,"* that is, the

Antichrist (I John 2:18) and what Muslim literature says about the *Mahdi*. Richardson's book is groundbreaking in prophetic literature, as there are no other available books that study and contrast Muslim end times predictions *and* Biblical end times prophecies.

Students of the Bible, understand the Antichrist won't be alone when he comes to power. He will be accompanied by a man that Revelation 19:20 calls the "False Prophet," also possessed and empowered by Satan, who will perform *"miraculous signs on his behalf,"* that is, on behalf of, and to build the authority and power of the Antichrist. The False Prophet's signs and astounding acts will deceive the inhabitants of the earth (Revelation 13:14). For example, he will be able to call fire down from the sky (Revelation 13:12). He will have the power to give breath to a statue of the Antichrist, *"so that it could speak and cause all who refused to worship the image to be killed"* (Revelation 13:15). Richardson writes: *"Imagine for a moment, a miracle-working evangelist who is completely possessed by Satan and refuses to take no for an answer at the threat of death. This is exactly what the False Prophet will be."*

Muslim literature and Muslims today also predict that Jesus will return to the earth at the time of what they call the "Last Day," a man whom their prophecies refer to as Isa al-Masih – Jesus the Messiah. But, the similarities end there! Muslims say that upon His return a.) Jesus will deny that He ever claimed to be the Son of God; b.) Jesus will *"espouse the cause of the Mahdi"* and will *"follow him"*; c.) Jesus will serve *"Allah Almighty"*; and d.) Jesus will *slaughter* those on the earth who remain faithful to His words in the Bible. Un huh.

Today a Kafir (infidel, non-Muslim believer) living in an Islamic nation can avoid death and physical persecution at the hands of Muslims by paying a Jizyah (poll) tax, annually. However, Muslim Last Day literature provides that once Jesus returns to earth the Jizyah tax will *no longer* be available, leaving only two options for Christians and Jews: become a Muslim *or* be decapitated. Incredibly, Muslims teach that the returned Jesus will lead an army that will kill tens of thousands of Jews–who are said to be followers of a man they say will be the *Antichrist.* Since the *Antichrist* parallels exactly the *Mahdi,* whom Muslims claim is their *Messiah,* whom do they see as their *Antichrist?*

Muslims, of course, do not perceive the *Mahdi* as the Antichrist, in spite of the obvious parallels and overlaps, and are offended by the suggestion (hence the Joel Richardson death threats). Instead, Muslim predictive literature and Muslims today say that the evil one to come will be a deceiver who will hold great power over the earth, and will be named *ad-Dajjal.* Muslims hold that the *Dajjal* is the false Messiah, or *Antichrist* (*Massih ad Dajjal*). He is described as being blind in one eye; with the word for infidel, "kafir", written between his eyes; and will claim to be divine. Muslims claim that the *Dajjal* will be Jewish, will be followed by Jews and women, and will falsely claim to be Jesus Christ. Thus, both the Bible and the Quran point toward a *coming evil world leader,* though the identity and nature of that person differ sharply, for obvious apparent reasons.

RADICAL ISLAMIC LEADERS HAVE GIVEN THE FINAL WARNING TO AMERICA

Twenty six days after 9/11, Osama bin Laden released the first of many videotapes to follow to al Jazerra, the Arab broadcast system based in Qatar. In it, he praised the 9/11 terrorists, claimed divine approval for 9/11 (*"God Almighty hit the United States at its most vulnerable spot. He destroyed its greatest buildings."*), and warned America there was more to come. He also said:

"As for the United States, I tell it and its people these few words: I swear by Almighty God who raised the heavens without pillars that neither the United States nor he who lives in the United States will enjoy security before we can see it (Muslim victory) as a reality in Palestine and before all the infidel armies leave the land of Mohammad, may God's peace and blessing be upon him. God is great and glory to Islam."

Bin Laden had earlier, in his *Fatwa* (Declaration of War) issued on August 1, 1996 claimed that his supporters *"love death as you love life."* He said that *"these youths know that their rewards in fighting you, the USA, is double than their rewards in fighting some one else not from the people of the book."* Muslims refer to Christian and Jews as being "People of the Book". He quoted Muhammad as saying *"so when you meet in battle those who disbelieve, then smite the necks",* saying that *there is nothing between us (that) needs to be explained, there is only killing and neck smiting."*

In January, 2006 bin Laden, after releasing no public statement for a year, released a new videotape, again through al Jazeera. In it, he made an attention-grabbing claim:

"The new operations of Al Qaeda have not happened not because we could not penetrate the security measures. It is being prepared, and you'll see it in your homeland very soon."

On September 8, 2007 bin Laden included in a rambling speech, full of theological allusions, this invitation:

"To conclude, I invite you to embrace Islam, for the greatest mistake one can make in this world and one which is uncorrectable is to die while not surrendering to Allah, the Most High, in all aspects of one's life – i.e., to die outside of Islam. And Islam means gain for you in this first life and the next, final life. The true religion is a mercy for people in their lives, filling their hearts with serenity and calm."

This "invitation" is more than just an effort to recruit converts to Islam. Before killing a kafir, an unbeliever/infidel, a Muslim *must first invite the kafir to embrace Islam.* Osama bin Laden has now done so, inviting Americans to convert to Islam. In addition, a Fatwa (a religious opinion on Islamic law) is necessary. In Attachment A, you can read the details of the Nuclear Fatwa granted by Nasir bin Hamid al-Fahd, and other Saudi Clerics, allowing the use of weapons of mass destruction to kill up to ten million Americans, sanctioned under Islamic law. Osama bin

Laden's 1996 Fatwa outlines his hatred of America and Israel, and prays for the destruction of both.

RADICAL ISLAMIC LEADERS WILL NOT BE CONCERNED THAT DESTROYING AMERICA WILL CAUSE A WORLD ECONOMIC DEPRESSION OR GREAT HARDSHIP FOR FELLOW MUSLIMS

One argument against the stated Islamic threat to destroy America is that no Muslim would purposely hurt or kill other Muslims. And, since many Muslims would die if America were massively attacked, and since Muslim economies would suffer should America fall, then it won't happen! This argument, which is wrong historically and theologically, and clearly, is contrary to current Muslim plans to conquer the world, regardless of the economic impact of America's destruction.

Historical – Muslims never have shied away from harming other Muslims.

Muhammad died in 632 AD. The third leader to succeed him was asked to resign by a group of Muslims. When he refused, he was killed. The fourth leader, Muhammad's cousin, Ali ibn Abi Talib, was chosen, but opposed by a family member of the slain third leader. After much disputing, by 660 AD the leadership had split between those who followed the third leader after Muhammad (Shiites) and those who followed the fourth leader (Sunnis). In the 14th century, a powerful Sunni leader, Ibn Taymiyah, established the principle that a Muslim could declare other Muslims as infidels, as Kafirs, and kill them. Centuries of bloodshed commenced and continue to date. For centuries, Muslims have been more than willing to kill other Muslims. Proof of this is borne out in newspaper reports from Iraq reporting on about Sunnis and Shiites killing each other. For example, a Sunni suicide bomber walked into a crowd of 1,000 mourners at the funeral of a Shiite leader in Pakistan recently, killing 30 and wounding 60. The terrorist and the

35

dead and wounded were all Muslims, just from the two branches of Islam.

This centuries old division in Islam is prophetically important. The prophet Daniel provides prophetic details as to the final or fourth great world empire. A major prophecy is that the fourth empire is in two manifestations–first the iron legs (Roman Empire – which beginning in the 3rd Century AD was led by two Emperors – East and West – hence the two legs of the prophecy) and then the two iron and clay feet (Revived Roman Empire). Daniel foretells: *"Just as you saw that the feet and toes were partly of baked clay and partly of iron, so this will be a divided kingdom; yet it will have some of the strength of iron in it, even as you saw iron mixed with clay"* (Daniel 2:41). Thirty years ago that meaning was subject to many interpretations, be it western/eastern Europe; free Europe/Communist Europe; Catholic Church/Orthodox Church, etc. But, today, we can more readily perceive that as strong as the Muslim move to conquer the world will be, it will be driven by the *two* divisions of Islam, the *Sunnis and the Shittes*, just as God disclosed through Daniel. Both branches of Islam will follow the powerful Antichrist/Mahdi, arising from and ruling over the two legs/feet of the revived Roman Empire.

Daniel was specific with regard to how the Fourth World Empire would not get along internally: *"And just as you saw the iron mixed with baked clay, so the people will be a mixture and will not remain united, any more than iron mixes with clay."* (Daniel 2:43). Daniel's prophecy may remind you of the prophecy in Genesis that the world has seen fulfilled for many centuries: *The angel* (speaking to Hagar, the mother of Ishmael, the father of the Arab nations) *added, "I will so increase your descendants that they will be too numerous to count." The angel of the LORD also said to her:*

"The angel of the LORD also said to her "You are now with child and you will have a son. You shall name him Ishmael, for the LORD has heard of your misery. He will be a wild donkey of a man; his hand will be against everyone and

36

everyone's hand against him, and he will live in hostility toward all his brothers. (Genesis 16:10-12)

Daniel also prophesied that the Fourth World Empire *"will be different from all the other kingdoms and will devour the whole earth, trampling it down and crushing it".* (Daniel 7:23). The Babylonian, Medo-Persian and Grecian empires were not primarily theologically based. They all had their own 'small g' gods, of course, but the primary reason for their drive to conquer was acquisition of land and treasure. On the other hand, the Fourth World Empire in the end times will be different from those which came before. Jihadists are convinced their role is to conquer the world, not for treasure or lands, but for Allah, killing all who don't follow Allah. Daniel's prophecy also tells us that this final world empire, which will be *"waging war against the saints and defeating them"* (Daniel 7:21) will be destroyed by *"one like the son of man, coming with the clouds of heaven...given authority, glory and sovereign power...his kingdom is one that will never be destroyed"* (Daniel 7:13-14).

Dr. Gunnar Heinsohn of the University of Bremen has estimated that since 1948, over 11,000,000 Muslims have been killed by other Muslims in various wars and uprisings (*Front Page Magazine,* October 8, 2007). It is estimated that over seventy Muslims died in the collapse of the Twin Towers, the Pentagon attack, and on the four airplanes on September 11, 2001. Countless thousands of Muslims have died in the over 11,000 Jihadist terrorist attacks across the world in the last few years, since 9/11.

THEOLOGICAL – The Islamic mindset is: if a Muslim is dwelling in nations or areas along with Kafir, then their death, along with the infidels, is permitted. Since 9/11, tens of thousands of Americans have converted to Islam (*New York Times,* October 21, 2001). A similar phenomenon has occurred in Europe (*London Times,* January 7, 2002). A large majority, by some estimates as high as 85%, of American Muslim converts have been in the inner city, with close to a half-million in the Chicago area and close to one million in

New York. As large as these numbers may be, Islamic law allows these Muslims to face death, along with the Kafir infidels with whom they dwell.

The Jihadist mindset and unfailing commitment is to replace every single national government in the world with a Muslim government, with Sharia law replacing all former national laws. *"Muslim nations are very special because they have a command from Allah to rule the entire world and to be over every nation in the world."* (Mawlana Abul Ala Mawdudi, quoted by Dr. Gabriel, *Islam and Terrorism*).

TO CONQUER THE WORLD – Given Jihadists' ultimate, unshakeable commitment to conquer the world, and knowing that bringing America to its knees will mean the rest of the nations of the world will fall like ripe plums into Muslim hands, no student of history, or of Islam, seriously thinks there will be any hesitancy against destroying America, even if it means the death of Muslims living in America. That concern would rank twelfth on a list of ten reasons not to bring down the nation Jihadists call *"the Great Satan"*.

ECONOMIC IMPACT - The United States buys almost three quarters of a trillion dollars ($738,000,000,000.00) more from overseas suppliers than it sells in exports (balance of trade deficit). Overall, the US buys about $ 2.5 Trillion dollars in goods and services produced by the other nations of the world every year. With the United States gone as the world's economic engine, the remaining nations of the world will, in varying degrees, immediately suffer from staggering financial depression. The financial credit crisis that started in mid-September, 2008 in the United States, soon reverberated in stock markets across the world. America's stock markets declined by 38% in 2008, but most of the world's major stock markets fell by closer to 50% for the same period. The destruction of the American engine of enterprise will bring down markets, corporations, and individuals worldwide.

Why would radical Muslim leaders want to bring such economic misery on the rest of the world? First, it won't affect those individual Muslim conspirators all that much, as they either have sufficient financial resources to suffer through the worldwide depression or, alternatively, they will live aesthetic lives in the caves of Pakistan and Afghanistan, not requiring huge financial resources. Secondly, and most important, *they won't care.* Jihadists have a singular goal that they believe their Allah has demanded of them. They also believe that their Allah has provided to them the weapons to accomplish that singular goal. The Jihadists will readily conclude that, if it is necessary to destroy the world's richest consuming nation (and also the world's only military superpower), in order to conquer the rest of the nations in the world for Islam, so be it. If one thinks like the Jihadists, one understands their actions, past, present, and future, from the belief that Muhammad has demanded:

"I command by Allah to go fight all the people of the world until they confess there is no God but Allah, and I am his messenger..." (From the Hadith recorded by Sahih Al-Bukhari, *Islam and Terrorism,* Dr. Gabriel).

RADICAL ISLAMIC LEADERS ARE NOW ONLY BEING RESTRAINED BY GOD'S PROTECTIVE HAND, WHICH HE CAN LIFT AS HE CHOOSES

Why didn't al Qaeda attack America after 9/11 through the balance of the Bush administration? Some will claim, and possibly correctly, that American intelligence stopped terror plots. Others may say, as bin Laden claims, that al Qaeda is just waiting for the right time to deliver either another major attack, or more likely, its final attack. Whatever those claims may be, the scriptural truth is that God decides when nations suffer calamities, just as He decides when nations are blessed.

More than 200 years ago, Benjamin Franklin stood before the Constitutional Convention and said, *"I have lived,*

Sir, a long time and the longer I live the more convincing proof I see of this truth: that God governs the affairs of men. If a sparrow cannot fall without His notice, is it possible that an empire can rise without His aid?" Franklin was obviously making reference to Jesus' words: *"Are not two sparrows sold for a penny? Yet not one of them will fall to the ground apart from the will of your Father. And even the very hairs of your head are all numbered. So don't be afraid; you are worth more than many sparrows".* (Matthew 10.29-31).

Why is America still standing? Only by the grace of God. How much longer will it stand? Only God knows, but He has given us insight through His prophetic Word. We now turn to that prophetic Word.

Chapter Four

THE MYSTERY OF THE IDENTITY OF THE DAUGHTER OF BABYLON

"The woman was clothed in purple and scarlet, and adorned with gold and precious stones and pearls, having in her hand a gold cup full of abominations and of the unclean things of her immorality, and on her forehead a name was written, a mystery, "BABYLON THE GREAT, THE MOTHER OF HARLOTS AND OF THE ABOMINATIONS OF THE EARTH." (Revelation 17:4,5 NASB)

In 2003, Dan Brown turned the literary world upside down with *"The Da Vinci Code."* The novel fictionalized a world in which ancient clues, long hidden, are progressively discovered by his compelling characters, revealing the future. Millions were fascinated as they followed the clues hidden in ancient buildings, statues, frescoes and crumbling writings. Brown pretended to reveal long-hidden conspiracies, such as a supposed secret society, the Priory of Sion, allegedly from the eleventh century. But he admitted in later interviews, what others quickly discovered, that the core conspiracy in his book wasn't ancient or long hidden at all, but instead a hoax created in 1956 by Pierre Plantard. It's fascinating reading, but pure fiction.

What if, on the other hand, there are clues that have been hidden for 3,500 years, in ancient writings, penned by several different writers who lived centuries apart, in some cases, which read together, reveal future events, with 100% accuracy? Well, those clues would be worth studying, would they not? In this Chapter we will examine the prophetic end times verses of the world's best selling book to discern what the Author has revealed about the future, and specifically, the future of the world's only superpower.

Besides referring to the end times nation that is rich and powerful, and that will fall in a moment as *"The*

Daughter of Babylon," the Bible also refers to this end times nation as: BABYLON THE GREAT. Those capital letters are as the words are set forth in Revelation 17:5. John refers to Babylon the Great as *"a mystery."* In Revelation 14:8 we read: A second angel followed and said, *"Fallen! Fallen is Babylon the Great, which made all the nations drink the maddening wine of her adulteries."* Then in Revelation 17:1-2: *"One of the seven angels who had the seven bowls came and said to me, 'Come, I will show you the punishment of the great prostitute, who sits on many waters. With her the kings of the earth committed adultery and the inhabitants of the earth were intoxicated with the wine of her adulteries'* (referring three verses later to *"a mystery, BABYLON THE GREAT"* [capitalization in original]).

Why did God give the word "mystery" to John to apply to the identity of the future nation described several times in scripture as the Daughter of Babylon? First, what is a *'mystery'*? The Greek word *mysterion* (from the root word *muo* –to shut the mouth) is used 25 times in the Bible, always translated in English as a *"mystery."* A dictionary definition is *"anything that is kept secret or remains unexplained...something that arouses curiosity or speculation...a novel, short story, play or film whose plot involves (an event) that remains puzzlingly unsettled until the very end'."* Interestingly, dictionary definitions of the word mystery also refer to the mysteries of the events of the life of Christ, such as the Mysteries of the Passion, and of the Sacraments. Jesus also used the word: *"Unto you it is given to know the mysteries of the kingdom of God: but to others in parables; that seeing they might not see, and hearing they might not understand."* The Bible refers to several mysteries, including the mysteries of salvation (which the angels desire to look into – I Peter 1:12), the mysteries of providence (Romans 1:19-20) and the mystery of the gospel (Ephesians 6:19).

It's fair to say that for centuries, the scholars who studied the verses prophesying a future 'Daughter of Babylon,' were not only not in agreement as to the identity of the Daughter of Babylon, but also *not* in agreement that all of the verses mentioning her, referred to the same institution, nation or person. That's understandable. The writer of a good mystery drops clues throughout the play, some meaningful, as it turns out later, some down rabbit trails leading nowhere, but calculated to keep the reader from knowing the end *too soon*. But as the end of the play nears, secrets are revealed, story lines converge, important clues are confirmed as such, and the mystery is solved.

Agatha Christie was a master at dropping clues. In *Murder on the Orient Express,* Hercule Poirot discovers in the victim's train compartment a monogrammed handerkerchief, a pipe cleaner, and a button from the Conductor's uniform. He studies bits of a burned letter. A scarlet kimono, previously seen on a woman retreating down the train's passage, shows up in Poirot's own luggage. The twelve stab wounds on the victim vary by intensity, some by right handed and some by left handed persons. By the end of the story, many of the noises and clues are found to have been unrelated to the murder, which turns out to have been caused by *all* of the suspects. Applause. The mystery was solved by Poirot's proper analysis of the correct clues.

With the occurrence of events in our world, the Lord is showing us more and more of the solution to the "*mystery*" of the identity of the Daughter of Babylon. The identity of the players on the end times stage, how they interact, and when, are all elements of the mystery that God is now progressively revealing in our time. Since 9/11 the world has become aware that what was previously seen as a pesky fringe group of radicals blowing up nightclubs in far away lands, is in reality, instead, a major player on the stage for the drama of the end times. Who could have known?

Paul wrote this concerning Biblical mysteries eventually revealed:

"Now to him who is able to establish you by my gospel and the proclamation of Jesus Christ, according to the revelation of the mystery hidden for long ages past, but now

revealed and made known through the prophetic writings by the command of the eternal God, so that all nations might believe and obey him—to the only wise God be glory forever through Jesus Christ! Amen." (Romans 16:25-27)

"Even the mystery hidden from ages and generations, but now is made manifest to his Saints." (Colossians 1:26)

Thus, Biblical mysteries don't stay mysteries forever. Before the curtain comes down, as in any good staged mystery, all clues finally make sense, all secrets are revealed and the mystery is, finally, explained. A good mystery, then, is one which is *"puzzlingly unsettled until the very end."* No one likes watching a mystery movie and having it ruined by someone who blurts out the secret of the ending in the beginning. Likewise, the mystery of the identity of the Daughter of Babylon has been reserved for the end times, as the other events that must occur before the end comes, have begun to occur. Many American Christians, upon reading this book, will be surprised to learn that what they had understood for many years–that America is nowhere found in scripture–is, in fact, wrong. God has given us as *clues* to His *"mystery"* as to the identity of the Daughter of Babylon. These clues tell us that America occupies a predominant position in Biblical end times prophecies, only now being increasingly revealed as we near the end. Like any good mystery.

THE FINAL WORLD WAR WILL INCLUDE ALL NATIONS

There is no mystery about which nations will be involved in the world's final war. The final battle of human history, which John referred to in Revelation 16:16, will take place at Armageddon. Zechariah tells us in 12:3 that *"On that day, when all the nations of the earth are gathered against her, I will make Jerusalem an immovable rock for all the nations. All who try to move it will injure themselves."* Look again at that prophecy. The final world war against

44

Israel will involve not *some* of the nations of the world, but *all* the nations of the world. If that battle were today, that would *include* the United States of America, Israel's historically closest ally. But . . . America invading Israel? Not going to happen. So how will such a battle shape up? If America is off the playing field, and the other nations of the world have a common religion (Islam) and a common goal (the destruction of Israel and conquering the whole world for Allah), the invasion of Israel by all of the (remaining) nations of the world makes perfect sense. As we near the time of the fulfillment of these prophecies, the solution to *the mystery of Babylon* is becoming more obvious, sad to say.

How many times have we heard a Christian say, 'well, of course, America's not mentioned in the Bible.' It is true that the current name of the United States of America does not appear in the Bible. The nation was named, after all, after the two continents of America, which were named after Amerigo Vespucci, who wasn't even born until 1454 AD, thirteen centuries after the New Testament was written. The Lord could have named the nation centuries before it was named. He named Cyrus, the future founder and king of the Persian Empire, two hundred years before he was born. But had He revealed America's name centuries ago, the very act of doing so could have easily warped the naming decisions, not only for our nation, but for others, which came along later in time. The real question, therefore, is not is America 'named' in the Bible, but instead, is America designated, portrayed or described in prophetic sections of God's Holy Word?

Our God knew from the beginning of time what He would do in the world during the Day of the Lord, the End Times and the Last Days. The varying roles of many nations in the world during those last days are described in considerable detail in both the Old and the New Testament.

WHAT NATIONS ARE NAMED IN SCRIPTURE?

So, which current day nations are described in scripture, without any doubt? Israel, of course, is the predominant nation in the last days. The final battle, the battle of Armageddon, is fought in Israel, as the nations of the world descend on her to try and destroy this pesky little nation, once and for all (Rev. 16:16). It doesn't work out well for them, of course, as the Lord Jesus will return and smite the invading nations, felling them with one word (Rev. 19:21). But, more to come on that in greater detail later.

China is shown as an invading army of two hundred million (Rev. 9:16 and 16:12–"*the Kings of the east*"). When Revelation was written, the total population of the world was only a fraction then, of the number of soldiers in this prophesied future mega-army. No other nation in the world then, or for that matter now, could mount such an army, except China's reserve armies today.

Russia is also clearly described in prophecy. Ezekiel in 38:2 prophecies that a future nation will join with others in a pre-Armageddon invasion of Israel, which will be considered in depth, in Chapter 5. In addition, the nations of the revived Roman Empire, that is, modern day Europe, are set forth in Daniel 7 and Revelation 12, 13 and 17. The role of the European Union in the end times is addressed in chapter 12. Other nations, such as Syria, Persia (Iran), Libya, Egypt, and others, are also mentioned in end times prophecies.

But, what about America? It is inconceivable to think that the most important single nation in the world would not be included in end times prophecies, with details as to what that nation would face in the last days. Would the Creator of the universe, who knows all things from the beginning to the end, not foretell that in the final days, in which He brought back Israel into the Promised Land, a nation would exist that is the world's most important military, financial and cultural power? Of course, He knew America before He caused her to be born, just as He knows each of us before we are birthed

(Psalm 139). He would not ignore such a nation in his prophesied narrative of what will happen in the last days.

As we enter further into the end times, we can rationally conclude, that America has a major, even a pre-imminent role in the events of the last days, before the return of Christ. Sadly, though, America's role appears to come to an abrupt end *before the final years* of the end times. So, surprising as it may seem to some, the Author of the Word has provided to us a great deal of detail about the United States of America in the end times. Frankly, that's what we would expect from the Creator of the Universe. Daniel described God, as *"the revealer of mysteries"* and *"a God in heaven who reveals mysteries"* (Daniel 2:28 and 29).

The following prophetic verses all deal with a nation described directly and implicitly as the *"Daughter of Babylon"* or *"Babylon the Great."* For Bible scholars, and those interested in studying the Hebrew and Greek words used in the original source documents, a Hebrew and Greek Annotation of selected Daughter of Babylon verses can be found at www.endofamericabook.com.

These are the prophetic verses describing the end of a rich and powerful end times nation:

Psalm 137:8
Isaiah 13; 21:1-10; 47 and 48
Jeremiah 50 and 51
Zechariah 2:7
Revelation 17 and 18

These prophecies total 223 verses–223 amazing verses.

Some, who have seriously studied these prophetic verses, have concluded they refer to events to take place on the site of ancient or historical Babylon, even concluding that *the ruins* of Babylon, which Saddam Hussein partially restored, will be the Daughter of Babylon. Some, on the other hand, have interpreted these verses as referring to an end times Church or denomination. In the years since the 17th century authors interpreted the verses, primarily those from Revelation, as referring to the Roman Catholic Church. The clash of interpretations is quite stark; do these end times verses, yet unfulfilled on their face, refer to modern day Iraq, do they describe modern day America, or is there another possible nation to which they could refer?

So, let's examine the prophetic verses centered on the *Daughter of Babylon*, in light of the whole of scripture, and compare them with current events. If there is a match, and no other scriptures are contradicted, then we should pay close attention. Really close attention.

IDENTITY CLUE 1:
IS THE DAUGHTER THE SAME AS THE MOTHER?

It may seem apparent, but no, the daughter is not the same as the mother. If the Lord intended these *'Daughter of Babylon'* verses to be understood as synonymous with Babylon, he could have easily omitted the modifying phrase "Daughter of" and just given us 'Babylon', instead. Clearly, we are meant to understand that the *Daughter of Babylon* has many characteristics of ancient Babylon, but is not, in fact, *the same* as historical Babylon, nor, for that matter, modern day Iraq, which contains the rubble of ancient Babylon, as we shall see in some detail as we look at the detailed descriptions of this end times prophesied nation.

The Bible makes this point even clearer by including in Jeremiah: *"Your mother will be greatly ashamed, she who gave you birth will be humiliated"* (Jeremiah 50:12). The word Jeremiah used, which is translated in the NIV as *"ashamed,"* and in the KJV as *"confounded"* (#954 *buwsh*), also has the meaning of *"paleness and terror"* and *"to men overwhelmed with unexpected calamity"* and to be *"troubled, disturbed, confused."* (Gesenius Lexicon). These words would certainly describe the reaction of America's *"mother"* and closest ally if its descendent nation were destroyed.

There is no recorded "mother" of ancient Babylon, as the nation was settled by early descendents of Adam and Eve, who, under the leadership of Nimrod, tried to reach up to heaven with their towers, and were scattered by dispersion according to language. If the Daughter of Babylon verses are actually about ancient Babylon, why does one of those verses refer to a non-existent *"mother"* of Babylon, as there is no recorded history of a "mother of Babylon"? Interpreting the verses as referring to the Catholic Church or, as one writer conjectured – to "corrupt Christianity" in the last days, is fraught with problems, as there is no "mother" of the Church in the world today who would be distressed by its fall.

On the other hand, if these prophetic verses in reality refer instead to the United States of America, is it possible for one to identify a *"mother"* of America, who will be ashamed and humiliated at what happens to that nation's "daughter"? Not a very tough question, right? This nation's Revolutionary War was not fought against any other nation except America's *"mother,"* the nation of Great Britain. When history is reviewed, only a handful of nations can be said to have a *"mother."* The United States is obviously one of those nations.

When the Lord gave to Jeremiah the revelations that he recorded, and we read, in the Book of Jeremiah, He only caused Jeremiah to use the phrase *"Daughter of Babylon"* twice, once in Jeremiah 50:42, and the second time in Jeremiah 51:33. This is not a casual or accidental use of the name. A close study of Chapters 50 and 51 reveals 99 verses, almost all of which could not apply to ancient Babylon, but do apply to the nation Jeremiah refers to as the *Daughter of Babylon.*

Jeremiah refers to Nebuchadnezzar, an ancient King of Babylon, 35 times out of the 90 times he is mentioned in the full Bible. The name of Nebuchadnezzar is dropped into Jeremiah only twice – in 50 (50:17) and 51 (51:34). The use of the name might cause some to initially think Jeremiah's use of the ancient name in these two end times chapters may mean they are really about the past, not the future. Like a good mystery, though, both references to Nebuchadnezzar are included in statements about how Israel had been attacked in the past. Historically true. But, neither verse says the prophecies in Chapters 50 and 51 are *about* ancient

Babylon. On the contrary, a close study of the 99 verses confirms they are for the future end days. Jeremiah 50:40, for example, states that the Daughter of Babylon will be destroyed "*as God overthrew Sodom and Gomorrah.*" That type of dramatic destruction never happened to ancient Babylon, but it will happen to the Daughter of Babylon.

IDENTITY CLUE 2:
"THE HAMMER OF THE WHOLE EARTH"

"*We will use nuclear weapons whenever we feel it necessary to protect our vital interests.*" United States Secretary of Defense Robert S. McNamara, September 25, 1961

Jeremiah 50:23 describes the nation in Chapter 50 and 51 that he labels the Daughter of Babylon as "*the hammer of the whole earth .*" That's quite a phrase. God also says the Daughter of Babylon is His "*war club*" with which nations and kingdoms are destroyed. (Jeremiah 51:20). To how many nations could the phrase "*hammer of the whole earth*" have ever applied? Well, certainly, the original Babylonian empire, the Medo-Persian empire, the Grecian empire, the Roman empire, the British empire, the Napoleonic empire, the Prussian empire, and others. At one point in time, each of these empires, and some other smaller empires, to varying extents, could have been described accurately as "the hammer" of at least a part of the earth.

What is the one unifying truth about each one of these "*hammers of the whole earth*"? It's a relatively important fact. None of these empires is still an empire, in any sense of the word 'empire'.' Does anyone in the world today look at France or Italy or England, for example, as a major world power which could pound their "*hammer*" and significantly affect the other nations of the world? Since Revelation 17 and 18 have not yet been fulfilled, they must apply to either a current or future "superpower" or "hyper power," but not a *past* empire, because the prophesied events of Revelation 17 and 18 have not yet been fulfilled in any nation. John wrote in Revelation 17:18, in relation to Babylon the Great, *"The woman you saw is the great city that rules over the kings of the earth."* That's a superpower.

Since, as we have seen, we are the generation that has witnessed the re-budding of Israel, the prophesied fig tree (Matthew 21:18-32), the Daughter of Babylon events are infinitely more likely to occur *in our generation,* rather than, say 200 years from now. That would be several generations after the passing of the generation that saw Israel brought back miraculously, to its God-given land. Therefore, it may be legitimately assumed that the Daughter of Babylon prophecies are for our times, the times of a re-born State of Israel. Apart from America, is there any other nation, any other nation, on the entire planet, which you could label as *"the hammer of the whole earth,"* without causing people to snicker? France can't control its own streets. The Soviet Empire is no longer. If one were to opine that the Daughter of Babylon is, in reality in our times, a reference to a restored city on the site of ancient Babylon, concluding then that those restored mud and brick buildings are really what Jeremiah meant when he described the *"hammer of the whole earth,"* would not be a currently defensible position. Neither the Vatican nor any other Christian denomination has a military budget. No Church or Christian denomination could conceivably be described today as *"the hammer of the whole earth".*

America has been spending every year, over $700 Billion Dollars (that's over half a trillion dollars), for military purposes, including expenditures in Iraq. America spends 40% of what the rest of the world, in total, spends every year for military purposes. More importantly, America spends 80% of all funds spent by all nations on military research and development. Thus America's capability to hammer an enemy is a gap which grows larger every year. No other nation is now even close to American military spending. America today has 850 military bases located in various parts of the world. That's *850.* How many military bases does

China have outside of China? How many does Russia have? Or any other nation?

When God revealed through Daniel (Daniel 2), that there would be four world empires, with the fourth empire coming in two phases, the last in the end times, He made no mention of the *"hammer of the whole earth"* reigning at the *same time* as the revived Roman Empire. Not there. What may we conclude from this? The *"hammer of the whole earth"* will not be around to assert its powerful title and position; otherwise, how could the two legs of Daniel's statute lay claim to being a world empire in the end times if it existed along with a competing *"hammer of the whole earth"*? We can legitimately conclude that the Daughter of Babylon, an end times world superpower, according to the Word of God, will be *gone* from the world stage *before* the fourth world empire based in Europe arises, and from which comes its leader, the Antichrist. From a timing viewpoint, this means that waiting for the Antichrist to become known *before* fleeing the Daughter of Babylon would be foolish, and would not be a correct analysis of the timing of prophecy.

What is most striking about these prophecies is not that in the end there will be a nation seen by the world as *"the hammer of the whole earth."* What grabs one's attention is that God tells us this world superpower with military authority over the earth will, at some point, be instantly destroyed. Not in a five year, lingering war; not in a several month conflict; not even destruction over several days, but instead in a single day, in an hour, in a moment. *"How is the hammer of the whole earth cut asunder and broken? How does Babylon become a desolation among the nations?"* (Jeremiah 50:23) *"Babylon is suddenly fallen and destroyed."* (Jeremiah 51:8 a) *"Therefore, shall her plagues come in one day, death and mourning...?"* (Revelation 18:8). *"For in one hour your judgment has come"* (Revelation 18:10) *"In one hour such great wealth has been brought to ruin"* (Revelation 18:17). *"In one hour she has been brought to ruin"* (Revelation 18:19) *"But these two things shall come to thee in a moment in one day, the loss of children, and widowhood."* (Isaiah

47:9a – KJV). In the history of the world, how many world empires or nations have been totally destroyed, in one day, in one hour, in one moment?

America's power position as *"the hammer of the whole earth"* extends to more than military power. America tells other nations what to do and how to do it. For example, America forced the UBS AG Bank in Switzerland to close all of the offshore accounts in the Swiss Bank held by U.S. citizens, as part of an IRS *"tax investigation which challenges Switzerland's famous banking secrecy laws."* (Reuters, January 9, 2009). The U.S. was able impose its will and force this traditionally independent country to act, even though Switzerland has maintained its banking activities in a strictly confidential manner, for *centuries*. As set forth in detail in Chapter 8, America has been instrumental in the change in leadership of a number of foreign nations. A fair analysis would have to conclude that America is by far the only real candidate for the position of *"hammer of the whole world."*

Who else thinks that America is the *"hammer of the whole earth"*? Here are the words of Osama bin Laden from a videotape released on September 8, 2007:

"To preface, I say: despite America being the greatest economic power and possessing the most powerful and up-to-date military arsenal as well; and despite it spending on this war and its army more than the entire world spends on its armies; and despite it being the major state influencing the policies of the world, as if it has a monopoly on the unjust right of veto; despite all of this, 19 young men were able – by the grace of Allah, the Most High- to change the direction of its compass."

IDENTITY CLUE 3:
A LATTER DAY NATION

"Behold, the hindermost of the nations shall be a wilderness, a dry land and a desert." (Jeremiah 50:12 (b) – KJV). It was only about 500 years ago that the new world was discovered by the 'civilized world.' And it's only been

about 230 years since our founding fathers declared that we were a separate nation. In the approximate 6,000 years of recorded human history, such a short period of existence would qualify as "hindmost" or "hindermost." We've been in existence as a nation less than 5% of recorded human history. European, Middle Eastern or Asian cities all have ancient buildings in which humans have lived and died for *millennia*. America is quite clearly the 'new kid on the block.'

The dictionary defines 'hindermost' as 'a variant of hindmost; farthest to the rear; last.' (American Heritage Dictionary). The Hebrew word used in Jeremiah 50:12, "*achariyth,*" appears 61 times in scripture, translated 31 times as end, and 12 times as latter. In the KJV it is never translated as "least" as does the NIV. The same word, *achariyth,* for example, is translated in Isaiah 2:2 as "last": "*It shall come to pass in the last days.*" In Daniel 10:14 the angel's words are translated, including the same word, *achariyth,* as: "*Now I am come to make thee understand what shall befall thy people in the last days.*" The NIV version of Daniel 10:14, translates *achariyth* as the "*future,*" not the 'least.' Such a translation is not only contrary to other interpretations of *achariyth,* it is also inconsistent with the other Daughter of Babylon verses, which tell us that the nation is the world's preeminent superpower, not the 'least' nation.

What this verse means, without any meaningful contrary interpretation, is that the Daughter of Babylon is not an ancient nation (nor the 'least' of the nations). That, alone, rules out interpreting Babylon, or Iraq, as the object of these prophecies. Also, weakest wouldn't work for "*the hammer of the whole earth.*" Would it be the poorest? The Daughter of Babylon prophecies identify this nation as extremely wealthy : "*The merchants of the earth grew rich from her excessive luxuries*" (Revelation 18:3(b) and "*All your riches and splendor have vanished, never to be recovered*" (Revelation 18:14(b)). So, 'weakest' or the 'poorest' can't apply. This identity clue could hardly apply to the Catholic Church which has been in existence over 2,000 years.

IDENTITY CLUE 4:
A NATION OF WEALTH AND LUXURY

Besides the foregoing prophecies which reveal the Daughter of Babylon will be a nation of great wealth, these verses further address the issue of great national wealth:

"...because ye are grown fat as the heifer at grass..." (Jeremiah 50:12(b)).

"...a sword is upon her treasures..." (Jeremiah 50:37(b))

"You who...are rich in treasures..." (Jeremiah 51:13(a)).

"The woman was dressed in purple and scarlet, and was glittering with gold, precious stones and pearls" (Revelation 17:4(a)).

"Give her as much torture and grief as the glory and luxury she gave herself" (Revelation 18:7(a))

"When the kings of the earth who committed adultery with her and shared her luxury..." (Revelation 18:9(a))

"Woe! Woe, O great city, dressed in fine linen, purple and scarlet, and glittering with gold, precious stones and pearls! In one hour such great wealth has been brought to ruin!" (Revelation 18:16)

"Woe! Woe, O great city, where all who had ships on the sea became rich through her wealth"! (Revelation 18:18(b))

Of all of the varied prophetic identity clues describing the Daughter of Babylon, this element, great national wealth, has the most pointers, as we see from the ten confirmatory verses. If these verses apply in our time, what are the facts?

Which nation is the world's richest? Saudi Arabia? It has significant oil and wealth. Iraq? How much is its oil worth? Iran? China? India?

Nation	Gross National Product
Gross World National Product	48.245 trillion
United States	13.194 trillion
China	2.644 trillion
India	0.087 trillion
Saudi Arabia	0.349 trillion
Iran	0.222 trillion
Iraq	.016 trillion (84th in world)

(Source: International Monetary Fund)

America has an astounding 27.3% of the world's total gross domestic product, with 4.5% of the world's population. This means Americans are 6 to 7 times (600-700%) wealthier than most earthlings. The GDP of the United States is roughly equivalent to the total GDP of every single nation in the European Union, added together.

Again, is there any other country in the world that one immediately thinks of, *except America*, even in the current recession, which so aptly matches the phrase 'wealthy nation'? This identity clue describes in detail a nation of luxurious wealth, but not a Church, even one with appreciable assets. Further, Revelation 18 describes the merchants of the world weeping over the loss of their major trading partner. Why would they weep and wail over the fall of a Church? The Daughter of Babylon is not a Church.

IDENTITY CLUE 5:
A MULTI-ETHNIC "MELTING POT" OF A NATION

Jeremiah writes about the Daughter of Babylon: *"A sword is upon... the mingled people that are in the midst of her"* (Jeremiah 50:37). What nation's people could accurately be described as *"mingled,"* or a population with a mixture of various kinds of people? Many nations have more than one national stock of residents within its borders, but how many have the extraordinary mixture of many nations, many races, and many peoples?

"E Pluribus Unum" is Latin for "Out of Many, One." E pluribus unum is a motto found on the Great Seal of the United States, and adopted by an Act of Congress in 1782. It also appears on the seal of the President and on the seals of the Vice President of the United States, of the United States Congress, of the United States House of Representatives, of the United States Senate, and on the seal of the United States Supreme Court. The motto also is found on most United States currency.

In 1782 J. Hector St. John de Crevecoeur, in Letters from an American Farmer wrote:
"...whence came all these people? They are a mixture of English, Scotch, Irish, French, Dutch, Germans, and Swedes... What, then, is the American, this new man? He is neither a European nor the descendant of a European; hence that strange mixture of blood, which you will find in no other country. I could point out to you a family whose grandfather was an Englishman, whose wife was Dutch, whose son married a French woman, and whose present four sons have now four wives of different nations. He is an American, who, leaving behind him all his ancient prejudices and manners, receives new ones from the new mode of life he has embraced, the new government he obeys, and the new rank he holds. . . . The Americans were once scattered all over Europe; here they

are incorporated into one of the finest systems of population which has ever appeared."

The term "melting pot" came into general usage after it was used as a metaphor describing a fusion of nationalities, cultures and ethnicities in the United States after the term was used in the 1908 play entitled "The Melting Pot", where the immigrant protagonist declared: *"Understand that America is God's Crucible, the great Melting-Pot where all the races of Europe are melting and reforming! A fig for your feuds and vendettas! Germans and Frenchmen, Irishmen and Englishmen, Jews and Russians—into the Crucible with you all! God is making the American."*

Jeremiah has given us a major identity clue when he tells us that the Daughter of Babylon is a melting pot of *"mingled"* people. This clue wouldn't apply to a global Church denomination even if it has members in many nations. The word Jeremiah used is translated as *"mingled"*, which doesn't apply to *scattered* persons in many nations.

IDENTITY CLUE 6:
YOU WHO LIVE ON MANY WATERS

Jeremiah 51:13 provides another critical clue of the identity of the Daughter of Babylon: *"You who live by many waters and are rich in treasures, your end has come, the time for you to be cut off."* Ancient Babylon, a quick review of a map will confirm, did not live by many waters, just the River Euphrates.

All nations have rivers, lakes and streams, but the continental United States has been blessed with an abundance of fresh water lakes (such as the Great Lakes which are themselves 20% of the world's fresh water lakes, the Great Salt Lake and the lakes created by the Corps of Engineers), wide rivers (the Mississippi, the Ohio, the Missouri, the Colorado, the Hudson, the Potomac, the Rio Grande, the Columbia, etc.), and is surrounded by *both* the Atlantic and Pacific Oceans, a location shared only by Canada and a handful of Central American nations.

97.5% of the water on the Earth is salt water, leaving only 2.5% as fresh water, of which over two thirds is frozen in glaciers and polar ice caps. The remaining unfrozen fresh water is mainly found as groundwater, with only a small fraction present above ground or in the air. (*Scientific Facts on Water: State of the Resource*, GreenFacts Foundation). America occupies less than 2% of the world's total land mass (9,629,000 sq. miles vs. 510,072,000 sq. miles- The World Factbook, 2002), yet it has a high percentage of the world's fresh water supply, due to the Great Lakes, and its many rivers, lakes and reservoirs.

Revelation also makes reference to the location of the Daughter of Babylon in relation to the world's navigable waters: *"Every sea captain, and all who travel by ship, the sailors, and all who earn their living from the sea, will stand far. When they see the smoke of her burning, they will exclaim, 'Was there ever a city like this great city?' They will throw dust on their heads, and with weeping and mourning cry out: 'Woe! Woe, O great city, where all who had ships on the sea became rich through her wealth! In one hour she has been brought to ruin!* (Revelation 18:18 and 19). *"...and the merchants of the earth grew rich from her excessive luxuries."* (Revelation 18:3b)

These prophetic verses certainly would apply to the United States. Twenty-two of our states have ports or harbors through which flow the world's goods for our consumption. There are over 400 coastal and inland ports throughout the United States. The U.S. Census Bureau has identified two hundred and forty national trading partners of the United States using those ports. Some of the largest U.S. ports are located on inland waterways, including Houston, Texas; Mobile, Alabama; New Orleans, Louisiana; and Portland, Oregon. The port city farthest from the ocean, Fairmont, West Virginia, is 2,085 miles via an inland waterway. America is truly a nation dwelling on many waters.

The statement in Jeremiah 51:13 that the Daughter of Babylon will *"live by many waters"* is similar to the statement in Revelation 17:1 that Babylon the Great *"sits on many waters."* John later, in Revelation chapter 17, says the Angel who gave John the prophecies that he recorded, also told him *"the waters you saw, where the prostitute (Babylon the Great) sits, are peoples, multitudes, nations and languages"* (Revelation 17:15). By the same symbolism, *"live by"* and *"sit on"* many waters, we have two insights into the Daughter of Babylon: a.) the nation will be physically located *"by many waters,"* and b.) the nation will sit on, or be over in strength and authority, the many nations of the world.

IDENTITY CLUE 7:
CENTER OF WORLD COMMERCE

Revelation Chapter 18 details the many goods which are sold through the Daughter of Babylon's ports. The lengthy list appears in Revelation 18:11-13. Take any one of those goods listed by John two thousand years ago, and ask this question: is any other nation the center for world trade in those commodities, *except* for the United States? Where else does one find exchanges as important as the New York Stock Exchange, the American Stock Exchange, the New York Mercantile Exchange, the New York Cotton Exchange, the Chicago Board of Trade, the Chicago Mercantile Exchange and numerous other exchanges for currency, coffee, sugar, tea, cocoa, soybeans, oats, wheat, cattle, hogs, lumber, diamonds, iron, ivory, marble, spices, cosmetics, steel, tin, zinc, rubber, etc. Those exchanges, through which the world's commerce is passed daily, are all located *in one country.* It's not Iraq, nor in Rome.

Outside of North America, there are 82 stock exchanges, some quite small, such as the Cayman Islands Stock Exchange. Very few have anything close to the influence on the world's economies enjoyed by American exchanges. It has been accurately said that if America's economy sneezes, the world catches a cold. Would American stock exchanges even hiccup if the Bermuda Stock Exchange, or the Kuala Lumpur Stock Exchange or the Lisbon Stock Exchange had a valuation and trading downturn? Not likely. But let the Dow Jones plunge and markets all over the world also plummet. Some economists have advocated *the decoupling of economies*, but the crash in global markets, preceded by the financial crisis in the United States, is a stark reminder of the inter-dependence of the nations of the world, increasing ever since the first and only decoupling occurred when God scattered the residents of the original Babylon.

Through America's ports and harbors flow billions of dollars of products made by others, and sold in America for consumption by Americans. In 2007 the trade deficit was $712 Billion dollars. That's almost three-quarters of a Trillion dollars. Of the total U.S. international waterborne trade, the United States imports approximately 76 percent of value of total trade, and exports 24 percent.

Since the total amount of imported goods flowing onto our shores is over a Trillion dollars, we can understand why the world will be shaken to its core when the world's largest buyer of its goods is no longer buying. Tens of millions of laborers across the world will be quickly thrown out of work, with all that will entail for their national economies. The world's financial superpower, which made the merchants of the world *"rich through her wealth"* (Revelation 18:19), will one day, in a day, no longer be buying their goods. Chapter 10 examines the impact of the fall of the Daughter of Babylon on the world's remaining nations, politically and financially.

In the above quoted verses John refers to that *"great city,"* rhetorically asking *"was there ever a city like this great city?"* Some have wondered why John didn't say "nation" or "country," instead of "city." The issue requires brief examination.

First, all scripture must be considered together, as no verse is of *'private interpretation.'* An examination of the several Daughter of Babylon verses shows that the verses describe a nation, *with numerous cities*. Isaiah warns the Daughter of Babylon that she will no longer be called the *"queen of kingdoms"* (Isaiah 47:5), indicating that she is more than a single community. Jeremiah warns that *"the LORD Almighty, the God of Israel, says: "I will punish the King of Babylon and his land..."* (Jeremiah 50:18), implying that more than a city will fall. Four verses later in 50:23 he notes *"How desolate is Babylon among the nations!"* He then settles the issue by recording God's words to the Daughter of Babylon: " *I will kindle a fire in his cities, and it shall devour all 'round about him ,"*(Jeremiah 50:32b). Later in 51:43 he writes: *"Her cities are a desolation, a dry land, and a wilderness."* That's *"cities,"* plural. Needless to say, a city may have suburbs, but only nations have *"cities."*

What did John have in mind in referring to that *"great city"*? Tonight's broadcast news will use phrases like this: *"Washington strongly reacted today to Moscow's invasion of Georgia...,"* or *"London today took sharp exception to the bombing in Jerusalem..."* Nations are frequently referred to, particularly by other countries, by the name of their capital city, or a leading prominent city. The 'Big Apple,' as New York is known, was one of two primary targets for Al Qaeda on September 11, 2001, in addition to our nation's Capitol. Both Washington, D.C. and New York City are quintessential targets for those who seek America's destruction.

IDENTITY CLUE 8:
THE GREAT VOICE

"Because the Lord hath spoiled Babylon, and destroyed out of her the great voice..." (Jeremiah 51:55)

A distinguishing characteristic of the Daughter of Babylon, Jeremiah tells us, is that this end times nation has a *"great voice,"* albeit a great voice that the Lord will eventually allow to be silenced. The world, particularly since the successful conclusion of the Second World War in 1945, has listened, and listened carefully, to what America has to say. The world's newspapers may not print much of what the Prime Minister of New Zealand says, or report on a news conference held by a member of the British Parliament, but the world's media will certainly relay pronouncements by the "leader of the free world" and frequently, statements made by members of the United States Congress.

Until the advent of immediate global communication, the 'great voice' was relayed through wire transmission and re-printed. Today, within seconds, the President of the United States can be on television screens in every corner of the globe, in homes, offices, stores, restaurants, mud huts, ships at sea, cell phones, in tens of millions of locations. The residents of the world, let's face it, have good reason to want to hear what *"the great voice"* has to say on any given day. What the leaders of America decide, and what America does, have wide and far-ranging impact on the lives of the people of the world. This single nation directly affects the personal economies of the people of the world, as the global downturn that followed the U.S. credit crunch that started in September, 2008, dramatically confirmed. America can change the geopolitical environment in any given area of the world by launching or defending against a military attack. As the world's only remaining superpower, the United States can impose its will on nations, or peoples within those nations. America's voice is 'great', in large part, because of its great wealth and because the nation is the 'the hammer of the whole earth' (Jeremiah 50:23). Another aspect of its status as 'the great voice,' is America's use of its voice as the cultural and entertainment leader of the world.

IDENTITY CLUE 9:
"THEY ARE MAD UPON THEIR IDOLS"

"...for it is the land of graven images, and they are mad upon their idols" (Jeremiah 50:38b)

What is America's currently most watched television program? Is it NBC News? Or 'In Touch Ministries' with Dr.

Charles Stanley? No, and really, it could not have been more appropriately named. AMERICAN IDOL draws more viewers than any other program, week after week. In the most recent season over *624,000,000 votes were cast over the course of the season for all contestants.* In the Old Testament, Israelites persisted in ascribing to hand carved idols powers and abilities that only God retains. In our day, we provide to actors and sports figures, not only mega wealth, we also ascribe wisdom to these human idols. We listen attentively to the political and governmental views of people who are paid to be something they are not. Voters are actually swayed in determining how they vote by what an actor or sports figure may say, or whom he or she may endorse. We are "mad upon our idols."

Our media also lavish mega attention on our idols, devoting countless hours of coverage to actors and sports figures, much of the coverage about how they get into trouble. Some networks admit to trying to include some daily snippet of "news" about Britney Spears, or Lindsay Lohan, or some other troubled famous young actor, co-enabled by the coverage and public attention, into their behavior. Some of the nation's bestselling magazines and weekly newspapers exclusively report on the varied activities of public figures, almost all in the entertainment industry. *People Magazine* recently paid a movie star $4.1 million dollars. To make a movie? No, $4.1 million dollars was paid for the right to publish pictures of her new baby. America's media covered the unfortunate death of singer Michael Jackson non-stop for days on end. We are "mad upon our idols."

If it all ended on our shores, that would be serious enough, indeed, as our idol worship of famous, rich actors and sports figures is not a sign of an emotionally healthy or self-reliant, let alone morally strong, nation. But what we have done as a nation, that is much worse, in the grand scheme of things, is that we have exported our idol worship to large portions of the globe. Today one can watch the latest American situation comedy (laced with repetitive, pervasive sexual content) in nations in most areas of the globe, appropriately translated with the local language. One can watch the latest movie from Hollywood on a silver screen in movie theaters in any developed nation. The only significant exception to access to American 'entertainment' is in predominantly Muslim nations, where this form of 'entertainment' is not available. One of Islam's most effective criticisms of America is that we are sex-crazed and morally reprehensible. If one were to base one's opinion of a nation on its movies and television shows produced about itself and its citizens, then the point is made.

In the balance of verse 51:7, though, Jeremiah gives us a further insight into the influence of the Daughter of Babylon on the people of the world:

"Intoxicating all the earth, the nations have drunk of her wine; therefore the nations are going mad."

If America has gone *"mad upon her idols"* (Jeremiah 50:38c), why would anyone be surprised that the citizens of the world, besotted with the same tainted and corrupt American 'entertainment,' would also be "going mad"? (Jeremiah 51:7d) Why would we be surprised that the people of the world, viewing how we portray ourselves in the entertainment media, hold America in such low esteem?

Those who might assert that the Catholic Church is meant by these verses, due to its portraying Biblical figures and saints in paintings and statues miss the point. For most, these are *symbols* of faith, not *objects* of faith. Unlike ancient Israel, worshippers today don't believe that a statue itself performs miracles. Errant Israelites actually called on their idols to do what only God can do.

How do the Daughter of Babylon's idols, and her idol worshippers, end up?

"Therefore behold, days are coming when I will punish the idols of Babylon; and her whole land will be put to shame, and all her slain will fall in her midst." (Jeremiah 51:47)

IDENTITY CLUE 10:
THE DAUGHTER OF BABYLON MOUNTS UP TO HEAVENS

Here is a fascinating verse, in that it was written over 2,600 years before man perfected flight: *"Though Babylon should mount up to heaven, and though she should fortify the height of her strength, yet from me spoilers come unto her, saith the LORD."* (Jeremiah 51:53)

The King James Version translates the Hebrew word *"alah"* as *"mount up"* to heaven. The New International Version translates the same word as *"reaches"* the sky. The New American Standard translates it as *"ascend to"* the heavens. Until 1961, most persons didn't seriously consider that space flight was possible. In a 1961 speech, President John F. Kennedy changed the nation's focus: *"I believe that this nation should commit itself to achieving the goal, before this decade is out, of landing a man on the Moon and returning him safely to the Earth."*

The Apollo 11 mission was the first manned mission to land on the Moon. Launched on July 16, 1969, it carried Commander Neil Armstrong, Command Module Pilot Michael Collins and Lunar Module Pilot Edwin 'Buzz' Aldrin. On July 20, 1969, Armstrong and Aldrin became the first humans to land on the Moon, while Collins orbited above. No other nation has landed on the Moon. Satellites and space stations in orbits around the earth, yes, but no other nation has *'mounted up'* or *'ascended'* so far into the heavens, except for America, making this identity clue fascinatingly applicable only to one nation. Needless to say, neither Iraq nor any Church has accomplished such a deed.

IDENTITY CLUE 11:
WHERE THE NATIONS GATHER

"...and the nations shall not flow together any more unto him" (Jeremiah 51:44c – KJV)

"...and the nations will no longer stream to him" (Jeremiah 51:44c – NAS)

In either translation, the identity clue verse says that *before* the fall of the Daughter of Babylon the nations of the world *"flow together"*, *"stream to"* this end times nation. The described gathering of nations could only have application to two nations, if the meaning is, at it appears, that the world's nations gather in order to meet with each other in a formal, deliberative sense, not just a commercial or social sense. This is reasonable, in that all nations engage in trade with other nations.

The first possible application would be the League of Nations, which was formed as a result of the Treaty of Versailles of 1919, ending the First World War. The headquarters of the League moved to Geneva, Switzerland, where the first General Assembly of the League was held on November 15, 1920, with representatives from 41 nations in attendance. The League proved incapable of preventing aggression and war in Europe in the 1930s. The onset of the Second World War proved that the League had failed in its primary purpose—to avoid any future world war. Thus, the United Nations replaced it after the war ended in 1945.

On April 25, 1945, the UN Conference on International Organization began in San Francisco. The UN came into existence on October 24. Fifty one countries were signatories. Today, one hundred and ninety one nations are members of the United Nations.

The United Nations Headquarters were constructed in New York City in 1949 and 1950 beside the East River, in an area historically called 'Turtle Bay,' on seventeen acres of land, the purchase of which was arranged by Nelson Rockefeller. The purchase was funded by his father, John D. Rockefeller, Jr., who donated the site to the City of New York for the UN headquarters. Only three nations voted against locating the United Nations headquarters in the United States. France and the United Kingdom were two of the objecting nations. Apart from a suggestion that the United

Nations headquarters would be located in Ontario, Canada, the United States was the only site seriously considered. San Francisco, Chicago and Philadelphia were all then in the running as sites for the UN headquarters.

Therefore, Switzerland could accurately be described as a nation to which the rest of the nations "streamed" or "flowed together." However, Switzerland is quite an unlikely candidate to be the Daughter of Babylon. Somehow the description of the Daughter of Babylon as *"the hammer of the whole earth"* doesn't fit for a nation that has never been in a foreign war, nor ever invaded another nation. No one appears to have seriously suggested that Switzerland is the future nation that Jeremiah, Isaiah, Joel, John and Zechariah all wrote about. In addition, although Church leaders gather in Rome, Jeremiah wrote that *"the nations"* would flow or stream together at the Daughter of Babylon, not prelates.

Thus, we can identify which end times country the Prophets *did* write about. That end times nation would clearly appear to be located on Turtle Bay, on the East River in New York City, where 191 nations of the world regularly *"stream"* and *"flow together."* There is no other such nation.

IDENTITY CLUE 12:
SHE HAS BEEN PROUD AGAINST THE LORD

"...for she has been proud against the LORD, against the Holy One of Israel" (Jeremiah 50:29d)

". . . 'See, I am against you, O arrogant one,' declares the LORD, the LORD Almighty, 'for your day has come, the time for you to be punished." (Jeremiah 50:31)

"And the most proud shall stumble and fall..." (Jeremiah 50:32a)

This clue as to the identity of the future Daughter of Babylon is, admittedly, a bit touchy. Almost every one loves their own country, for obvious reasons. I love America, all the Christians I know love America. If you are an American, you likewise undoubtedly love your country. Gospel concerts frequently include songs praising America. Our home nation is where we live, work, recreate and enjoy life. That's where our loved ones are generally located. If one doesn't love their own country, there must be something wrong with them, we would generally conclude. That analysis and line of reasoning applies when the one who doesn't love his/her country, lives in the same country we live in. Unpatriotic, we say. Ungrateful, we assume. But, as Christians, like Abraham, we need to remember the location of our true home:

"By faith Abraham, when called to go to a place he would later receive as his inheritance, obeyed and went, even though he did not know where he was going. By faith he made his home in the promised land like a stranger in a foreign country; he lived in tents, as did Isaac and Jacob, who were heirs with him of the same promise. For he was looking forward to the city with foundations, whose architect and builder is God." (Hebrews 11:8-10)

But, go outside of the 'it's our country, love it or leave it' syndrome for just a moment. How would we judge a Russian resident of Moscow, for example, who was critical of the nation's high rates of alcoholism or abortion, or who didn't back the nation's invasion of Chechnya? Since we don't live there, and we're not invested in any way, in Russia, so to speak, we could understand the angst against the Russian nation by one of its citizens. Having stepped back then, for this foreign analysis, is there anything about America that could lead *other nations* to conclude we are overly proud or arrogant?

Everyone knows someone who is arrogant. But arrogant persons hardly ever recognize it in themselves. They may feel self confident, or self assured, but they would generally never conclude that they were prideful or arrogant. After 9/11 the nation was flooded with bumper stickers across the land proclaiming THE POWER OF PRIDE. There were lots of things that could have been, and should have been, placed on America's auto bumpers, but trumpeting our *pride* probably wasn't the ideal choice of words.

Isaiah, Jeremiah, and John, in Revelation, all give us an insight into how the Daughter of Babylon manifests her arrogance:

The Message (NavPress) gives us a contemporary interpretation of Isaiah's biting criticism of the nation that Isaiah calls the *"Virgin Daughter of Babylon"*:

"You said, 'I'm the First Lady. I'll always be the pampered darling.'...Well, start thinking, playgirl. You're acting like the center of the universe, smugly saying to yourself, 'I'm Number One. There's nobody but me. I'll never be a widow, I'll never lose my children.'...You were so confident and comfortable in your evil life, saying 'No one sees me.' You thought you knew so much, had everything figured out. What delusion! Smugly telling yourself, 'I'm Number One. There's nobody but me.' (Isaiah 47:7, 8,10)

In the New Testament, John tells us: *"In her heart she boasts, 'I sit as queen; I am not a widow, and I will never mourn.'* (Revelation 18:7)

Seven hundred years before John wrote these words about the Daughter of Babylon the prophet Isaiah wrote: *"You said, 'I will continue forever–the eternal queen! But you did not consider these things or reflect on what might happen."* (Isaiah 47:7) *"Sit in silence, go into darkness, Daughter of the Babylonians; no more will you be called the queen of kingdoms."* (Isaiah 47:5)

Here then is a critical connection between an Old Testament prophet and the Prophet John in the New Testament. Both described the Daughter of Babylon with the same noun – *'a queen'.'* This is relevant because historical Babylon had long faded into history by the time John wrote his words under the power of the Holy Spirit. The prophecies concerning the *coming* Daughter of Babylon were exactly that–prophecies about a future nation, not a nation that no longer existed. These verses tie together the several verses in

Isaiah, Jeremiah, Joel, and Zechariah with the prophecies of John, seven centuries later, and all of them about a future nation called the *"queen of kingdoms."* Is there any nation in our world, in our time that this title fits more appropriately than the world's only remaining superpower, the United States of America? America is the *"queen of kingdoms."*

IDENTITY CLUE 13:
JEWISH POPULATION

"In those days, at that time," declares the LORD, "the people of Israel and the people of Judah together will go in tears to seek the LORD their God. They will ask the way to Zion and turn their faces toward it...Flee out of Babylon; leave the land of the Babylonians," (Jeremiah 50:4-5)

Jeremiah tells us that the timing of the destruction of the Daughter of Babylon, which he sets forth in great detail in Jeremiah 50 and 51, will be *after* Israel is back in the land of Israel (Jeremiah 50:4,5), which officially occurred in 1948. From the dispersion of Israel in 132 AD until 1948 there could be no Destruction of the Daughter of Babylon, because there was no nation of Israel. But not all Jewish people live in Israel. Interestingly, God gives His Jewish people the same warning to flee from the Daughter of Babylon that He gives believers in His Son. Thus, the Daughter of Babylon must have *a significant Jewish population.*

Chapter 13 examines the nine separate calls given by God, through three different writers, both in the Old and New Testaments, to His people, to *flee* from the Daughter of Babylon before its destruction. Seven of God's warnings to flee the Daughter of Babylon are addressed simply to His people. One such warning is in Revelation 18:4, and is linked to the Old Testament's almost identical warnings, thus clearly referring to believers in the Lord Jesus Christ. Two other warnings to flee the Daughter of Babylon, however, stand apart, as specifically addressed to His Jewish people: *"Come, O Zion! Escape, you who live in the Daughter*

71

of Babylon!' (Zechariah 2:7). The warning to flee the Daughter of Babylon couldn't be any plainer than Zechariah's words. God, likewise, in Isaiah 48:20, warns the Jewish residents of the Daughter of Babylon to flee: *"Leave Babylon, flee from the Babylonians! Announce this with shouts of joy and proclaim it. Send it out to the ends of the earth; say, 'The LORD has redeemed his servant Jacob'."*

These calls to flee are highly relevant because of the Jewish population today in America, which exceeds that of Israel and Russia, nations with the second and third largest Jewish populations. The estimate of the Jewish population of the world is 13.2 million. The American Jewish population is 6.15 million, with 5.6 million living in Israel and 800,000 in Russia. How many Jewish residents live in Iraq, historical Babylon? On June 1, 2008 the *New York Times* reported that the Jewish population in Iraq in 1936 was 120,000; that 100,000 moved out of Iraq between 1949 to 1952, most moving to the newly formed State of Israel; and that the Jewish population in Iraq currently is almost zero, estimated by the Jewish Agency of Israel at only seven persons. God's two separate warnings, through Zechariah and Isaiah, to His Jewish people must be meant for the over six million descendants of Jacob who live in the United States, versus the seven individuals who reside in Iraq, ancient Babylon.

In light of the fact that America is the home of a larger number of descendants of Abraham, Isaac and Jacob than even modern day Israel, God's warnings to Zion to flee the Daughter of Babylon, along with the other seven warnings for Christians to flee, certainly appear to be His compassionate call on his people to avoid coming destruction and death. Though there are Catholics of Jewish heritage, the warnings addressed to Jews to flee from the Daughter of Babylon can't really be made to apply to a denomination. On their face they are warnings to flee a nation, not a Church.

IDENTITY CLUE 14:
DEEP WATER PORT NATION

Revelation 18:17-19 gives us a dramatic picture of how the crews of the ships off the coast of the Daughter of Babylon will react when it's destroyed: *"Every sea captain, and all who travel by ship, the sailors, and all who earn their living from the sea, will stand far off. When they see the smoke of her burning, they will exclaim, 'Was there ever a city like this great city?' They will throw dust on their heads, and with weeping and mourning cry out: 'Woe! Woe, O great city, where all who had ships on the sea became rich through her wealth! In one hour she has been brought to ruin!'"*

At least two facts may be deduced from these verses: The merchants of the world would require a *deep water port* in which to bring the world's goods for purchase and consumption by the residents of this great nation. Neither Iraq nor Vatican City have deep water ports. A restored Iraq can not be the nation contemplated in these prophetic scriptures, nor the Catholic Church, but the description is quite apt when applied to port-heavy America.

IDENTITY CLUE 15:
THE KINGS OF THE MEDES WON'T DESTROY
THEMSELVES

Jeremiah gives us a significant clue as to the source of the devastating disaster that will come upon the Daughter of Babylon: *"The LORD has stirred up the kings of the Medes, because his purpose is to destroy Babylon."* (Jeremiah 51:11b). The Bible includes references to the Medes and the Persians (Daniel 5:28 and Esther 1:19). In the 6th century B.C., the Median kingdom included what is now Iran, Turkey, Iraq and surrounding areas. The Medo-Persian empire, a powerful dual empire, lasted until its conquest by Alexander the Great in 330 B.C. The area, for centuries, has been populated by Muslims.

When God removes His protection from the Daughter of Babylon, He will stir up the kings of the Medes to destroy the Daughter of Babylon. Those persons would be from the area that today includes Iran and Iraq. Would the leaders of either nation seek to destroy historical Babylon in today's Iraq? Obviously, Iraq won't seek to destroy itself. Iran and Iraq in 1980-1988 engaged in a debilitating war, but have since that time avoided any further direct wars. In fact, the President of Iran, Mahmoud Ahmadinejad, visited Iraq engaging in friendly discussions with the Prime Minister. That same Iranian President has announced that he intends to *"wipe Israel from the face of the map."* When the world reacted, he suggested that Israel's Jewish population should move to Canada. In June, 2009 Tehran's streets were filled with demonstrators protesting the elections Whichever Muslim President of Iran is in office, its Ayatollahs, who are in ultimate control of Iran, are committed to advancing their global goals.

The Kings of the Medes will also be stirred up by God, along with Russia, and Libya, and others, to invade Israel. How will the Daughter of Babylon react to the invasion? Will the Daughter of Babylon come to the aid of Israel? Why will God stir up of the Kings of the Medes? Jeremiah tells us that God will use the Medes as His 'war club' against the Daughter of Babylon. Why? Answers to all of these questions are set forth in the next Chapter which details what the Daughter of Babylon will do to deserve destruction. A major player in that destruction will be the Medes, today's Iran – a radical Muslim nation, which, not coincidentally, is officially committed to the destruction of Israel and America.

IDENTITY CLUE 16:
A LAND OF ENTERTAINMENT

John tells us in Revelation 18:22 that when the Daughter of Babylon falls: *"The music of harpists and musicians, flute players and trumpeters, will never be heard in you again. No workman of any trade will ever be found in you again."* He then writes that *"By your magic spell all the nations were led astray"* (Revelation 18:23d). Many have observed that Hollywood has the unique talent to 'weave magic spells' in its movies. But that will come to an end, apparently, as Jeremiah tells us that *"Her images will be put to shame and her idols filled with terror"* (Jeremiah 50:2d). Price Waterhouse Coopers projects that Americans will spend $495 Billion on entertainment in 2013. No other nation on earth spends so much of its national treasure on entertaining itself.

IDENTITY CLUE 17:
HISTORICAL BABYLON IS GONE AND WON'T BE BACK

The roots of historical Babylon are given to us in Genesis 10, where we learn that one of Noah's sons, Ham, had a son, Cush, who bore a son named Nimrod. Nimrod, who was the founder of the kingdom of Babylon, is described in scripture as evil, his name meaning, 'rebel against God.' Sorcery and witchcraft are historically traced back as commencing with Nimrod, who decided to build a tower to reach up to God (Genesis 11:4). He is the world's first recorded empire builder, as Genesis 10:10 tells us that *"the beginning of his kingdom was Babel..."* God quickly dispensed with Nimrod's rebellion by causing families and tribes to speak different languages, which led most of them then, to be scattered upon the face of the earth (Genesis 11:9).

God established the first distinct nations, beginning at about 4500 BC in an area in which an early city was known as Babylon. The city grew over time, and by about 1700 BC, flourished under the reign of Hammurabi, who developed the world's first written legal code, pre-dating Moses by about 200 years. Nebuchadnezzar II built Babylon into a magnificent city. Its hanging gardens ranked as one of the Seven Wonders of the World. He ruled for 43 years, until he died in 562 BC. Babylon took Israel captive during his reign in 600 BC, where Israel languished for seventy years. Persia, under Cyrus, conquered Babylon in 539 BC (fulfilling the *'handwriting on the wall'* –Daniel 5), and Babylon remained under Persian rule, until 332 BC, when Alexander the Great conquered Babylon. As rivers swelled and desert sands shifted, Babylon crumbled. Colonial powers carted away Babylon's artifacts. The Germans took the Ishtar Gate, the French grabbed ceramics, and the Turks used the bricks, some of which still bore Nebuchadnezzar's name, to build dams on the Euphrates.

For many centuries, Babylon lay in three mounds of rubble, named by the Arabs as the Babil, the Kasr, and the Amran. The city was eventually overgrown and some questioned if it ever existed. In 1914 German archeologist, Robert Koldewey, excavated the ruins, confirming its historicity. While alive and in power, Iraq's despot Saddam Hussein initiated efforts, in 1985, to re-build some of the mounds of rubble at the location of ancient Babylon into a tourist center, with buildings designed to resemble some of those of ancient Babylon. Hussein built one of his numerous palaces overlooking the site, some 55 miles south of Baghdad.

The International Herald Tribune reported on April 21, 2006, that the *"crumbling mud-brick buildings"* in the area Hussein was trying to re-build in Babylon, *"look like smashed sandcastles at the beach.* The paper observed that Babylon had been *"ransacked, looted, torn up, paved over, neglected and roughly occupied...soldiers had even used soil thick with priceless artifacts to stuff sandbags".* The Mayor of a nearby village, Hilla, told the newspaper that he still had hopes that Babylon could some day have *"restaurants, gift shops, long parking lots...and maybe even a Holiday Inn."* Some unnamed Iraqi officials are quoted as saying they would still like to turn Babylon into *"a cultural center and possibly even an Iraqi theme park."* One Bible commentator wrote recently, that it was *"enormously significant"* that the U.S. had agreed to invest $700,000 (that's thousands, not millions or billions – enough to buy a couple of nice houses) into re-building Babylon as a 'tourist attraction.' He wrote

76

that ancient Babylon would become *"the wealthiest and most powerful city on the face of the planet."* In arriving at this conclusion he has interpreted the Bible's Daughter of Babylon verses as applying to the site of ancient Babylon.

Some sincere, solid expositors of the Word, read the Bible's Daughter of Babylon verses, and insist these verses really mean ancient Babylon, not the Daughter of Babylon, and that ancient Babylon will be re-built, and fulfill the prophetic verses relating to the Daughter of Babylon. In arriving at this conclusion, to be consistent, they must also argue that restored ancient Babylon will become: wealthy (*"you who are rich in treasures"*); powerful (*"the hammer of the whole earth"*); somehow build deep sea ports, though Babylon is no where near the sea; somehow be located on *"many waters,"* though it's only on the River Euphrates; become the world's *"great voice"*; attract the world's great merchants, and become the center of the world's trade and commerce; attract the world's nations who will flow into Babylon and congregate together; switch from possibly the world's oldest nation, to one of the youngest (*"hindermost"*); become a nation of many mixed peoples, instead of the three main people groups now populating Iraq (Sunni, Shihite and Kurd); allow large numbers of Jewish persons to immigrate to Iraq (un-huh); and develop a space program (*"reaching up to the heavens"*). Iraq is rich in oil, but it has not been able to convert that oil to building any meaningful financial, commercial or industrial infrastructure. Even if it began to do so in a meaningful way today (not likely, given the internal disintegration and external threats from Iran), how many decades or centuries would it take to meet the Biblical prophecies of the Daughter of Babylon?

All of these end times prophecies will occur in a town now consisting of a ram-shackle collection of *"crumbling mud-brick buildings,"* the highest hope for which, is that a nearby Mayor wants to see a Holiday Inn built? Not a realistic likelihood for the next century or two.

John, in Revelation 18:9 prophecies that when Babylon falls, *"the kings of the earth...shall bewail her, and lament for her, when they shall see the smoke of her burning,"* and in 18:11, *"the merchants of the earth shall weep and mourn over her; for no man buyeth their merchandise any more."* Obviously, if the entire nation of Iraq, let alone Babylon (whether with a Holiday Inn or even a full theme park), were to fall today, the kings and the merchants of the world would not be shedding tears and mourning over the loss. Even if Iraq stabilized, it would have a long way to go. Ancient Babylon is not the Daughter of Babylon

IDENTITY CLUE 18:
ONLY AMERICA SITS ON THE SEVEN MOUNTAINS/CONTINENTS OF THE EARTH

The Apostle John, in Revelation, describes Babylon the Great as riding on a beast with seven heads, which are described as seven hills or mountains. Through the ages, some have said this is an indicator that Babylon the Great is really the Catholic Church, because it is headquartered in Rome, which has seven hills. Those who have been to Rome, know from personal observation, that the "Seven Hills of Rome" are more like knolls, not what we would normally call a very large hill, and certainly not a mountain. Strong's Exhaustive Concordance shows the Greek word (Greek word number 3735) used in Revelation 17:9, to mean *"mountain,"* and is the same word used in Matthew 4:8 when Satan tempted Jesus on an *"exceeding high mountain."* Thus, the argument that Babylon the Great must be the Catholic Church, because it is based in a town with seven small hills, is more than a questionable application, particularly when the other clues as to the identity of Babylon the Great just don't apply to the Catholic Church.

The attempt to make Babylon the Great a denomination, instead of a nation with cities, located on many waters, with a deep water port, etc., appears to have had its start in a book on the subject, *The Two Babylons,* written by Rev. Alexander Hislop, published in 1858. Hislop claimed the Roman Catholic Church was a Babylonian

78

mystery cult, basing the foundation of his argument almost solely on Revelation's reference to seven mountains which he connected with the fact that Rome was called the 'City of Seven Hills'. For decades since, under Hislop's influence, the Bible's Daughter of Babylon/Babylon the Great prophetic verses have been interpreted to apply to the Catholic Church.

What the reference to Babylon the Great, riding on a beast with seven mountains, could refer to instead, however, is the fact that the earth has seven major land masses, or continents, containing various heights of mountains: Europe, Africa, Asia, North America, South America, Australia and Antarctica, each rising up out of the depths of the seas. Since the Daughter of Babylon/Babylon the Great is described as the end times *'hammer of the whole earth,'* its depiction as riding on, or having power or authority over, the seven continents of the earth makes sense. No prior world empire could make this claim. The Bible only describes one entity, Babylon the Great, as riding upon the back of the whole world. Only America can claim such sweeping influence over the globe. In addition, since Revelation 17:3 and 17:7 refer to Babylon the Great sitting upon or riding on a beast, a dominant position of Babylon the Great is clearly being depicted. Until America's victory over the Axis Powers in 1945, such a description of this relatively new nation would not have been accurate. Since that time, and particularly with the disintegration of the Soviet Union, it has become a recognized reality.

Serious Bible students will note that Revelation 17:9 specifically says *"the seven heads* (of the beast on which Babylon the Great rides) *are seven mountains, on which the woman sits."* The fact that the very next verse tells us *"and there are seven kings,"*, is not a contradiction of the description of the seven heads of the beast as mountains, as verse 9 is quite specific in that regard. Verse ten notes, *"and"* there are seven kings, five of which are fallen, one is and one yet to come. Babylon the Great rides upon the mountains of the continents of the world, not just seven knolls in Rome, and therefore readily applies to America.

IDENTITY CLUE 19:
ANCIENT BABYLON HAS ALREADY BEEN PUNISHED FOR CONQUERING JERUSALEM

Those who argue for the interpretation of the identity of the Daughter of Babylon as being revived Babylon in the same location, in Iraq, must also argue that a modern re-built Babylon will pay for the sins of ancient Babylon for invading and conquering ancient Jerusalem. There is, however, a scriptural problem with the argument. In Jeremiah 21, Judah's King Zedekiah asked Jeremiah what would happen, as Babylon's King Nebuchadnezzar was making war against them. The answer the Lord gave to King Zedekiah, through Jeremiah, was unpleasant, as the Lord informed Israel's King that Judah would be conquered due to its unabated sins. The Lord states that it is He, Himself, who will fight against Judah: *"I myself will fight against you with an outstretched hand and a mighty arm in anger and fury and great wrath. I will strike down those who live in this city—both men and animals—and they will die of a terrible plague"* (Jeremiah 21:5 and 6). The Lord did this through the human agency of an invading Babylon army. Verse 21:7 reads *"After that, declares the LORD, I will hand over Zedekiah king of Judah, his officials and the people in this city who survive the plague, sword and famine, to Nebuchadnezzar king of Babylon and to their enemies who seek their lives."*

Later, after the seventy years of captivity in Babylon, Babylon was dealt with in punishment for what it did to Judah, which God allowed. *"And it shall come to pass, when seventy years are accomplished, that I will punish the king of Babylon, and that nation, saith the LORD, for their iniquity, and the land of the Chaldeans, and will make it perpetual desolations."* (Jeremiah 25:12) God punished ancient Babylon by taking Babylon into captivity for destroying

Jerusalem, which happened to Babylon after Israel served its seventy year sentence in captivity in Babylon. Nebuchadnezzar's son succeeded him, but he was assassinated within two years. Within only twenty-one years of Nebuchadnezzar's death, Babylon was conquered by Persia under Cyrus, just as God had prophesied through Isaiah (Isaiah 45:13).

Therefore, arguing that a modern day Daughter of Babylon arising again in Iraq will be destroyed because ancient Babylon conquered Jerusalem over 2,600 years ago, ignores the fact that God tells us in His inspired Word that He has *already punished* ancient Babylon for what it did to Israel Thus, the argument that the Daughter of Babylon will fall, because of what ancient Babylon did to Judah, won't wash. The Daughter of Babylon will fall because of what the Daughter of Babylon does. The next chapter expands on the sins of the Daughter of Babylon.

IDENTITY CLUE 20
PAST USE BY GOD OF THE DAUGHTER OF BABYLON

Of all of the several identity clues, this may be the saddest. Jeremiah makes a statement about the Daughter of Babylon that at first reads like a compliment: *"Babylon has been a golden cup in the hand of the LORD."* (Jeremiah 51:7a). The most important aspect of this verse is that it applies, in all translations, to a future end times nation in the *past tense.* This nation *has been* a golden cup in the hand of the Lord. A half century ago, America contributed over 80% of all money given to, and used in foreign missionary activities. Modern missions were founded in this nation during the mid 1860's, and then spread around the world. It is without question a true statement that America *has been* a golden cup in the Lord's hand for great good, for many people.

American Christians have written, printed and distributed around the world, millions and millions, hundreds of millions, of Bibles, tracts, commentaries, Bible studies, and other Christian literature, in every known language, and in many languages previously unknown. The Jesus Film Project has shown *The Jesus Film* in every nation, translated into 1,043 languages and dialects, with over 6 billion viewings over the last 30 years, mostly funded by American Christian contributors. Truly, America has been a golden cup in the hands of the Lord.

However, times change, people change, and nations change. America, the formerly great missionary nation, is no longer viewed as holding a golden cup used of the Lord, but by the time of its fall, instead, will be seen in this manner: *"For all the nations have drunk the maddening wine of her adulteries. The kings of the earth committed adultery with her."* (Revelation 18:3). The kings of the earth could hardly have been said to have committed adultery with a Church or denomination.

IDENTITY CLUE 21
HOW MANY NATIONS ARE SWORN TO DEFEND ISRAEL?

The Daughter of Babylon's treachery against Israel is shown dramatically in these verses:

"O Daughter of Babylon, doomed to destruction, happy is he who repays you for what you have done to us." (Psalm 137:8)

"A dire vision has been shown to me: The traitor betrays, the looter takes loot. Elam, attack! Media, lay siege! I will bring to an end all the groaning she caused." (Isaiah 21:12)

"Before your eyes I will repay Babylon and all who live in Babylonia for all the wrong they have done in Zion, declares the LORD." (Jeremiah 51:24)

"May the violence done to our flesh be upon Babylon, say the inhabitants of Zion. "May our blood be on those who

live in Babylonia," says Jerusalem. Therefore, this is what the LORD says: "See, I will defend your cause and avenge you;" (Jeremiah 51:35-36)

Name the nations of the world that have military defense agreements with Israel, under which the nation promises to come to Israel's assistance, "on an urgent basis," if Israel is attacked militarily. That's right, just one nation. The United States of America. Neither ancient Babylon, nor today's Iraq, in which ancient Babylon is located, did or would come to Israel's defense if attacked.

Why is this a truly important identity clue? Chapter Five sets forth in detail what the Daughter of Babylon does, and does not do, when Israel is invaded. If a nation didn't have a military defense agreement with Israel, i.e., all of the nations of the world except for America, then *not* coming to Israel's aid wouldn't be an issue. Only America, of the nations of the world, matches this identity clue. To read what America has promised Israel, in writing, it will do, read the U. S. – Israel Defense Agreement in Attachment B.

DO THESE IDENTITY CLUE VERSES FIT ANY OTHER NATION?

It's worth asking why God would hide clues in several different Old and New Testament books, penned by different writers, and which are not easily discerned? Good question. He could have just had one of the prophets in the Bible write something like:

JEREMIAH 53

1. This is the word the LORD spoke through Jeremiah his prophet concerning the great end times nation, that will come to be known as America, 2. to the daughter of the nation that will be called Britain. 3. The nation that will be the hammer of the whole earth reaching up into the heavens. 4. The nation to whom the nations will flow and gather together.

5. America will be a rich, sumptuous nation overflowing with wealth and splendor, dwelling on many waters. 6. A nation to be one of the youngest of the world's great nations. 7. One nation formed out of many nations, melted together in a pot. 8. The center of the world's trade in fine goods among nations. 9. Speaking its Great Voice to all people in all lands, and carrying its culture, in which it is mad on its worldly idols, to all who have eyes to see and ears to hear. 10. The land that had in the past, been used by the LORD as a golden cup. 11. A land with many descendants of Abraham, Isaac, and Jacob. 12. And a land with deep water ports to, which the merchants of the earth sell and buy their goods. 13. To this nation, here is what the LORD says will be your future.

Besides the fact that Jeremiah has only 52 chapters, could God the Holy Spirit have led Jeremiah, or any other Biblical prophet, to have written such specific words? Of course, He could. He has given us many of the elements in the paragraph above, just without any specific identification of the referenced nations by name. He certainly has the ability to know and reveal the future. As previously noted, for example, He revealed the name of Cyrus, the coming future king of Persia, two hundred years before Cyrus was born. King Josiah was named and identified by God three hundred years before his birth (I Kings 13:2 – II Kings 23:15-18).Why not just lay it all out in one really specific book of the Bible, naming the future names of yet unformed nations, in unmistakable detail?

TIME LINE CLUES

Bible scholars have observed that the Book of Revelation's prophecies are not set forth in a strict chronological order, though chapters 19-22 do progress in order once Jesus returns to earth (Revelation 19:11-16). There is however contained within the Book of Revelation a mini series of prophecy clues, in one part of one chapter, which, like a good mystery, give us an insight into solving the mystery. A revealing lineage of events is found in Revelation Chapter 14. In verse 7 the angel proclaims that *"the hour of His judgment is come"*. The next verse, 14:8, proclaims: *"Fallen! Fallen is Babylon the Great, which made all the nations drink the maddening wine of her adulteries."* Following verse 8, verses 9-12 prophesy details concerning the Antichrist, the mark of the beast, those who worship him, etc. The final battle of Armageddon and widespread deaths accompanying it follow in verses 14:14-20.

Thus, John presents a time line of the end times, in chronological order: a.) God proclaims that judgment time has arrived (not the final Great White Throne Judgment in heaven, but judgment on the earth of earth's inhabitants); b.) Babylon, as a part of that judgment, is destroyed; c.) the Antichrist *follows* the fall of Babylon, as his allied forces take over Europe (Revived Roman Empire nations) under the threat of doing to them what was done to Babylon if they don't agree to his leadership over their nations; d.) the final battle of Armageddon commences; and e.) Jesus returns to earth, to reign. Therefore, even though John was given to write the Book of the Revelation in a manner that was not from chapter 1 through 22 chronological, the above section of prophecy contained within chapter 14 is helpful in unlocking the clues and solving the mystery of the identity of the Daughter of Babylon/Babylon the Great. (See Attachment C for a listing of end times events.)

Jesus was asked why He frequently spoke in parables, speaking in stories, instead of just stating His message straight out? *"The disciples came to him and asked, 'Why do you speak to the people in parables?' He replied, 'The knowledge of the secrets of the kingdom of heaven has been given to you, but not to them. Whoever has will be given more, and he will have an abundance. Whoever does not have, even what he has will be taken from him. This is why I speak to them in parables: 'Though seeing, they do not see; though hearing, they do not hear or understand."* (Matthew 13:10-13). Thus, not everything that God has chosen to reveal in His Word is revealed in a manner that is crystal clear, and not subject to any interpretation. The decision as to what is stated flat out, and what is wrapped in mysteries, is God's alone. Prophetic truth is revealed, but not always in a way that everyone can instantly understand, or even agree as to its meaning.

If the forgoing identity clues are not convincing that America is the future, prophesied Daughter of Babylon, consider a thought Paul gave us in Philippians 3:15b: *"And if on some point you think differently, that too God will make clear to you."* Prayerfully ask Him to reveal his meaning in these verses, for, *"If any of you lacks wisdom, he should ask God, who gives generously to all without finding fault, and it will be given to him"*. (James 1:5)

Chapter Five

WHAT WILL THE DAUGHTER OF BABYLON DO TO DESERVE DESTRUCTION?

"Flee from Babylon!
Run for your lives!
Do not be destroyed because of her sins.
It is time for the LORD's vengeance;
he will pay her what she deserves."
(Jeremiah 51:6)

By this chapter of the book, the reader may have concluded that the prophetic verses describing a future nation labeled by God as the Daughter of Babylon are one of the following:

a.) most likely describing the United States of America;

b.) describing some other nation;

c.) not sure.

For those who have concluded that the Daughter of Babylon is in fact America, the next most obvious question would be, what does this great end times nation *do* to deserve destruction? Further study and analysis of the whole of scripture also seems to indicate we should now be looking for *three* future unfolding events which will *precede* the downfall of the Daughter of Babylon. The three future occurrences that scripture tells us we should be expecting and watching for are:

1.) Israel will be *"at peace"* for the first time since its founding in 1948;

2.) The Daughter of Babylon will severely *persecute* many of God's people;

3.) The Daughter of Babylon will *betray Israel*, by not coming to its defense when a Russian-Muslim coalition invasion of Israel occurs, causing many in Israel to die.

Though all three are prophesied to occur, of these three, only one is stated in scripture as *the reason for the destruction* of the Daughter of Babylon. The common link, between the second and third listed future occurrences, is a precious liquid, i.e., human blood,.the shedding of innocent human blood. Chapter Ten examines the scriptural significance of shed blood, and God's demand that there be an accounting for shedding innocent blood. Chapter 17 explores the significance of Israel making peace with its Muslim neighbors, and what that will mean in terms of *when God's people should flee* the Daughter of Babylon. Consider the verses that disclose the future of the Daughter of Babylon's betrayal of Israel, and its persecution of God's people.

The Betrayal of Israel in the Russian-Muslim Invasion of Israel

"May the violence done to our flesh be upon Babylon," say the inhabitants of Zion. "May our blood be on those who live in Babylonia," says Jerusalem.
(Jeremiah 51:35)

Unlike the other quoted five prophets who gave us verses detailing a future Daughter of Babylon, the Lord did not use the prophet Ezekiel to give us any *direct* references to a future nation known as the "Daughter of Babylon." But in many ways Ezekiel's prophecies are just as important. Ezekiel gives us critical information as to *why* the Daughter of Babylon will ultimately be destroyed. His prophecies tie directly into the prophecies of Jeremiah and John, both of whom tell us specifically, the *reason* for the fall of the Daughter of Babylon.

Ezekiel writes that God "*scattered (Israel) among the nations*" (Ezekiel 36:19), they "*were soon to come home*" (Ezekiel 36:8), and God would "*multiply men upon you, all the house of Israel, even all of it, and the cities shall be inhabited and the wastes shall be built...and I will settle you according to your old estates, and will do better unto you than at your beginnings*" (Ezekiel 36: 10-11). Not only did God keep these promises, we know that Israel was re-born as a nation on May 14, 1948, but He also caused them to search out the names of the towns and villages in the areas where they settled. They used the same names in the same areas, thus settling according to their old estates. ("*I will settle you according to your old estates*" – Ezekiel 36:11). How many nations have been wiped out, the people scattered across the face of the earth, and then, almost 2,000 years later, their descendants returned to the very same area, re-forming their nation with the same national identity and the same name? Only Israel can make that claim.

ISRAEL IS RE-GATHERED, AS PROPHESIED

In Chapter 37 Ezekiel records a dramatic vision from the Lord of a valley full of dry bones, upon which sinews appear, and then flesh, and then breath, as the dry bones become people who "*lived, and stood up upon their feet, an exceedingly great army.*" The Lord then explains to Ezekiel the meaning of the dry bones vision: "*Then he said to me: "Son of man, these bones are the whole house of Israel. They say, 'Our bones are dried up and our hope is gone; we are cut off.' Therefore prophesy and say to them: 'This is what the Sovereign LORD says: O my people...I will bring you back to the land of Israel. Then you, my people, will know that I am the LORD ...and you will live, and I will settle you in your own land. Then you will know that I the LORD have spoken, and I have done it, declares the LORD.'*"(Ezekiel 37:11-14). Lest anyone miss what He was telling Ezekiel, in verse 21 it reads: "And say to them, *'This is what the Sovereign LORD says: I will take the Israelites out of the nations where they have gone. I will gather them from all around and bring them back into their own land."* Other prophets also record in detail that Israel would, in a future day, be re-gathered to its Promised Land.

Israel's miraculous return to its land is dramatic proof that Biblical prophecies are being fulfilled in our time. God said He would bring Israel back into the land He gave them, after their long dispersion (which they called their *diaspora*) and He did it, just as He said. In Ezekiel 38:8, God prophecies that, after its dispersion, Israel would be *"a land...whose people were gathered from many nations to the mountains of Israel, which had long been desolate."*

ISRAEL WILL BE AT PEACE

Scripture also reveals that Israel will, once back in the land, enter into peace treaties. Re-read that sentence. *Peace* and *Israel* in the same sentence? Since Israel was re-born in the land in May, 1948, it has not experienced peace, but instead, violence, hatred, and opposition from its Muslim neighbors, and frequently, from its Muslim inhabitants, as 16% of the residents of Israel are Muslim (*CIA Factbook*). However, scripture tells us that a time will come when Israel will dwell securely in the land, under a purported peace treaty with her enemies. This peace treaty, which will be broken as Russia and the listed Muslim nations invade and attempt to annihilate Israel, is not the same peace treaty that Daniel prophesied (Daniel 9:27) will be signed by the Antichrist with Israel. The second end times peace treaty will be broken by the Antichrist during the Tribulation.

Yes, it's a 'future fact' that Israel, as in the past, will fall for the same illusory offer from man, and depend on man, instead of God, for its security, and will do so twice in the end times. How will that work out? Great! That is, for a while. God tells us that Israel will be *"a land that has recovered from war"* (Ezekiel 38:8), that Israel will be inhabited by *"a peaceful and unsuspecting people"* (38:11), and that Israel's people will be *"living in safety"* (38:14).

How will that "peace" come about? Chapter 13 explains efforts by the United States to force Israel to trade its 'land for peace,' a plan initiated by President Bush (41), pushed by President Clinton, revived and given strong American pressure by President Bush (43), advancing the plan through the Annapolis Conference in 2007, and which became the subject of significant pressure by President Obama on Israeli Prime Minister Benjamin Netanyahu. Chapter 14 shows how America's pressure on Israel to do something God said *not to do*, give up its God-given *land*, resulted in the fulfillment of Genesis 12:3–that those who curse Israel are cursed.

It was Netanyahu, who, in his first term as Israeli Prime Minister ten years ago, gave up Hebron (where Abraham and many of the patriarchs are buried) to Palestinian control. Also, it was Israel's 11th Prime Minister, Ariel Sharon, who ran for office against giving up any *land* and who then reversed course, giving up the Gaza Strip to Palestinian, and now Hamas', control. In doing so, he agreed to the expulsion of 9,480 Jewish settlers from 21 settlements in Gaza in mid-August, 2005. (Chapter 13 looks at events occurring in America at the same time as the Gaza evacuation.) Israeli soldiers bulldozed every Jewish settlement structure, except for synagogues, which were then promptly blown up by the Palestinians, upon taking over the *land*. Rabbi Yosef Dayan imposed an ancient curse on Sharon for giving up the *land,* known as a *Pulsa di Nura,* which included a request that the Angel of Death take Sharon's life. About 100 days later, Sharon suffered what was thought to be a minor stroke, which was soon followed by a second stroke, other complications and ultimately, over several months, he was declared to be in a persistent vegetative state.

What would it take to arrive at such a treaty? Frankly, not much. Most of the original Jewish freedom fighters who fought to establish Israel against all worldly forces, are now dead. The David Ben-Gurions and Moshe Dayans are gone. The next generation of Israeli leadership in the 70's through the 90's were tough, disciplined and resolute in preserving control over the land that God placed in their hands. Those leaders are now no longer in power. Recently, Israel was led by Prime Minister Ehud Olmert, who is, to put it charitably, no David Ben Gurion. He made it clear that he would deal away the *land* that the Lord granted to Israel, even saying in his final days in office that to attain peace with the Palestinians, Israel would have to withdraw *"from nearly all of the West Bank as well as East Jerusalem."* Olmert was forced to resign due to corruption charges, before he could bargain away Israel's *land.* Land for peace has failed repeatedly for Israel, but Israel evidently keeps hoping that maybe, this time, it will work. Israel's treaty partners have been consistent, consistent in breaking their word.

In mid 2008, Israeli Prime Minister Olmert made it clear that he would agree to abandon part of the *land*, in order to get a peace treaty with Israel's enemies. Like most leaders, Olmert was just reflecting what his constituents seemed to want. In polls of Israeli voters, a majority said they favored giving up the *land* for the *promise* of peace, though the percentage that favored doing so declined sharply among those Israelis describing themselves as *"religious."*

Therefore, if the elected leaders of Israel, the voters and residents of Israel, Israel's major military partner, the United States, as well as Europe, the United Nations, even the Pope, *all want a peace treaty*, a peace treaty may well happen, at any given short-term time. Once signed, Israel can breathe a sigh of relief, as the missiles and bombs stop falling, and Israel actually comes to believe that its people are safe and secure. However, from the beginning of its existence, God warned Israel against relying on treaties with other nations, instead of relying on Him. (Exodus 23:32) Israel didn't listen, and always suffered for it. Today is no different. If you had a customer who entered into multiple contracts with you, and over time, *breached* every single contract, *every one*, how smart would you be to give consideration, real serious consideration, to signing *another contract?* Your family and friends might recommend a guardianship. However, the appointment of a guardian for an entire nation is not a legal or feasible alternative. Thus, there are many indications that Israel may *soon* enter into another peace treaty.

ISRAEL WILL BE AT WAR

What God revealed to Ezekiel about Israel did not end with Israel's return to the Promised Land, nor with Israel falling again for a peace treaty to attempt to secure its safety. In Ezekiel Chapters 38 and 39, God reveals to Israel eye-opening details about a future major invasion of Israel, after Israel's return to the *land* and re-establishment as a nation. The first end times peace treaty, like all of Israel's prior peace agreements, will be broken. Ezekiel reveals to us a number of specifics as to how Israel's first end times peace treaty will be breached. He even lists the identities of the nations that will seek to conquer, kill and destroy Israel.

God revealed this to Ezekiel as to the coalition of invading nations:

"After many days you will be called to arms. In future years you will invade a land that has recovered from war, whose people were gathered from many nations to the mountains of Israel, which had long been desolate. They had been brought out from the nations, and now all of them live in safety." (Ezekiel 38:8).

There are three significant prophecies in this one verse:

a.) Israel *will be back*, after a long time, gathered from the nations to which its people had been previously dispersed;

b.) A time will come, after the re-gathering, of recovery from war and its people living in *safety*;

c.) An *invasion* of arms, breaking the peace.

Which nations will invade Israel and break the peace? Ezekiel gives us abundant clues as to the modern day identity of the invaders. The first listed, apparently the lead invading nation, is: *"Gog, of the land of Magog, the chief prince of Meshech and Tubal."* Magog was a grandson of Noah, who settled north of the Black Sea (Gen.10:2; I Chron.1:5). His offspring were the Scythians, forebears of the Russians. Tubal was a grandson of Noah who settled northeast of the Black Sea (Gen. 10:2; I Chron. 1:5). The 'Siberian Capitol' of Russia was named for him, and called *Tobalsk.* So who was Meshech? He, also, was a grandson of Noah, who settled north of the Black Sea (Gen. 10:2; I Chron 1:5). The capitol of Russia, *Moscow*, was named after Meshech. There shouldn't be any question about the identity of Gog, as God the Holy Spirit gave to Ezekiel every needed clue to show us the identity of this great nation, which nation didn't yet exist when Ezekiel wrote these verses.

In addition, Ezekiel informs us that along with Gog (Russia) in the future invading force, will come several other nations, including Persia, Cush, Put, Gomer and Beth Togarmah (Ezek. 38:5 and 6). Persia is modern day Iran. Cush refers to modern day Ethiopia and Sudan; Put is today's Libya; Gomer was a part of modern day Turkey; and Beth Togarmah occupied part of today's Turkey and Eastern Europe, which was under Soviet domination for half a century (an area with a high percentage of Muslim residents). It is no *coincidence* that Ezekiel, writing centuries *before* Muhammad was even born, listed as the future invading nations, *only* nations that today are *Muslim,* or have large numbers of Muslim residents, such as Russia. There are no Western European nations included in Ezekiel's list of invaders.

Ezekiel even tells us *why* the Russians and Muslim nations will invade Israel. First, God will put *"hooks in their jaws"* and drag them into the invasion of Israel (Ezekiel 38:4). Why? Not because He is against Israel, but because *"I am against you, O Gog, chief prince of Meshech and Tubal"* (Ezekiel 38:3). How will God 'encourage' the invading nations? *"On that day thoughts will come into your mind and you will devise an evil scheme. You will say, '...I will plunder and loot and turn my hand against the...people gathered from the nations'..."* (Ezekiel 38:10-12).

"Sheba and Dedan" (areas that were in what is now known as Saudi Arabia) and the merchants of Europe and its *"young lions,"* implying Canada, Australia and, yes, the United States, will quickly challenge Russia and the invading Muslim nations and ask: *"Art thou come to take a spoil...to take a great spoil?"* (Ezekiel 38:13 KJV). It is of more than passing interest that centuries ago, a Jewish Prophet listed the names of nations that will object to such a future invasion, and that the list includes the primary nations one would expect today would raise the loudest objections. No one should doubt that the Russian bear is capable of such an invasion. In this regard, one also should not forget that Russia invaded Georgia in 2008, exquisitely timing the invasion for the first day of the Olympics in China, as the world's attention was diverted, and the leaders of Russia and the United States were both seated a few feet away from each other in the grandstands in Beijing.

"Spoil" certainly sounds a lot like OIL, though capturing Israel's industrial and commercial infrastructure would be of inestimable value. Today, Israel has no producing oil wells. However, a huge natural gas deposit was discovered in January, 2009 a few kilometers off of the Israeli coast near Haifa, estimated at $15 billion in value, making it one of the largest natural gas finds in history, and potentially making Israel energy independent. Drilling for oil continues in other areas of Israel. Author Joel Rosenberg speculates that Deuteronomy 33:24 (Asher will *"dip his foot in oil"*) will mean that Israel will discover massive quantities of oil, which will entice Russia and the listed Muslim nations to invade, to seize the sp(oil). But, whatever the then current price of oil, the internal rationale for Russia and the invading Muslim nations to invade, will be economic in large part, in order to take Israel's spoil. To grab the spoil they must, by necessity, also destroy Israel's military might. They come to

Israel to *"wipe Israel off of the map,"* as promised by Iran's President Ahmadinejad. How will that work out for them? Not so well.

The Lord also tells us that His purpose in all of this is so *"the nations may know me when I show myself holy through you before their eyes"* (Ezekiel 38:16). He tells us that through the aborted invasion He will *"make myself known in the sight of many nations. Then they will know that I am the LORD."* (Ezekiel 38:23). Just as importantly, if not more so, once Israel sees God come to its defense by destroying over 83% of the invading armies (since no other nation, including its military treaty partner, the United States, will come to its defense), then *"the house of Israel shall know that I am the LORD, their God, from that day and forward."* (Ezekiel 38:22). Spiritually at that time the Lord tells us that He will *"pour out My spirit on the house of Israel"*. (Ezekiel 39:29).

Could the invasion of Israel happen today? There is no verse making the discovery of oil an event that must occur *prior* to the invasion. What must occur, though, as we saw in the verses above, is that Israel needs to be *at peace* with its neighbors *prior* to the Russian/Muslim invasion. Ezekiel gives us the time sequence: Gog/Russia will say, *"I will invade a land of unwalled villages; I will attack a peaceful and unsuspecting people—all of them living without walls and without gates and bars."* (Ezekiel 38:11). When Ezekiel wrote these words people didn't build unwalled villages in his part of the world. It didn't make any sense to do so, because without walls, one could never rest at night, or be secure in the day, for that matter. Ezekiel is *not* recorded as asking: *"Unwalled villages? Who would live in such a place? You said it, LORD, so I'll write it down, but unwalled villages?"*

With regard to timing, the Russian/Muslim invasion could not have been, and historically did not happen, during a time when villages were walled. Flash forward to our time, though, and one will see unwalled village after unwalled village across the Middle East. Ezekiel buries the next time clue in the middle of verse 38:11: *"I will invade a land of unwalled villages; I will attack a peaceful and unsuspecting people—all of them living without walls and without gates and bars."* That description just can not apply to Israel today. The southern part of Israel in 2008 suffered missile bombardment for several months. Iran has regularly threatened to push Israel into the sea. A Russian/Muslim invasion today is not a likely event because it would *not* come as a surprise to a *"peaceful and unsuspecting people."* So, until Israel is at *"peace"* and, as a consequence, *"unsuspecting,"* we won't witness Ezekiel's prophesied Russian/Muslim invasion.

AMERICA'S WRITTEN PROMISES TO DEFEND ISRAEL

On April 14, 2004 President George W. Bush provided an important letter to then Prime Minister Ariel Sharon. The letter was given to Sharon by Bush to help Sharon justify his unilateral withdrawal of 9,480 Jewish residents and the Israeli Army from Gaza, as part of a future 'peace' effort to create a new separate Palestinian state, as part of a 'two state solution'. Sharon relied on Bush's letter. In the letter, Bush made four promises to Israel:

1.) The borders of the new Muslim state to be created would *not* encompass the entire West Bank (referring to Israel as "Judea" and "Samaria," including Jerusalem), despite Muslim leaders demanding the complete withdrawal from the areas Israel captured when it was invaded in 1967;

2.) Jewish towns and villages in the West Bank would be incorporated into the borders of Israel;

3.) Muslims would have to forego their demand to be given the right to immigrate to Israel;

4.) Israel's existence as a Jewish state would be assured.

Unfortunately, four years later, in 2008, the Bush administration abandoned these assurances made to Prime Minister Sharon in 2004. Secretary of State Rice told reporters in Israel on the occasion of Israel's 60th Anniversary as a re-born State that the 2004 letter *"talked about realities at that time. And there are realities for both sides...*" In an interview in the Oval Office with David Horowitz, editor of the Jerusalem Post, President Bush had to be reminded of the letter by his National Security Adviser, Stephen Hadley, who said in briefings that *"Israel has tried to overstate the importance of a rather vague letter."* (*Jerusalem Post*, May 14, 2008).

Apart from this critical letter, the Bush administration largely ignored Israel for most of its first seven years, discovering it as a final eighth year issue. Secretary of State Rice was a regular commuter to Israel, all the while "pushing" Israel to give up land to obtain a peace treaty.

However, prior to the Bush assurances, so hastily withdrawn, Israel has for some appreciable length of time enjoyed the military protection umbrella of American support. The United States of America, on March 26, 1979, guaranteed Israel that if she were to be *militarily invaded,* America would *militarily respond.* Israel bargained for this American military commitment and treaty promise as a condition of the Camp David peace agreement with Yassar Arafat and Anwar Sadat of Egypt, brokered by then President Jimmy Carter. The President of the United States of America on that date signed a *Memorandum of Agreement between the Governments of the United States of America and the State of Israel.* (Full two page text in Attachment B). The Agreement begins with these critical words: *"Recognizing the significance of the conclusion of the Treaty of Peace between Israel and Egypt and considering the importance of full implementation of the Treaty of Peace to Israel's security interests.* In other words, the military treaty between Israel and America came about because Israel in 1979 was willing to withdraw from the Sinai Peninsula making peace with Egypt, which had invaded earlier in 1948, 1968, and 1973, *because* America was willing to make certain promises to come to Israel's defense militarily, *were Israel to be invaded* again in the future.

The March 26, 1979 Agreement between Israel and America states in quite simple, easily understood terms that if Israel's *"security"* is *"threaten(ed),"* including *"an armed attack against Israel"* that the United States *"on an urgent basis"* will *"be responsive to military and economic assistance requirements of Israel ."* That's not very subtle diplomatic language for 'if you are invaded militarily, we'll respond militarily.' Frankly, it might have been better from a Genesis 12:3 perspective (*"I will bless those who bless you, and curse those who curse you"*) if the 1979 military defense agreement with Israel had been 202 pages, with multiple sub-parts, and several whereas clauses, instead of two pages which can't be easily misinterpreted. Any lawyer will tell you that the most difficult contract to defeat by finding a 'loophole' is a contract that is short, simple, and straight forward. That's exactly what America signed with Israel about thirty years ago.

AMERICA WILL BETRAY ISRAEL

When Gog/Russia, Iran, Sudan, Ethiopia, Libya, and other Muslim nations come out of their homelands to invade and destroy Israel, they will do so with the full knowledge that America has *promised* to come to Israel's defense and that America has committed to be *"responsive to (the) military...assistance requirements of Israel."* Why then, one might well ask, would these nations launch such an attack in the face of such a clear promise to defend Israel, a promise solemnly made by the *"hammer of the whole earth,"* the world's only remaining superpower? The simple answer is, we don't know. Whether these nations gain inside knowledge that Israel's only earthly defender will fail to keep its word, or by some other means the invaders gain knowledge that Israel's only earthly defender will not launch a military response in the face of its invasion, we are not told. What we do have reason to believe, though, is that Israel's only earthly defender *will* abandon her, that it *will* betray Israel and that it will NOT come to Israel's defense in the face of this mighty invading army.

'The Message' translation of Lamentations 4:17 reads:

"We watched and watched,
wore our eyes out looking for help. And nothing.
We mounted our lookouts and looked
for the help that never showed up."

This verse implies that some time passes as the Russian-Muslim coalition comes against Israel. It is further supported by the Prophet Joel (1:1-2:17) who prophecies a land invasion into Israel that clearly takes time, before God removes *"the Northern Army"* from the strategic position it will gain between the Dead Sea and the Mediterranean Sea (Joel 2:20). The relevance of these prophecies is twofold:

a.) America will have more than sufficient time to come to Israel's defense, Israel wearing its eyes out "looking for help", as Israel's only military treaty partner decides what to do.

b.) Nuclear weapons won't be used on Israel. In this invasion the non-use of nuclear weapons makes sense as the invading army comes to take a spoil, kill Israelites and take their land. Nuclear weapons would render the land unusable for years, and would cause radioactive fallout that would drift outside of Israel over the invaders' homelands. Why is Iran working feverishly to develop nuclear weapons it won't likely use on Israel? It may have another enemy in mind for their use.

Jeremiah's Chapters 50 and 51, which are devoted to the end times Daughter of Babylon, prophesy that the failure of the Daughter of Babylon to come to Israel's defense when it is attacked, is the *reason* for God's vengeance on the betraying nation:

"Since this is the vengeance of the LORD, take
vengeance on her; do to her as she has done to others."
(Jeremiah 50:15)

*'The LORD has vindicated us; come, let us tell in Zion
what the LORD our God has done.'* (Jeremiah 51:10)

*"Before your eyes I will repay Babylon and all who live
in Babylonia for all the wrong they have done in Zion,"
declares the LORD."* (Jeremiah 51:24)

*"May the violence done to our flesh be upon Babylon,"
say the inhabitants of Zion.
"May our blood be on those who live in Babylonia,"
says Jerusalem. Therefore, this is what the LORD
says: "See, I will defend your cause and avenge you..."*
(Jeremiah 51:35- 36)

*"Babylon must fall because of Israel's slain,
just as the slain in all the earth
have fallen because of Babylon."* (Jeremiah 51:49)

*"A destroyer will come against Babylon;
her warriors will be captured,
and their bows will be broken.
For the LORD is a God of retribution;
he will repay in full."* (Jeremiah 51:56)

Isaiah and the writer of Psalm 137 also state how God will view the betrayal of Israel:

*"O Daughter of Babylon, doomed to destruction,
happy is he who repays you
for what you have done to us"* (Psalm 137:8)

*"A dire vision has been shown to me:
The traitor betrays, the looter takes loot.
Elam, attack! Media, lay siege!
I will bring to an end all the groaning she caused."*
(Isaiah 21:2)

"I will take vengeance;
I will spare no one." (Isaiah 47:3)

How likely is it that America will break its word to defend Israel? Chapter 14 analyzes what America has done *to* Israel to pressure it to give up His land, since President Bush (41) to President Obama. Suffice it to say that America has been taking actions that are contrary to God's word on this issue, at our peril.

GOD IS SERIOUS ABOUT ISRAEL

God is quite serious about Israel, and His promise to bless those who bless Israel, and conversely curse those who curse Israel. When Israel is invaded, it will be in dire nation-destroying circumstances. Israel will face Russia, Iran, and several Muslim nations, obviously intent, by their launched invading forces and *"great army,"* on *"wiping Israel from the map."* Worse yet, though Israel possesses powerful armaments, they're not inexhaustible. To survive, Israel will need help, a great deal of help. Israel will look to her only earthly defender, the only nation on the globe that has promised to come to Israel's defense if Israel is faced with *"an armed attack"* – the United States of America. No other nation has made such an agreement with Israel. The whole world will also turn its eyes on America, expecting a strong response from the nation which has not shrunk from using its military force in many distant lands in the past.

And there at that point in time, we read a shocking prophecy. *No nation,* Ezekiel tells us, *will come to Israel's defense.* None. . . thereby proving for the umpteenth time that Israel should not lean on man and man's promises, only on God and His promises. Chapter 9 explores God's prophecies telling us how He will deal with the end times power that betrays His chosen people. But, without the military might of its only earthly defender, how will Israel survive complete destruction? Good question. Ezekiel spells it out:

"*This is what will happen in that day: When Gog attacks the land of Israel, my hot anger will be aroused, declares the Sovereign LORD. In my zeal and fiery wrath I declare that at that time there shall be a great earthquake in the land of Israel. The fish of the sea, the birds of the air, the beasts of the field, every creature that moves along the ground, and all the people on the face of the earth will tremble at my presence. The mountains will be overturned, the cliffs will crumble and every wall will fall to the ground. I will summon a sword against Gog on all my mountains, declares the Sovereign LORD. Every man's sword will be against his brother. I will execute judgment upon him with plague and bloodshed; I will pour down torrents of rain, hailstones and burning sulfur on him and on his troops and on the many nations with him. And so I will show my greatness and my holiness, and I will make myself known in the sight of many nations. Then they will know that I am the LORD.'"* (Ezekiel 38:18-23)

That will surely be an 'urgent basis military response." As we have seen, God has always, and will always, deal with the nations of the world in the *same way* they deal with Israel. This pattern of divine action directly fulfills His blessings/curse promise in Genesis 12:3, which He confirmed was for the Isaaic descendants of Abraham (Genesis 17:19-21) and the Jacobic descendants of Abraham (Genesis 27:37), not the Ishmaelite descendants of Abraham (Arabs and eventually Muslims). (Genesis 21:10-12)

How severe will God's divine intervention appear to be in the protection of Israel? Five-sixths (84%) of the invading great army will fall "*on the mountains of Israel*" and "*on the open field.*" (Ezekiel 39:2-4) The destruction of the Russian/Muslim invading army won't stop with its armed forces. "*I will send a fire on Magog and on those who live in safety in the coastlands, and they will know that I am the LORD.*" (Ezekiel 39:6) Thus, Russia, and the invading Muslim nations, will suffer divine intervention in their homelands in such a way that they will have no doubt that the heavy destruction comes from the hand of the Lord.

Ezekiel then gives great detail as to the clean up and burial of the massive fallen dead invaders. He tells us that the burial process will involve many men hired specifically to engage in the *"continual task of passing through the land to bury."* It will require seven months to bury the dead. (Ezekiel 39:12) Ezekiel prophecies that the slain will be buried in an area that will be called the *"Valley of Hamon-Gog,"* literally 'the place of many dead Russians.' (Ezekiel 39:11).

IS THIS ARMAGEDDON?

Some commentators have wrapped the Russian/Muslim invasion into the final battle at Armageddon. That's easy to do because both are end times battles and both take place in and near Israel. However, a close analysis shows us that these are two distinctly different end times events.

Russian/Muslim Invasion	***Armageddon***
Location of Battle:	
Northern Mountains of Israel (Ezekiel 38:8)	Jerusalem (Revelation 16:16)
Participants:	
Six Specific Listed Nations (Ezekiel 38: 1-6)	All of the World's Nations (Revelation 16:14)
Results of the Battles:	
Russian/Muslim armies routed; (Ezekiel 39:4)	Christ and the 'armies of heaven' return to stop world carnage; (Revelation 19:19-21)
Destruction in Russia-'fire on Magog'; (Ezekiel 39:6)	Satan bound; (Revelation 20:1-3)

Israel buries the dead – 7 months;
(Ezekiel 39:14)

Christ begins 1,000 year reign;
(Revelation 20:6)

Israel uses booty for 7 years;
(Ezekiel 39:9)

Jesus reigns in the Temple;
(Isaiah 2:1-3)

Israel builds the Temple
(Ezekiel 40-48)

Interpreting the Russian/Muslim invasion as a part of the final battle of Armageddon is just not consistent with what scripture states will happen after the Russian/Muslim invasion, that *after* the God-thwarted attack, Israel buries the dead for seven months and uses the captured armaments for fuel for seven years. These are clearly two different battles, with different participants, in different locations and with decidedly different results. David Jeremiah, in his recent book (*What in the World is Going On?*, Thomas Nelson, 2008), agrees that the invasion of Israel by Russia and its Muslim allies *"will precede the Battle of Armageddon, (and) will be a massive, Russian-led coalition of nations coming against Israel like swarms of hornets against a defenseless child."*

Following the details of the aborted Russian/Muslim invasion in Ezekiel chapter 38-39 we find detailed architectural plans for the third Temple in Ezekiel chapters 40-48. That is not a coincidental placement. Once Israel survives the Russian/Muslim invasion, especially in the way she will be protected by what will clearly be seen world-wide as divine intervention, Israel will quickly move to build the Temple. It will be like a 'world war memorial' to Israel's victory. Why is the building of the Temple important?

First, the Temple must be in place for the coming Antichrist to commit an abomination of desolation (Daniel 9:27; Matthew 24:15). There is no possible way Israel could today build, let alone even *plan* to build a Temple, without widespread rioting, death and destruction on the Temple Mount. Years ago, when Prime Minister Ariel Sharon merely *walked* on the Temple Mount, it started several years of rioting and bloodshed. But with the more than impressive God-caused Israeli victory over the armed forces of Ezekiel's seven listed nations, Israel will have a window of opportunity to re-build the Temple.

Secondly, the Temple must also be in place for Jesus to reign from the Temple Mount as Isaiah prophesied. Some have speculated that the Dome of the Rock must first be destroyed in order to build Israel's Third Temple. That's not necessarily true. In the mid 1970's the *Jerusalem Post* revealed that excavations of the eastern portion of the current Temple Mount confirm that the Temple of Solomon was likely in that location, and not where the Dome of the Rock is sited. Thus, the Temple could be built without destroying the Dome of the Rock, and would fulfill the prophecy, that the Court of the Temple would be occupied by gentiles (Revelation 11:2).

Two of the three events that must take place before the fall of the Daughter of Babylon, i.e.: 1.) the persecution of God's people and 2.) the betrayal of Israel, may be *linked*. God may well expect that His American Believers will take Him at his Word, believe His Word, and conclude that His people have an obligation to: 1.) bless Israel (Genesis 12:3), 2.) pray for the peace of Jerusalem (Psalm 122:6) and 3.) insure that their nation keep its sworn covenant treaty obligations to come to Israel's defense if Israel is attacked (Romans 1:31). The failure of His people to do so may be tied to their own persecution and martyrdom. What has His church in America, with very limited exceptions, done to help, defend, pray for, and bless Israel? God is a God of linkage.

WHAT WILL GOD DO TO THE LEADER
OF THE DAUGHTER OF BABYLON?

Interestingly, the Daughter of Babylon prophetic verses include a focus on the leader of the Daughter of

Babylon. Jeremiah refers to the Daughter of Babylon's leader twice as the "*king of Babylon*":

> "*Therefore this is what the LORD Almighty, the God of Israel, says: "I will punish the king of Babylon and his land..."*(Jeremiah 50:18)

> "*The king of Babylon has heard reports about them, and his hands hang limp. Anguish has gripped him, pain like that of a woman in labor.*" (Jeremiah 50:43)

The leader of the Daughter of Babylon is also referred to indirectly in other verses. Jeremiah writes that "*Bel*" will be "*put to shame*" (Jeremiah 50:2) and he quotes God as saying: "*I will punish Bel in Babylon*" (Jeremiah 50:44). Who is Bel? The name is only used three times in the Bible, these two uses and once in Isaiah 46, in the verses preceding Isaiah 47, which is centered on the Daughter of Babylon. What do these three uses of the name 'Bel' imply? The Biblical commentaries are in agreement that Bel is a contraction of Baal, the principal god of Babylon, signifying 'lord,' and also known as Marduk, their sun god. In fact, Jeremiah links Bel with Marduk in 50:2:

> "*Babylon will be captured;*
> *Bel will be put to shame,*
> *Marduk filled with terror.*"

Three times Jeremiah tells us that God will "*punish Bel in Babylon*" (Jeremiah 51:44); "*will punish the idols in Babylon*" (Jeremiah 51:47); and tells us that "*But the days are coming, declares the LORD, when I will punish her idols.*" (Jeremiah 51:52). Ponder that for a moment. Human beings may wrongly believe that idols have power or feelings so that "*punishing*" the idol would mean something. But that concept is antithetical to the sole God of the universe. So, why would He tell us that He will "*punish Bel of Babylon*" and "*punish the idols of Babylon*"? The references to the Bel

107

of Babylon and to Babylon's idols appear to be to a person, a leader, or leaders of Babylon.

When ancient Babylon became the capital of Mesopotamia, Marduk, the leading god/idol of Babylon was elevated to the level of Supreme God. So it would be a reasonable interpretation of the use of Marduk in Jeremiah 50:2 (the only time the word is used in the Bible),to conclude that it is a reference to the leader of the Daughter of Babylon. Jeremiah also tells us that the King of Babylon will react in *"anguish and fear"* when he hears of Babylon's impending/immediate demise. Who will the leader of the Daughter be at the time of its destruction? That we don't know, of course, but the leader of the Daughter of Babylon who is punished, is the same leader of the Daughter of Babylon who leads the nation in *the betrayal of Israel,* by refusing to keep the nation's obligation to help Israel resist the Russian/Muslim invasion . That is the leader, the Bel of Babylon, whom God will punish for the betrayal of Israel, whom God calls the *"apple of his eye"* (Zechariah 2:8). The punishment, as we know from the other Daughter of Babylon verses, *doesn't end* with the punishment of the Daughter of Babylon's *leader.* Jeremiah 50:18 confirms to us:

"I will punish the King of Babylon and his land..."

WHAT ABOUT HOPE?

A major sub-theme of *America at the Crossroads* was that as bad as things seemed in America there was still hope. Hope that if we heeded God's call to repentance (II Chronicles 7:14), that we would be healed, and we would survive coming difficult times. That message is still operative, as America can still be healed, if we humble ourselves, pray, seek God's face and turn from our wicked ways, He *will* heal our land. That's His promise, and He will do it – that is, if we do what He has commanded us to do.

Is it too late, even at this stage in human history? No, it's not too late, until, as Casey Stengel might say, *until, it's too late.* Israel was healed on one occasion, as they cried out to God and repented, as the Philistines were coming over the sand dunes to destroy them. America can *still* be healed. There's *hope* that we can survive the evil plans of those who seek to destroy us as a nation. However, hope can only remain as a viable reality for a finite period of time. God is patient, but He's not a doddering fool, forgetting what He has commanded.

America has been blessed materially beyond all other nations. God has called on our blessed nation for decades to come back to Him. Each year, each day, we have ignored His loving entreaties to repent and be healed. So, what should He do? Cancel His call to repentance? Overlook fifty million slain innocent children? Ignore America's betrayal of Israel, when it happens? He actually covered this question in two of the Daughter of Babylon prophetic verses in Jeremiah:

> *"Babylon will suddenly fall and be broken. Wail over her! Get balm for her pain; perhaps she can be healed.*
> *" 'We would have healed Babylon, but she cannot be healed; let us leave her and each go to his own land, for her judgment reaches to the skies, it rises as high as the clouds.' "* (Jeremiah 51:8-9)

Jeremiah prophetically saw and recorded the Trinity discussing the future fall of the rich, powerful, influential end times Daughter of Babylon. *"We"*, the members of the Trinity say, *"would have healed"* the Daughter of Babylon, even decreeing that she *"can be healed"*. That's the *"hope"* part. There is hope that she *"can be healed"*, the members of the Trinity even saying *"we would have healed Babylon"*. Those words almost seem to be said with great remorse, such as anyone has felt who has ever wanted to help someone out of a major problem, but the troubled person didn't want help. *"We would have healed Babylon"*. That's true, still, today. We can be healed, if we *want* to be healed.

There is no contradiction between verse 8: *"perhaps she can be healed"* and verse 9: *"she cannot be healed"*. The

109

word *"perhaps"* is the reason there is no contradiction. *"Perhaps"* refers to God's stated condition for national healing, spiritual repentance. There is now, even now, hope that we can be healed. But, sadly, prophetically, we must conclude that what we witness every day in our nation will be borne out in the days ahead as we face what we deserve. There is in all of this, not only the obvious bad news of coming destruction prophesied by five Prophets, there is also the *good news.* God loves His people so much, that even when we don't please Him, He is still willing to offer us an escape, a warning to flee and survive and live, in spite of the fall of our nation. We ignore that *good news* at our peril.

WHAT ABOUT THE RAPTURE?

A minister friend upon hearing about the Daughter of Babylon prophecies as applied to America asked, *"But won't we all be gone in the Rapture?"* If only it were so. The Daughter of Babylon prophecies are all world events that will happen *before* the following prophetic events:

a.) the rise of the Antichrist and False Prophet;
b.) the second peace treaty with Israel;
c.) the Rapture of the Church;
d.) the seven year Tribulation period;
e.) the Second Coming of Christ.

The Daughter of Babylon will be removed from the world stage *before* the above listed prophetic events. In fact, it is the *removal* of this rich, powerful and influential end times nation that precipitates and leads to the rise of the Antichrist (see Chapter 12 for details). *Until* the rise of the Antichrist there won't be a second peace treaty with Israel, nor the seven year Tribulation period which starts with the signing of the treaty. Thus, though escaping the destruction of America by way of a heavenly Rapture would be much preferable to living through it, scripture doesn't support that option. God's people, as throughout history, will live in perilous times, with accompanying persecution.

Jesus tells us that if He does not return towards the end of the tribulation that no flesh would be spared:

"For then there will be great distress, unequaled from the beginning of the world until now—and never to be equaled again. If those days had not been cut short, no one would survive, but for the sake of the elect those days will be shortened." (Matthew 24:22)

Using the sound, discerning minds that God has given us, if America in the end times is in the same position as the other nations of the world, that is, that Jesus will return for His own, and rapture them out of the world, otherwise no one would survive, then why are God's people *called out* of the Daughter of Babylon *nine times* in scripture? Why would God specifically tell His people, Christians and Jews, to *"flee"* the Daughter of Babylon, foreseen by five Prophets? Why not just let them stay in the Daughter of Babylon and be *raptured* like everyone else? The answer is logically clear, because the Daughter of Babylon is *not around* as a country at the return of Jesus, but destroyed some time *before* His return. God doesn't do things that make no sense. He would not tell millions of His people to pack up and flee from their native land for no reason, if they were about to be raptured out of the world anyway.

Clearly, He moves His own, Christians and Jews, out of the rich, powerful nation he calls the Daughter of Babylon, in order to preserve their lives from the coming destruction that the nation will have invited upon itself. Thus, God calls on His people to flee *well before* the return of Jesus, because Jesus will not return until the Antichrist is in power, and the Antichrist will not be in power until the *"hammer of the whole earth"* is gone from power. Then, when the rapture *does* come, His people, by then relocated in other nations than their native America, will be *alive to be raptured*, along with the other believers in the world. Immediately before

Jesus returns His people will be on the brink of being slain by those committed to their beheading and death. That's why He says that His return will be necessary, otherwise, widespread death would destroy them. Whether one believes that the rapture will come before, during, or after the tribulation is not at issue, because the need to escape from America will come well before the Antichrist, the tribulation and the rapture.

Chapter Six
THE DAUGHTER OF BABYLON'S PERSECUTION OF GOD'S PEOPLE

"Intolerance of Christianity will rise to levels many of us have not believed possible in our lifetimes, and public policy will become hostile toward evangelical Christians, seeing it as the opponent of the common good...Evangelicals will increasingly be seen as a threat to cultural progress. Public leaders will consider us bad for America, bad for education, bad for children and bad for society." (Michael Spencer, CS Monitor)

"I was angry with my people...
and I gave them into your hand."
(Isaiah 47:6)

"Do not prophesy," their prophets say. "Do not prophesy about these things; disgrace will not overtake us." Should it be said, O house of Jacob: "Is the Spirit of the LORD angry? Does he do such things?" "Do not my words do good to him whose ways are upright?... Get up, go away! For this is not your resting place, because it is defiled, it is ruined, beyond all remedy. If a liar and deceiver comes and says, 'I will prophesy for you plenty of wine and beer,' he would be just the prophet for this people! (Micah 2:6,7,10,11)

As we have just read, the betrayal of Israel is the *ultimate reason* given in scripture for the destruction of the end times, "Mother of Abominations" nation, also labeled the Daughter of Babylon. Scripture discloses to us that this rich, powerful, influential, fallen end times nation will *persecute* God's people. Why?

Two of the instances in which the "Daughter of Babylon" is referred to in the Bible are found in Isaiah 47:1 – *"Go down, sit in the dust, Virgin Daughter of Babylon; sit on the ground without a throne, Daughter of the Babylonians. No more will you be called tender or delicate,"* and in 47:5 *"Sit in silence, go into darkness, Daughter of the Babylonians; no more will you be called queen of kingdoms."* The very next verse of Isaiah 47 contains the disclosure that God will become *"angry"* with His *"people"* who reside in the Daughter of Babylon and He then will give His people into the hand of the Daughter of Babylon (Isaiah 47:6). At the same time, He also warns His people to get out of, to flee, the Daughter of Babylon.

First, it should be asked, why does God become *"angry"* (His word choice) with His people in the end times? We are not told, actually, the reason in these sections of scripture that directly reference the Daughter of Babylon. Some insight on this question, however, may be gleaned from the Apostle John's *Book of The Revelation.* John describes seven epochs of the Church in Revelation 2:1 through 3:22. The final stage of the Church, described as the Church of Laodicea (Revelation 3:14-19) is not a very winsome description of a rich, self-indulgent church, neither hot nor cold for the Lord, which thinks it has no need of anything, but is, in reality, *"wretched, miserable, poor, blind and naked."* John records the Lord as saying to the Church at Laodicea that *"As many as I love, I rebuke and chasten."* So, why would God be angry with His own people living in the nation He called the Daughter of Babylon? Why is God angry? We can surmise that His people must not be obedient to His Word, for if we were, He would not be *"angry."*

Secondly, notice that one of the key problems with the end times Church of Laodicea is that the Church is *"blind."* If the American church is part of the church of Laodicea, and there are multiple reasons to conclude that we are, and we are therefore *"blind,"* it is clear that we won't even see, let alone understand, our true spiritual condition. How can we see what we have become if we're *"blind"*? Some may argue that the major changes that have swept over most of the individual churches in America may not be in obedience to God's will. Let's be honest. Has the Church influenced the popular culture of America since the 60's or has the popular culture influenced the Church? Chuck Colson has observed that *"the culture is religion incarnate."* Chew on that thought for a minute. Our culture reflects and puts flesh on our religious beliefs. We rail against our declining culture, but if our culture is a reflection *of us*, as Christians, then who's to blame for our declining culture? Has the church in America become *"Christianity Light,"* or like the new Coke product, *"Christianity Zero?"* Reflecting our condition as a body of believers, recently in the same week a U.S. Senator and a Governor, both recognized Christian leaders, admitted extramarital affairs. *"For it is time for judgment to begin with the family of God; and if it begins with us, what will the outcome be for those who do not obey the gospel of God?"* (I Peter 4:17)

A recent George Barna poll revealed that only 1% of Christians interviewed in his poll subscribed to all thirteen listed basic doctrinal principles of our Christian faith, only one percent. Colson notes that in most churches today, *"Biblical illiteracy is rampant."* As I detailed in *America at the Crossroads* (Tyndale House, 1979), cultures historically have only improved when God's people get serious and experience spiritual revival. America has not witnessed a nationwide revival since early in the 20th century, over one hundred years ago. Americans really shouldn't be too surprised, as our culture continues to spiral downward. These words may incite anger, but if we are *"blind"* to our true spiritual condition as an end times Church, our prayer should be that we see our true spiritual condition, *as God sees it.*

Are we blind to how far we are from 'hitting the mark'? The literal translation of the word "sin" is missing the mark. Since current polls and demographic studies show that Christians living in America are divorcing, abusing, over-indulging, bankrupting or adultering at rates that don't differ from non-Christians, we have to ask we must admit our blindness.

America also has sinned grievously since 1973 in allowing, by law, the killing of fifty million American babies in, and emerging from, their mothers' wombs. Does anyone seriously think that this carnage would have been allowed to happen if the Church had arisen with one voice and said 'we will not abide the legalized murder of our children in the womb'? David Bereit, Founder of Forty Days for Life, points out that any abortion clinic in America should have a sign in their window that reads "THIS ABORTION CLINIC IS MADE POSSIBLE BY THE INACTION OF CHRISTIANS IN THIS COMMUNITY." When the Lord looks upon the Church in America today what does He see? Perhaps it's not unlike what the Apostle John saw when the Church of Laodicea was revealed to him.

CAN PERSECUTION BE HELPFUL?

Author and columnist, Mark Steyn has observed, "*Most mainline Protestant churches are, to one degree or another, post-Christian.*" Some openly violate God's Word on key moral issues; some teach the Bible is advisory only; too many ignore the prophetical verses in Scripture as a quaint anachronism; and many are making no visible difference in the lives of those in their community who might actually be interested in knowing more about Christ's substitutionary death on their behalf. How many churches share the Gospel of Jesus Christ out in the community? How many, instead, are modern versions of what used to be the local rarified exclusive, members only, country clubs, with a steeple on top? Steyn does notes that, fortunately, there is still in America a "*strain of evangelical Protestantism,*" and decries the fact that Europe lacks any discernable evangelical movement. If it's true that the churches in America still have a substantial number of committed believers, then why would God be *angry* with "His people" and allow His people to be persecuted by the government of the Daughter of Babylon?

Oppression of believers throughout the centuries has improved the spirituality of the oppressed. A little righteous anger from above isn't the worst thing that can happen. God has a plan for His people who are living in the Daughter of

Babylon, and it involves their believing His Word and acting on it, and *escaping* from terrible, deadly times. It is a basic premise that only God's people who believe His Word will decide to take Him at His Word, act upon it, and be protected as a result. Those who don't believe His Word is true, and that it *can't* be relied upon, shouldn't complain about what happens to them, if their disregard of His warnings proves to be a fatal error. This, then, may be an important reason why our loving Father will permit His people to be persecuted by the government of the Daughter of Babylon. He knows the only way many Christians and Jews actually will pull up their American roots and flee to another country is when their government *makes their life here too miserable to stay.*

WHAT WILL HAPPEN TO BELIEVERS?

What happens to God's people when He turns them over to the Daughter of Babylon? Jeremiah prophecies that *"strangers"* will *"come into the sanctuaries of the LORD's house,"* leading God's people to be *"confounded"* and held to *"reproach"* and to *"shame."* (Jeremiah 51:51) This verse could have dual application. It could refer to uninvited trespassers coming into the church and disrupting God's people in their worship. Interestingly, the sanctity of the church appears to have changed, and changed dramatically, immediately after election day, November 4, 2008. At first hundreds, and then thousands, of protestors surrounded churches and Mormon Temples in California. Also, certain evangelical pastors were provided with police protection. The protests arose from the campaign for California's Proposition 8. The measure, which defined marriage as exclusively between a man and a woman, was voted for by a majority of California voters on November 4, 2008.

The protest then spread to Salt Lake City on November 14th, where more than 3,000 people swarmed downtown Salt Lake City to march past the Mormon temple and church headquarters, protesting Mormon involvement in support of

Proposition 8. Signs by protestors read: *"I didn't vote on your marriage,"* *"Mormons once persecuted . . . Now persecutors,"* *"Jesus said love everyone"* and *"Proud of my two moms."* (*The Salt Lake Tribune*, November 15, 2008). Soon, via the internet, supporters of same sex marriage organized protestors in all 50 states. On Saturday, November 16[th,] tens of thousands of people, by one Fox News estimate a million protestors, marched in protest of the prior passage of Prop 8, in every state, including 10,000 in San Francisco. One protestor, John Aravosis, an influential Washington, D.C.-based blogger, told the Associated Press, *"The main focus is going to be going after the Utah brand; We're going to destroy the Utah brand. It is a hate state."* One newspaper columnist who attacked the Mormon Church for succeeding with Prop 8 in voting homosexuals, in his words, *"into second class status,"* also wrote that the protests, bomb threats and marches against the Mormon Church were justified. His rationale? *"So, you leave the sanctuary for the kitchen, you get the heat."* (*Indianapolis Star*, Dan Carpenter, December 7, 2008)

At about the same time, protestors targeted Mt. Hope Church, a large evangelical Assemblies of God-affiliated church in Lansing, Michigan. A homosexual activist group, Bash Back, on Sunday, November 16[th,] came into the Michigan church and disrupted services. They threw fliers, unfurled a banner, set off a fire alarm, shouted slogans at churchgoers, and had same sex couples kissing each other at the front of the Church. A statement released by church officials said they believe *"homosexuality to be a sin, just as fornication, stealing, drunkenness and lying are sins. No sin greater than the next."* In an online news release, called Bash Back, described Mt. Hope as *"a deplorable anti-queer mega church."* The police were called, but the protestors had vacated the church by the time police arrived. The name of the group and the timing of the disruptive protest could well indicate more protests in churches may be expected in the future. In Mid-December, 2008 Alaska Governor Sarah Palin's Wasilla Bible Church was firebombed, causing $1 million in damages. Was this an act by those protesting Governor Palin's management of state government, or instead her Christian views on social issues? The number of churches that have been burned has increased alarmingly, and could portend more burnings in the future.

In discussing gay activists, it is important to understand that there are *no* prophetic verses saying the fall of the Daughter of Babylon will be *because* of homosexual activity. Persons may read the prior discussion about gay activists' attacks on the church, and incorrectly write that this book is a 'gay-bashing' diatribe. Not true. What is true, however, is that:

a.) Jesus prophesied that the end times would be like *'the days of Lot'* (Luke 17:22-30) in which Sodom and Gomorrah were destroyed during a time of rampant homosexuality;

b.) For three millennia the laws of the nations of the world reflected concern over being destroyed, as were Sodom and Gomorrah, as the nations of the world banned same-sex activities as criminal acts ("Sodomy" laws); and

c.) It has only been since the early 1960's that it accurately can be said, with *repeal* of those thousands of laws in all non-Muslim nations, that our days are becoming like *"the Days of Lot,'* just as Jesus said they would.

Since Jesus said these days would come upon the earth in the end times, why isn't the Daughter of Babylon destroyed *because* of same-sex activities? The answer is, because those verses aren't found in the Bible. The Daughter of Babylon falls *because* of its betrayal of Israel and the shedding of blood in Israel. (*"Babylon must fall because of Israel's slain..."* Jeremiah 51:49). So, what can we conclude then, about Jesus telling us that the last days would be like *the Days of Lot*? This fulfilled prophecy is just one more proof of His divinity and ability to 'tell us ahead of time,' as He said. It also could indicate a source of much of the persecution of the Church in the last days by those who can't abide God's people refusing to agree that gay activists' lifestyles are *acceptable*, and who *won't agree* that same-sex activities are *not* sinful, as stated in scripture.

TURNED OVER TO THE GOVERNMENT

Since random trouble-making individuals coming in the church would normally be considered trespassers, and therefore, could be removed by the authorities, these prophecies may have a second application. They may foretell governmental interference with the Church, by law and edict, and possibly much worse.

Note that when God turns over His people, He turns them over *to* the Daughter of Babylon, which is a *nation*. So, God's people will be turned over into the hands of the government. Historically, Christians who are severely mistreated and oppressed, have generally suffered at the hands of a government, or by permission of the government. Though quite serious, it also has been potentially survivable, with Christians meeting in house churches, in secret churches or private, hidden Bible studies. But the persecution of God's people by the Daughter of Babylon will get worse. In Revelation 17:6 John tells us it was revealed to him that Babylon, in the end times, will be *"drunk with the blood of the saints, and with the blood of the martyrs of Jesus."* In Revelation 18:24 John reveals that in Babylon *"was found the blood ... of saints."* Being turned over to the Daughter of Babylon by a God who is *"angry"* with His *"people,"* is not a terribly appealing prospect. But, there it is, black letters on white paper.

Some may say at this point, 'whew', we're so far from oppression, and the martyrdom of Christians and Jews, that we have no worries. Consider these three points: First, discrimination against Christians in the workplace, in the classroom, in public places, in virtually every area of the nation has been ongoing now for some time, and is not decreasing in scope or intensity, but actually increasing. This author has represented Christians who were fired and lost their jobs, or disciplined, or retaliated against, or demoted, or worse, only because they were Christians. To read about the current wide spread level of anti-Christian discrimination, which has not been declining, visit the websites of the:

Alliance Defense Fund (www.alliancedefensefund.org),
the Rutherford Institute (www.rutherford.org),
and the American Center for Law and Justice (www.aclj.org).

Don Wildmon details the facts of Christian persecution in *Speechless, Silencing the Christians,* (Richard Vigilante Books, 2009). By God's grace, though, much of this activity, at this time, is generally without *official* government sanction. What will happen when God removes His hand of protection from His people, and we are open to attack by those who don't like God's people, and are acting on behalf of a government that authorizes the persecution *officially*?

Secondly, Christians are being martyred across the globe at alarmingly increasing rates. The *'Voices of the Martyrs'* website reveals just how serious this killing of our brothers and sisters in Christ has become.

Third, though oppression to the level of 'being thrown in jail' for one's Christian faith, may not yet be apparent in the United States, history confirms that religious oppression in any given nation can be just the passage of a few laws away. Within six years of Adolph Hitler's selection as Germany's leader, the nation was imprisoning and killing its own people.

It doesn't take a significant amount of discernment to conclude that Christians could be in for government sanctioned or directed investigations, harassment and civil suits or criminal charges. How could that be, one may ask? Remember Isaiah 47:6-*"I was angry with my people...and I gave them into your hand."* The *"your"* referenced here is the Daughter of Babylon mentioned in the preceding verse. When God hands over His people, in effect, that means He will withdraw His hedge of protection, and persons who are motivated to attack and hurt Christians, will freely be allowed to do so. That could be private persons, who are not restrained by the government in their attacks on God's people, and it can also mean official acts of the government. Whichever it is, most likely both, in looking back, it almost seems the 'hounds of hell' against the church were set loose in the last few weeks of 2008.

OUR GOVERNMENT IN ACTION

On January 20, 2009 America was given a new President. How that President views *the way in which* the federal government should treat Christians, and their tax-exempt churches and ministries, is just beginning to emerge. But there are some disturbing early indicators. Even under the George W. Bush administration, the Internal Revenue Service launched a publicly revealed investigation into a local church of which one of the candidates for President had been a member for twenty years, and also began an investigation of the denomination of that church. That kind of precedent could easily carry over to investigations of churches that may have opposed candidates for President, from the pulpit, or supported or opposed other public issues. Where that could lead should cause concern.

Senator Charles Grassley (R-Iowa) launched an investigation in 2007 demanding several national televangelists turn over previously private detailed financial information, revealing salaries, expenses, and related information. Others to his political left, may be even more motivated to attempt to shut down what they view as ministries abusing tax and financial disclosure laws. Judgment begins at the house of God. (I Peter 4:17)

In the 2008 campaign for President, a number of political positions were taken by religious figures that could lead to repercussions. The *New York Times* reported on October 2, 2005 that Bishop Joseph Martino of Scranton, Pennsylvania ordered every Catholic priest in his diocese to read a letter warning in a special homily that voting for a supporter of abortion (in 2008, that was Senator, now President, Barack Obama) amounted to *"endorsing homicide."* Bishop Martino wrote that *"being 'right' on taxes, education, health care, emigration and the economy fails to make up for the error of disregarding the value of human life. It is a tragic irony that 'pro-choice' candidates have come to support homicide–the gravest injustice a society can tolerate– in the name of 'social justice'."* Bishop Martino's letter attracted extra attention because Scranton is the boyhood home of Vice President Biden.

As mentioned, California Proposition 8 was placed on the ballot by voters who sought to reverse the 4-3 ruling of the California Supreme Court which set aside traditional marriage between a man and a woman. Prop 8 was heavily contested, with millions spent by both sides on television ads and other campaign techniques. In the end, supporters of traditional marriage were successful as Prop 8 passed. Within hours, tens of thousands of those who favor same-sex marriage organized protests, some violent. One same-sex marriage organization, Californians Against Hate, filed a Complaint with the California Fair Political Practices Commission calling for an investigation and $5,000 per incident fines against the Mormon Church for its involvement in promoting the successful adoption of Prop 8. Gay activists in California established a website showing the address and location on neighborhood maps of those who contributed money to passing Prop 8. (*Fox News*, January 14, 2009). What could be the possible motive for targeting these individuals?

The *New York Times* editorially asserted that Prop 8 *"wrote discrimination against one particular group of people into the State Constitution"* (November 29, 2008). Upholding the 6,000 year history of marriage between a man and a woman is *"discrimination against one particular group of people"*? Future attacks against churches of all types may well be inevitable.

Just before the November 2008 general election there was a nationwide effort by several Protestant pastors to exercise their First Amendment rights, and to speak from their pulpits about politics and about candidates for office, with most making it clear they did not favor the election of Senator Obama as President. Organized by the Alliance Defense Fund, the pastors spoke in open defiance of a portion of the IRS Code which states that a tax exempt organization *"does not participate in or intervene in (including the publishing or distributing of statements), any political campaign on behalf of (or in opposition to) any candidate for public office."* The IRS Code provision was adopted by Congress in 1954 upon the urging of then Senator Lyndon Baines Johnson. In the previous general election Johnson had been opposed by two non-profit 501(C)(3) organizations that urged voters to reject Johnson and his *"radical communist ideas."*

If a Texas Senator a half century ago decided to get even with 501(C)(3) tax exempt organizations because they opposed his election, what can be expected today? Those who raised the political sword in the 2008 election may be dealt with in the same manner. *"As you live by the sword you will die by the sword'* could be a misapplication of scripture that will come down on those who opposed certain candidates. Or, as the media have said: *"if you leave the sanctuary for the kitchen, you get the heat."* All of this assumes, of course, that the political and governmental views of Christians must stay in the sanctuary, and if brought out into the kitchen of the public square, they may expect to *"feel the heat"* of religious persecution, contrary to the plain words of the free exercise clause of the First Amendment.

Don't be surprised in the near future to see the following laws proposed and adopted, based on the erroneous argument that the so-called "separation of church and state" (which is no where in the United States Constitution) prohibits the government, federal, state and local from giving any support to religion, in any form whatsoever, directly or indirectly:

A.) RELIGIOUS BROADCASTING

"Without recourse to a vote, the president, or even just an unelected Federal Communications Commission commissioner, could drive conservatives and Christians off the air, as one more step in the new liberals' relentless campaign to drive Christian principles from public life." (Don Wildman, *Speechless, Silencing the Christians*, Richard Vigilante Books, 2009)

Expect to see an amendment to the Federal Communications Act (47 USC Sec. 151, *et seq.*) to prohibit the granting or renewal of licenses to "religious stations," radio and television, based on the argument that the public owns the broadcast spectrum, and any licensed use of any portion of the public spectrum constitutes an impermissible endorsement of religious expression by the government. It's only been by the grace of God that America's religious broadcasters have been allowed to operate as long as they have.

It will be ironic if such a major change in the Federal Communications Act occurs, as well-meaning Christians for several years have been duped into sending petitions to the Federal Communications Commission protesting a mythical petition by Madalyn Murray O'Hair (who has been dead since 1995) to suspend religious broadcasting. There never was such a petition, but don't be surprised if anti-Christian activists actually do file complaints against religious broadcasters. Also, expect certain members of Congress to introduce an amendment to the Federal Communications Act under which religious broadcasters would lose their licenses under such an amendment, in order to avoid the "entanglement of church and state." Also, we should expect re-adoption of the misnamed *"Fairness Doctrine."* This would have the effect of shutting down talk shows that include discussions of topics and officials not favored by those in power. Soon after the new Congress convened in 2009, U. S. Senator Debbie Stabenow of Michigan confirmed that *"it was time to bring back the Fairness Doctrine"* and that hearings would take place to adopt legislation to see *"accountability and standards put in place."* If the "Fairness Doctrine" is adopted, the free speech clause of the First Amendment would be effectively repealed.

B.) RELIGIOUS CONTRIBUTIONS

"Trend #5–Rising Intolerance of the Christian Worldview –In the days ahead, we are going to see a pronounced intolerance toward the Christian perspective. I believe the biblical worldview will be unwelcome in the discourse of determining U.S. public policy for national, state or even local legislation.. I expect some attempt will be made to eliminate income tax deductions for charitable contributions."(Money Matters, Crown Financial Ministries, CEO Chuck Bentley, *"Five Predictable Trends"*)

Expect to see a push to amend the Internal Revenue Code [26 U.S.C. 501(C)(3)] deleting from the list of specified organizations entitled to tax exemption for contributions under Section 501(C)(3) any organization which has a religious purpose. The argument is? Why should taxpayers have to pay for the costs of government, when contributors to religious tax-exempt organizations pay less individual income taxes due to the religious contribution deduction? That, it may be argued, is an illegal endorsement of religion by the state, which the Constitution will not countenance. Those pushing for this change in the law, will undoubtedly base their legal arguments for removing tax exempt status on *Bob Jones University v. United States*, 461 U.S. 574 (1983), in which the U. S. Supreme Court removed the tax exempt status of the religious school because it had policies *"contrary to established public policy."* They will likely argue that failure to hire those who support same sex marriage violates public policy. Substitute 'sexual orientation' for 'race' in the reasoning from the Opinion and entire ministries and churches will no longer be allowed 501(C)(3) status, if they refuse to hire on a quota basis, those whom they would not normally hire out of religious conviction. Expect a line in a future case patterned on *Bob Jones:* "...the government has a fundamental, overriding interest in eradicating (sexual orientation) discrimination..."

All states include in their state statutes an exemption from taxation of property owned by churches, qualified, ministries, charities, not-for-profits, schools, etc. Expect a movement to arise to exclude religious property tax exemptions, under the same church/state separation arguments. Though not widespread, and certainly not successful, over the last few years, there have been outbreaks of efforts by persons who want to repeal the exemption from property taxes of religious property, even though exempting religious buildings from such taxes has been traced as far back as pre-Christian Egypt. Property taxes are levied and collected at the local level. Because this is a local issue, in order to effect a national change, Congress could adopt legislation that would have the effect of penalizing states which don't repeal property tax exemption for religious purposes. It has done so in the past. For example, for states which allowed speed limits on highways, higher than considered prudent by Congress, federal funding was lost. 'With shekels come shackles.'

In January, 2009 the American Civil Liberties Union filed suit in Boston, charging that the U.S. Conference of Catholic Bishops, and the U.S. government, had violated the Constitution by granting money to the church to help women hurt by human trafficking. The ACLU said the church's refusal to work with subcontractors who provide abortions was a violation of the so-called separation of church. The pattern here is clear–the ACLU will sue whenever any tax dollars are granted to help solve human problems, *if* the grants go to *religious* organizations.

President Obama's proposed new federal budget, released in late February, 2009, included a provision that Americans who make a certain level of income will not be allowed to fully deduct contributions to churches and other charities, as in the past. A study, soon after the budget was released, showed that contributions from those affected taxpayers would decline by at least 26%, or a decrease of $81 billion a year. This proposal appeared to be aimed squarely at decreasing the amount that will be contributed to various ministries. The proposal may well have been the first shot in a drive to hobble institutions of faith. Shortly thereafter, a bill was introduced in the Connecticut General Assembly that would have taken away from the "Roman Catholic Church" management and financial control over any of the Church's congregations in Connecticut. Though a hearing on the bill was called off due to public outcry, the mere filing of such a bill speaks volumes about where anti-religious sentiment is headed in America.

C.) RELIGIOUS HATE SPEECH

In 2003 Sweden added *"sexual orientation"* to its *"hate crime laws."* Soon thereafter, in 2004, Pastor Ike Green was convicted in Sweden of a hate crime for giving a sermon, from the Bible, repeating what the Bible says on the subject of same gender sexual relations. Only after an international outcry was Pastor Green's conviction reversed by the Swedish Supreme Court, although in doing so, the Court labeled the Bible's views as *"offensive."* Canada also amended its national criminal code to add *"sexual orientation"* to its *"hate crime"* legislation. Pastors and teachers there have been charged with the crime of inciting hatred for preaching the Biblical prohibition of same gender sexual conduct (38 *Vanderbilt Journal of Transnational Law 443).* A federal Hate Crimes Act for America has been on the front burner of Congress for some time, and is slated for early passage. How long will it be in America before the *enforcers* of the Hate Crimes Act, federal employees of some newly created agency or recruited from an existing agency (such as the FBI or the Department of Homeland Security), receive the assignment, and begin to monitor what comes from the nation's pulpits? Churches are generally open to the public, to all who wish to attend, so it wouldn't take much effort to assign monitors to Sunday services, record the messages and file indictments for violation of the new Federal Hate Crimes Act.

Once started, where will it end? Isaiah and John give us some indication. Isaiah, 47:6, states: *"I was angry with my people and desecrated my inheritance; I gave them into your hand, and you showed them no mercy. Even on the aged you laid a very heavy yoke."* *"No mercy"* sounds chilling. John in Revelation 18:24 reveals that in the Daughter of Babylon was found the blood of saints, a Biblical phrase for Christians. Thus, oppression by the Daughter of Babylon/the American government, its lack of mercy and its heavy yoke laid upon God's people, will eventually result in spilled blood, as scripture prophecies.

How close may Christians, particularly pro life Christians, be to official oppression? The Department of Homeland Security, Homeland Environment Threat Analysis Division, Extremism and Radicalization Branch, on April 7, 2007, sent to law enforcement authorities across the nation a threat Assessment entitled: *"Rightwing Extremism: Current Economic and Political Climate Fueling Resurgence in Radicalization and Recruitment."* The Assessment was not to be released *"to the public, the media or other personnel who do not have a valid need-to-know."* The Assessment stated that *"rightwing extremism"* in the United States *"may include groups that are dedicated to a single issue, such as opposition to abortion or emigration,"* and *"disgruntled military veterans."* The Assessment was written so local officials could *"respond to terrorist attacks"* by American *"rightwing extremists."* This from a Department that officially does not use the word *"terrorist"* to describe Jihadists, but is not reluctant to use the term for single issue or military veteran Americans.

D.) THE SHEDDING OF RELIGIOUS BLOOD

There may be voices raised, petitions signed, and letters to the editor written, when broadcast licenses and tax exemptions are taken away. But physical protests in the street would most likely come when the feds haul our pastors out of our churches' pulpits. Just as inevitably, there would be violence, and then bloodshed. That won't happen, one might say. Tell that to the students at the Kent State massacre, or folks at the Waco debacle, or to the grandmothers arrested in Philadelphia for peacefully protesting social issues.

As to timing, therefore, it would be an appropriate analysis of the Daughter of Babylon prophecies to expect to see persecution, oppression, and the shedding of the blood of God's people *before* the destruction of the Daughter of Babylon. That's because the blood of the saints is cited by John as being found in the Daughter of Babylon at the time of her destruction. But the blood of the saints is *not* cited as the *reason* for the destruction of Babylon. The blood of the saints is observed in the Daughter of Babylon, as a nation, but no verse says that is why the nation falls. Remember that God says He will become angry with His own people, and He will turn His people over for punishment, just as He did with Israel, as set forth in the Old Testament prophets.

In many ways, the persecution of God's people by the Daughter of Babylon will be *a blessing*. What? One may ask. Persecution will be a *blessing*? Since the Daughter of Babylon verses warn God's people to flee from The Daughter of Babylon, what would be the most effective way to encourage God's people to actually move? When God was ready to move His people from Europe to settle North America, He didn't make things comfortable, but He instead sent/allowed troubles, persecution and sorrows. Why did the Pilgrims flee England? The Pilgrims, also known in England as Separatists, were opposed to governmental requirements that they attend official Church of England services, with a monetary fine for each missed Sunday and holy day. The penalties for conducting unofficial non-Church of England services included imprisonment and larger fines. Disobedient clergy were replaced, and prominent Separatists were confronted, fined, and imprisoned. Two leaders of the Christian movement, Henry Barrowe and John Greenwood, were executed for sedition, crimes against the state, in 1593. Many Christians were driven out of the country because of their beliefs.

After Stephen, the Church's first martyr, was executed, many Christians left Israel: *"Now those who had been scattered by the persecution in connection with Stephen traveled as far as Phoenicia, Cyprus and Antioch...telling them the good news about the LORD Jesus."* (Acts 11:19-20). Likewise, the increasing persecution of God's People in America should serve as a holy incentive to move, just as it was in the early Church. Notice that God used the exodus of early Christians from Israel to spread the Gospel into nations hundreds of miles away. He can do the same thing in the early 21st Century, as committed Christians settle into their new homes, and share their savior with their new neighbors.

It very well may become the case that American Christians and Orthodox and Conservative Jews are "encouraged" to leave our shores due to increasing persecution, church destruction, invasion of church services, imprisonment of pastors, rabbis and others, such as those who speak out against the 'official' government position on social issues. In that sense, what will happen to many Christians and Jews in the future can be the final 'nudge' which will lead many to move, and will literally save their lives when the Daughter of Babylon is destroyed.

Chapter Seven
HOW DOES GOD VIEW
THE DAUGHTER OF BABYLON?

"A second angel followed and said, "Fallen! Fallen is Babylon the Great, which made all the nations drink the maddening wine of her adulteries." (Revelation 14:8)

"Come, I will show you the punishment of the great prostitute, who sits on many waters. With her the kings of the earth committed adultery and the inhabitants of the earth were intoxicated with the wine of her adulteries." (Revelation 17:1)

"The woman was clothed in purple and scarlet, and adorned with gold and precious stones and pearls, having in her hand a gold cup full of abominations and of the unclean things of her immorality, and on her forehead a name was written, a mystery, "BABYLON THE GREAT, THE MOTHER OF HARLOTS AND OF THE ABOMINATIONS OF THE EARTH." (Revelation 17:4-5)

"And he cried out with a mighty voice, saying, "Fallen, fallen is Babylon the great! She has become a dwelling place of demons and a prison of every unclean spirit, and a prison of every unclean and hateful bird. For all the nations have drunk of the wine of the passion of her immorality, and the kings of the earth have committed acts of immorality with her, and the merchants of the earth have become rich by the wealth of her sensuality." (Revelation 18:2-3)

"...for He has judged the great harlot who was corrupting the earth with her immorality..." (Revelation 19:2b – NASB)

The following chapter has proved to be one of the more difficult portions of this book for the author to write, and perhaps difficult for the reader, as well. When reading the above verses from Revelation, in the 1970's, it was easy to conclude the verses must refer to some miserably corrupt institution or nation, but certainly not to our nation, our beloved United States of America. Few people disdain their own country, for obvious reasons. "Our nation, right or wrong," has been our unofficial motto for a long time. But now in the 21st century, by any societal indicia, America has become a decidedly changed country from just a few decades ago. The purpose of this portion of the book is not just to decry our obvious declining standards of morality, an easy task for any impartial observer, but also to see if we as a nation fit the description of the Daughter of Babylon found in scripture. The question is: do these additional scriptural clues to the identity of the Daughter of Babylon, centered on her *immorality* fit America?

Though Christians are loyal and patriotic Americans, our most important citizenship is as citizens of heaven, our true and future home. *"But our citizenship is in heaven. And we eagerly await a Savior from there, the LORD Jesus Christ"* (Philippians 3:20). As Congressman Mike Pence of Indiana frequently says: *"I am a Christian first, an American second and a Republican third."* Is it possible then for us as American Christians in the beginning of the 21st century to accurately view our nation? To see it not for what it *was*, but instead, for *what it has become*? To see our nation *as God sees it?*

In His Word, God sees the Daughter of Babylon for what it *had been* (past tense) and what it *will become*. He says the nation *"had been"* (past tense) *"a Golden Cup"* in His hand. However, by the time of Revelation 17:4 the Golden Cup is filled with filthiness and abominations. According to scripture, the Daughter of Babylon fills the earth with *"immorality,"* a word not very politically correct these days.

The common mantra of today is to not "legislate morality," though, of course, every law is a statement of what that nation's people believe to be moral or immoral. Not incorporating a nation's views of moral conduct in its laws would inevitably lead to a lawless society.

If we are a nation, in God's view, responsible for several abominations, we have an obligation to see and understand, with clear eyes, our *true condition* before God. Our prayer should be for wisdom asking God to show us the "*abominations*" of our nation in our times. Following are but a few that readily come to mind:

IMMORALITY IDENTITY CLUE A – ABORTION

Chapter 8 ("*God's Accounting for the Shedding of Innocent Blood*") explores in depth, the heinous sin of killing our nation's infants in the womb. Though many other nations, but not all, also allow abortion, it has been America which has *led* in the abortion movement. Once *Roe v. Wade* was handed down by the Supreme Court of the world's leading nation, abortions took off in nations across the globe. Prior to *Roe,* only two nations allowed strictly limited availability of abortion. After America approved abortion on demand, with no effective limit as to when in the gestation period abortion was allowed, and no restriction whatsoever on the reason for the abortion, the floodgates were opened in nations worldwide. John wrote in Revelation 17, that Babylon was the "*mother*" of abominations. In other words, an innovator and pioneer of promoting sin. Once America 'birthed' the killing of babies, others quickly concluded they should follow our lead and do the same.

Not content with just 'birthing' modern-day abortion on demand, America has taken an active role in pressuring other nations to change their laws to allow abortion on demand. Google any of the nations listed in Chapter 13 that *don't allow abortion* by law. The surrounding articles disclose that the Center for Reproductive Law and Policy, headquartered in the U.S., is involved in inducing those nations to change their laws, to allow abortion. What is a New York City based pro-abortion advocacy group doing in other nations lobbying them to repeal *their laws* against abortion? The Center, which is funded in large part by "*grants*" from unspecified sources, states on its website that abortion is "*a fundamental right that all governments are legally obligated to protect, respect and fulfill,*" promising to "*work toward the time when (abortion) is enshrined in law...throughout the world.*" It brags on its opening page that it is active in promoting abortion law changes from "*the poorest neighborhoods of Rio De Janeiro*" to "*the mountains of Nepal.*" Americans are thus telling foreign lawmakers that they must repeal their laws prohibiting abortion, such as Chile, whose laws have been on the nation's law books *for centuries.*

In the first week after becoming President, Barack Obama signed an Executive Order lifting restrictions on the use of American foreign aid dollars sent to other countries for "*family planning purposes.*" There are now no restrictions on these foreign aid recipients from promoting abortion, using American tax dollars. . . our tax dollars. America alone among the nations of the world, is the only nation sending its treasure, both private funds and public tax dollars, to the other nations of the world, to facilitate and encourage the killing of those nations' infants.

What other nation in the world can be said to be the "*mother*" of the *abomination of abortion,* more than America? We own the title.

IMMORALITY IDENTITY CLUE B - PORNOGRAPHY

America, by all accounts, produces and distributes more pornographic movies, magazines and DVDs than any other nation. Porn industry revenue exceeds $15 billion per year. Internet users can access 1.3 million pornographic websites. There were over one billion adult DVD/video rentals and over 13,500 hardcore pornographic titles produced and released in the most recent year surveyed (*Adult Video News* and *Internet Filter Review*). CNN news reported in January, 2009 that fully 25% of working Americans visit pornographic websites on their office computers while at work. One out of every six women, including Christians, struggles with an addiction to pornography (*Today's Christian Woman*, Fall 2003). Child pornography is a $3 billion annual industry (*Internet Filter Review*). China has announced that it is studying how to protect its people from pornography.

Christianity Today in March, 2008, reported that seventy percent of American men age 18–34 view Internet pornography once a month. The magazine warned: *"Don't assume that porn isn't a problem in the church. One evangelical leader was skeptical of survey findings that said 50 percent of Christian men have looked at porn recently. So he surveyed his own congregation. He found that 60 percent had done so within the past year, and 25 percent within the past 30 days. Other surveys reveal that one in three visitors to adult websites is a woman. Porn is gaining a stranglehold on mainstream American culture."* At a 2003 meeting of the American Academy of Matrimonial Lawyers, two thirds of the divorce lawyers who attended said the Internet played a significant role in divorces in the past year, with excessive interest in online porn contributing to more than *half* of the divorce cases. They also said that *"pornography had an almost non-existent role in divorce just seven or eight years ago."* (Divorcewizards.com) It's interesting that a major criticism Jihadists proclaim to the Muslim world is that America is a primary source of moral corruption through its *pornography.*

IMMORALITY IDENTITY CLUE C – ADULTERY/DIVORCE

America didn't invent adultery, nor divorce, both of which are criticized early in scripture. But, it has promoted, glamorized, and legitimized both. American movies are sub-titled and viewed all over the world. America's movies, since the mid-1960's, have increasingly depicted actors involved in sexual affairs outside of their marriages. Do we know that America's promotion of adultery in its movies is actually influencing people in other cultures? The American Legacy Foundation recently wrote, not about adultery, but about the influence of American movies on teen smoking:

"A second study out of Germany published in the American Journal of Preventive Medicine found teens who had seen the most smoking in movies (mostly U.S. movies) were twice as likely to have tried smoking as those who saw the least amount–results that mirror findings in the U.S. The researchers also determined that smoking in internationally distributed movies is associated with current smoking among German adolescents....This evidence should impel the film industry to take this issue seriously as it has apparent potential worldwide risks. It is time for the influencers in the movie industry to do what is right and implement evidence-based policies...that permanently and substantially reduce adolescent exposure to on-screen smoking. When we get smoking out of youth-rated movies in Hollywood, it will be felt all the way to Kiev, Cape Town, Shanghai, and Djakarta."

Smoking is not the issue (though some may claim that the health effects of American dollars spent on marketing and promotion of smoking worldwide, amounts to an abomination), but what is clear by analogy from this study, is that people who watch America's movies want to do what they see in America's movies. The nation has been in the forefront of promoting adultery, through its movies and television shows, which generally leads to divorce. America has one of the highest divorce rates in the world. The divorce rate in Britain has doubled since 1971; in Germany the divorce rate has doubled since 1960; and in Greece it more than doubled since 1970. To what do we attribute these startling increases? Global warming? Something in the air? Or maybe something on the *airwaves*? America has been the 'mother' of the promotion and glorification of adultery (leading to divorce), in spite of the Seventh Commandment's prohibition (Exodus 20:14). What other nation can make such a dishonorable claim?

IMMORALITY IDENTITY CLUE D – SAME SEX MARRIAGE

In 1986, the United States Supreme Court, in *Bowers v. Hardwick,* upheld the right of the States to adopt sodomy laws. Chief Justice Warren Burger wrote in his concurring opinion, that society had historically held negative attitudes toward homosexual sex, quoting Sir William Blackstone's description of sodomy as *"a crime not fit to be named."* The Chief Justice wrote: *"To hold that the act of homosexual sodomy is somehow protected as a fundamental right would be to cast aside millennia of moral teaching."*

Seventeen years later, in 2003, the Supreme Court directly overruled *Bowers v. Hardwick* in the case of *Lawrence v. Texas,* thus casting aside millennia of moral teaching. In the oral argument before the Court, Justice Antonin Scalia said from the bench that some were arguing that the case had nothing to do with same sex marriage. Scalia said, *"Don't you believe it."* Before *Lawrence,* same sex marriage was rarely, if ever, mentioned in public discourse. Scalia wrote in his dissent, that laws against persons of the same gender marrying were *"sustainable only in light of Bowers' validation of laws based on moral choices."* Scalia's prediction that the floodgates would open to same sex marriage with *Lawrence's* invalidation of sodomy laws proved to be correct. Massachusetts, Connecticut, Vermont, Rhode Island, Maine and Iowa have authorized persons of the same gender to marry. In 2008 California narrowly defeated an effort to authorize same sex marriage in the state. What just a few years ago was not even *discussed*, is now *the law* in some jurisdictions, and quite likely to be the law in other states, if not the entire nation, soon. Justice Scalia in his dissent wrote that the Court *"has largely signed on to the so-called homosexual agenda"*.

A major portion of the decision in *Lawrence* dealt with the history of the issue, with Justice Kennedy, who wrote the majority opinion, critical of former Chief Justice Burger's statement in *Bowers* that homosexuality was an historically condemned practice. Kennedy emphasized in his ruling a

1981European Court of Human Rights case, but ignored the historical record as to the original source of the term and the criminal act known as *"sodomy"*. In Genesis 19 God records how He dealt with a community in which *"all the men from every part of the city of Sodom—both young and old—surrounded the house"* in an attempt to rape male visitors to Lot's house. God's destruction of Sodom and nearby towns that apparently had fallen into Sodom's *"wicked"* ways, was so significant that: a.) it became the only crime in history named after a town; b.) for centuries, even millennia, until our time, same gender sexual acts were illegal, as law enactors apparently didn't want what happened to Sodom to happen to their communities; c.) some European nations prohibited persons engaged in same gender relations from owning property; d.) the British common law's prohibition against sodomy was carried to this country; and e.) at one point in time all American States had sodomy laws. Jesus warned that in the end times things would change on this subject, as they certainly have after 3,500 years. He said the last days would be like *"the days of Lot"* (Luke 17:26-30).

America continues to have the predominant global role on this issue. Though America was not the first to allow same sex marriage (Netherlands was first), it is leading the way, 'mothering' this issue to global prominence.

IMMORALITY IDENTITY CLUE E – VIOLENCE

Osama bin Laden, the originating source of the 9/11 attacks, in a speech broadcast on January 19, 2006 on the al Jazeera network, uttered a statement worth pursuing. He said that Americans should read a book entitled *Rogue State*. Bin Laden in his recorded speeches hasn't referred to any other published book, apart from the Quran. *"If you [Americans] are sincere in your desire for peace and security, we have answered you. And if Bush decides to carry on with his lies and oppression, then it would be useful for you to read the book 'Rogue State'.* One has to be curious why a little known American book about America would be cited by the world's best-known terrorist. The 388 page paperback is published by Common Courage Press of Monroe, Maine and authored by William Blum, a self-described investigative journalist.

Rogue State–A Guide to the World's Only Superpower is a broadside criticism of American foreign policy and military interventions from 1945 to the present. In Chapter 17 (*"A Concise History of United States Global Interventions, 1945 to Present"*), found on pages 163 to 220 of the book, Blum sets forth details of American interventions in various nations of the world, some of which we recall, and some of which are not so well remembered. He recounts these seventy American military and intelligence agency interventions since 1945:

China 1945-51; France, 1947; Marshall Islands, 1946-58; Italy, 1947-1970s; Greece, 1947-49; Philippines, 1945-53; Korea, 1945-53; Albania, 1949-53; Eastern Europe, 1948-56; Germany, 1950s; Iran, 1953; Guatemala, 1953-1990s; Costa Rica, mid-1950s, 1970-71; Middle East, 1956-58; Indonesia, 1957-58; Haiti, 1959; Western Europe, 1950s-1960s; British Guiana/Guyana, 1953-64; Iraq, 1958-63; Soviet Union, 1940s-1960s; Vietnam, 1945-73; Cambodia, 1955-73; Laos, 1957-73; Thailand, 1965-73; Ecuador, 1960-63; The Congo/Zaire, 1960-65, 1977-78; France/Algeria, 1960s; Brazil, 1961-64; Peru, 1965;Dominican Republic, 1963-65;Cuba, 1959 to present; Indonesia, 1965; Uruguay, 1969-72; Chile, 1964-73; Greece, 1967-74; South Africa, 1960s-1980s; Bolivia, 1964-75; Australia, 1972-75; Iraq, 1972-75; Portugal, 1974-76; East Timor, 1975-99; Angola, 1975-1980s; Jamaica, 1976; Honduras, 1980s; Nicaragua, 1979-90; Philippines, 1970s-1990s; Seychelles, 1979-81; Diego Garcia, late 1960s to present; South Yemen, 1979-84; South Korea, 1980; Chad, 1981-82; Grenada, 1979-83; Suriname, 1982-84; Libya, 1981-89; Fiji, 1987; Panama, 1989; Afghanistan, 1979-92; El Salvador, 1980-92; Haiti, 1987-94; Bulgaria, 1990-91; Albania, 1991-92; Somalia, 1993; Iraq, 1991-2003; Colombia, 1990s to present; Yugoslavia, 1995-99; Ecuador, 2000; Afghanistan, 2001 to present; Venezuela, 2001-2004; Iraq, 2003 to present; Haiti, 2004.

Rogue State author Blum sets out details for each of the 70 interventions, ranging from attempts, some successful, to depose national leaders, all the way up to full scale invasion and war. Obviously, some of the seventy were/are more extensive and intrusive than others, but Blum claims America did intervene, in various ways and to varying extents in each one of the seventy. This list does assist in confirming one thing-that Jeremiah's identity clue describing the Daughter of Babylon as the *"hammer of the whole earth"* (Jeremiah 50:23) certainly applies to America, in light of such an extensive series of interventions in the other nations of the world. No other 20th or 21st century nation can come close to making such a claim.

Many of these American interventions were for good and noble purposes. America's role in liberating oppressed people stands it apart from most nations who have used their military for purposes of conquest, not liberation. It would be dishonest to cast all of these American actions as objectionable, which appears to be why bin Laden raised *Rogue State* in his al Jazeera speech. On the other hand, if one were to stand back and try to dispassionately analyze such an extensive series of interventions in other nations, it would also be honest to conclude that America has spent a lot of its treasure in other nations, whatever the reasons. Jeremiah refers to the Daughter of Babylon as the *"arrogant one"* (Jeremiah 50:31), which is an interesting description, much heard on the Muslim street today to describe the world's only superpower. President Obama at the G-20 Conference in France in April, 2009, stated in his comments that America had, at times, been *"arrogant."*

But, would God allow a nation to fall if that nation, in its military and intelligence agency interventions, also did so frequently for *good purposes?* As noted, the reason God gives for the fall of this end times nation is the shedding of blood of God's people by it's betrayal of Israel. However, the Daughter of Babylon is criticized, in part, because it starts or 'mothers' many abominations, so it's appropriate to analyze what those abominations may be. We have scriptural guidance on this question. David was a man of war. He fought numerous battles that the Lord led him/allowed him to fight. However, because of that history of violence, when it came time to build the Temple, the Lord told David he would *not* be constructing it. Some have concluded that this was because of the volume of blood that David shed in his many wars.

There is no question that America has liberated the oppressed, has set captives free, and has defended those who were in danger of destruction at the hands of violent aggressors. It is also true that America has not always exercised discretion in how we did what we did. Some would give as an example invading Iraq, without any prior attack by Iraq on our shores. As patriotic Americans, we take pride in the many people freed by our troops, as was Europe from the powers of Nazi Germany and Asia from Imperial Japan. In an effort to see our nation as we are seen by others, and as our nation is viewed by our Lord, we must acknowledge that we have been, like David, violence prone.

In a moral equivalence argument that won't wash, Al Qaeda attempts to justify its terror by pointing out repeatedly, that America was the first and only nation to use nuclear weapons, and we used them on two cities populated for the most part by civilians. The Japanese surprise attack on Pearl Harbor led to approximately 3,300 casualties, mostly military personnel. American military casualties in the Pacific theater were approximately 100,000. U.S. nuclear weapons used on Hiroshima and Nagasaki led to approximately 220,000 casualties, almost all of whom were civilians. America dropped its atomic bombs on Japan in early August 1945, though Secretary of War Henry Stimson had concluded that, since 67 Japanese cities had been destroyed by firebombing, Japan could collapse within a matter of weeks (*World at War*, PBS).

In response, some may say that the Japanese civilian population '*deserved*' what it got. After all, 'it was their government that waged war in the world, and the Japanese people didn't *stop* it.' Applying the same logic to the 50 million Americans killed by abortion, one could similarly say: 'it was the government elected by Americans that allowed 50 million to die in abortions, and the American people didn't *stop* it.' So, will America, likewise, *deserve* what it will get?

On September 8, 2007, terrorist leader Osama bin Laden concluded his remarks with these words: *"The genocide of peoples and their holocausts took place at your hands: only a few specimens of Red Indians were spared, and just a few days ago, the Japanese observed the 62nd anniversary of the annihilation of Hiroshima and Nagasaki by your nuclear weapons."* Osama bin Laden has referred to his plan to destroy America as *"the American Hiroshima."*

IMMORALITY IDENTITY CLUE F – DRUG CULTURE

Any analyst of the illegal drug culture in the world today will acknowledge that *the* major driving engine of the illegal drug trade is the American consumer of drugs. Here is a portion of a blog from a South American crusader against drugs:

"If there were not so many consumers in the United States, then we would not produce so many drugs. We are simply supplying a product where there is a demand. It is as simple as the law of supply and demand! Your average campesino is only trying to make a living the best way he can. They do not use or consume drugs themselves after all. The sad fact of the matter is that too many Latin Americans, because of lack of education and underdeveloped Third World economies, have nothing better (or more profitable) to do with their time and industry than produce and smuggle illicit drugs. And the United States has the temerity to blame the Latin Americans for their own huge drug appetite! Everyone in the United States has been told that drugs are dangerous and yet people still buy and consume them to the tune of an estimated 57.3 billion dollars in 1995!

The 2009 CIA Factbook reports:

"The United States is the world's largest consumer of cocaine, Colombian heroin, and Mexican heroin and marijuana; major consumer of ecstasy and Mexican methamphetamine; minor consumer of high-quality Southeast Asian heroin; illicit producer of cannabis, marijuana, depressants, ...hallucinogens, and methamphetamine."

IMMORALITY IDENTITY CLUE G – WITCHCRAFT

It may be surprising to learn how many Witchcraft and Occult titles are carried in American bookstores. A search of 'Witchcraft Books' on Amazon.com produces 4,180 available titles. Likewise, typing in 'Occult Books' will show 6,040 books available for purchase. Law enforcement officers can vouch for the prevalence of evil witchcraft and occult practices in their communities. And should the astrology column be omitted from our local newspapers, there is a public outcry.

Isaiah, in describing the "virgin Daughter of Babylon wrote: *Keep on, then, with your magic spells and with your many sorceries, which you have labored at since childhood...Let your astrologers come forward, those stargazers who make predictions month by month, let them save you from what is coming upon you."* (Isaiah 47:12-13)

The application of the name of Babylon to America as Babylon's Daughter is appropriate. Nimrod was the founder of Babylon and of the black arts. *"Nimrod had his people build a number of ziggurats (temple-towers) for religious purposes. These were claimed to be staircases from earth to heaven, and were used for satanic worship and occultic initiation. The best known was at Babylon, and was called 'The Platform of Heaven and Earth.' This is the famous 'Tower of Babel'–(Babel means 'Gateway to God' as well as 'Confusion'). Josephus, the Jewish/Roman historian, records 'it was Nimrod who ... said that he would be revenged on*

God, if He should have a mind to drown the world again: for he would build a tower too high for the waters to be able to reach and that he would avenge himself on God for destroying their forefathers.' Nimrod rebelled against God, and determined to lead the people away with him. Together with his wife, Semiramis, Nimrod created most of what we know today as Occultism, including witchcraft, astrology, blood sacrifices and much more. Nimrod...required human sacrifices by fire, particularly of children... The overwhelming evidence is that Nimrod, Semiramis and many of the other priestly leaders were involved in direct Satanic contact and activity." (Selwyn Stevens Ph.D., *The New Age: The Old Lie in a New Package*, 1992)

IMMORALITY IDENTITY CLUE H – SUMPTUOUS, SELF-INDULGENT LIFESTYLES

America has 4.5% of the world's population. Americans consume 25% of the world's energy and 27% of the world's total annual output of goods and services. How does God view the Daughter of Babylon's living standards?

"You who live by many waters and are rich in treasures..." (Jeremiah 51:13)

"...the merchants of the earth grew rich from her excessive luxuries" (Revelation 18:3)

"Give her as much torture and grief as the glory and luxury she gave herself." Revelation 18:7

A recent article about the lifestyle of one of the emerging stock market 'Ponzi scheme scammers used language that could well apply, to varying degrees, to many in America:

" The Gatsbyesque mansion at the crest of a hill overlooking Titicus Reservoir, with the Palladian interior and library made from Cuban mahogany. The 250-acre horse

146

farm. It is the now-clichéd litany of excess and indulgence, leavened with a few lordly footnotes of charity and good work as if the biggest crooks of our time really did have it all – more pilfered riches than Croesus and the grateful respect of the little people for their generosity as well. Rich and beloved. Who could ask for more?" (*New York Times*, March 1, 2009, *When a Public Persona of Generosity Hits a Wall of Fraud Charges*).

America has established sumptuous, self indulgent lifestyles as the goal for the rest of the world. America largely invented, perfected and spread across the globe the art and practice of advertising goods and services to convince consumers they needed what they did not yet have. The emerging consumers of the world seek to be like us.

IMMORALITY IDENTITY CLUE I – OTHER ABOMINATIONS

Most people love their country; so honestly, looking at the errors of one's own homeland is not easy. Many American expatriates, who have chosen to live in other parts of the world, write that it was *only* from the viewpoint of living outside America that they could clearly see America's failures. Seeing America as it really is though, may be quite difficult, even for God's people. If we ask our loving Lord to open our eyes and show us the true condition of our church and our nation, we will better see the abominations of both.

As for the reference in Revelation 17 to Babylon as the *"Mother of Prostitutes,"* insight into its meaning is found in Judges 2:17:

"Yet they would not listen to their judges but prostituted themselves to other gods and worshiped them. Unlike their fathers, they quickly turned from the way in which their fathers had walked, the way of obedience to the LORD's commands."

What is meant in Revelation 17 goes beyond the physical act of prostitution, and applies to the spiritual aspects of turning away from the true God, *"to other gods."* The United States has turned away from the God who founded and birthed us, "to other gods.' Founded as a Christian nation, as our Supreme Court acknowledged over one hundred years ago (*Holy Trinity Church v. U.S.,* 12 Sup. Ct. 511 – 1892), we have become anything but.

Chapter Eight

JIHADISTS HAVE THE DESIRE, PERMISSION, AND PATIENCE TO DESTROY AMERICA

"The ultimate threat to the country is a 9/11-type event where the terrorists are armed with something much more dangerous than an airline ticket and a box cutter–a nuclear weapon or a biological agent of some kind that is deployed in the middle of an American city. That's the one that would involve the deaths of perhaps hundreds of thousands of people...I think there's a high probability of such an attempt." (Former Vice President Richard Cheney, two weeks after leaving office, February 4, 2009, Politico Interview)

"On Wednesday, in an interview with Politico, Dick Cheney warned of the possible death of 'perhaps hundreds of thousands' of Americans in a terror attack using nuclear or biological weapons. 'I think there is a high probability of such an attempt,' he said. When the interview broke and was read on the air, I was in a room off of a television studio. For a moment everything went silent, and then a makeup woman said to a guest, 'I don't see how anyone can think that's not true.' I told her I'm certain it is true. And it didn't seem to me any of the half dozen others there found the content of Mr. Cheney's message surprising. They got a grim or preoccupied look." (Peggy Noonan, Column in *Wall Street Journal*, February 7, 2009)

WHAT HAVE JIHADISTS SAID ABOUT DESTROYING AMERICA?

Answer: *"Many thanks to God, for his kind gesture, and choosing us to perform the act of Jihad for his cause and to defend Islam and Muslims. Therefore, killing you and fighting you, destroying you and terrorizing you, responding back to your attacks, are all considered to be (a) great legitimate duty in our religion. These actions are offerings to God."* ("*The Islamic Response to the Government's Nine Accusations*," written and released on March 1, 2009, by Khalid Sheikh Mohammed, Ramzi bin As-Shibh, Walid bin 'Attash, Mustafa Ahmed Al-Hawsawl and 'Ali 'abd Al-'Aziz 'Ali, Prisoners at Guantanamo Bay, Cuba–full text at www.the-end-of-america.com)

The best known Muslim terrorist in the world today is Osama bin Laden, who was born in Riyadh, Saudi Arabia in 1957. His father was a wealthy businessman with close ties to the Saudi royal family. Bin Laden was raised as a devout Sunni Muslim. Bin Laden studied economics at a respected university in Saudi Arabia, though he may not have finished his course of instruction. Bin Laden is reported to have married five women and divorced two. He has fathered anywhere from 12 to 24 children.

In 1996, bin Laden issued al Qaeda's first "*Declaration of War*" against America. He declared Jihad against Americans occupying the "*Land of the Two Holy Mosques*" (Saudi Arabia); and called on Muslims to expel the 'heretics' from the Arabian Peninsula. In 1998 bin Laden and leading Muslim militants declared the formation of a coalition called the International Islamic Front for Jihad Against the Jews and Crusaders to Fight America. Bin Laden was selected to head the Front's Council (*Shura*). The militants adopted a *fatwa* (religious opinion) outlining the Front's goals. Their *fatwa* called on all Muslims to "*kill the Americans and their allies – civilians and military,*" wherever they may be found.

Also in 1998 al Qaeda bombed two U.S. embassies in East Africa; then in 2000, bombed the U.S.S. Cole; and on September 11, 2001, nineteen al Qaeda terrorists, all from Saudi Arabia, hijacked four passenger planes, piloted two into the World Trade Center towers in New York City, one into the Pentagon, and a fourth plane crashed in rural Pennsylvania.

A Commander of al Qaeda, Abu Shihab el Kandahri, has clearly stated the intentions of al Qaeda to use *nuclear devices* to destroy America:

> *"In the name of Allah the most merciful. Thus, you are not mistaken in reading this text. This is the only way to kill the greatest possible number of Americans. The Americans have never experienced a threat like this one. During World War II, America used this (nuclear) weapon twice in three days following the successful Japanese attack on Pearl Harbor. Today, the United States uses the most powerful and advanced weapons against the peaceful citizens of Iraq and Afghanistan...from its hatred of Muslims. America has bombed Iraq with weaponry that will pollute the soil and underground water with radiation for thousands of years. It also enhances its bombs with depleted uranium to cause even greater harm to people and the environment...Therefore, an eye for an eye, a tooth for a tooth...The coming days will prove that Kaedat el-Jihad (an al Qaeda organization) is capable of turning America into a sea of deadly radiation, and this will prove to the world that the end is at hand...Yes, we will destroy America and its allies, because they used their power for evil against the weak. And, now the end approaches..."* (*The Day of Islam,* Paul L. Williams, Prometheus Books, 2007).

In a videotaped speech broadcast by al-Jazeera network on November 12, 2002, just over a year after 9/11, bin Laden praised the *"zealous sons of Islam"* for their terrorist killings in Bali, Yemen and other areas of the world. Bin Laden, in referring to the war in Iraq said, *"Why should fear, killing, destruction, displacement, orphaning and widowing continue to be our lot, while security, stability and happiness be your lot? This is unfair. It is time that we get even. You will be killed just as you kill, and you will be bombed just as you bomb. And expect more that will further distress you."* Al Jazeera is not available to be viewed by most Americans, but it is widely available on cable systems around the world.

151

Two years later, on October 29, 2004, bin Laden, wearing a golden turban and white robe in place of the guerrilla fatigues worn in his 2002 speech, released another videotaped al-Jazeera broadcast speech. He apparently intended to influence the Presidential election in the United States, to be held just days later. Much of his speech was an attack on then President Bush, calling him a *"liar in the White House."* Bin Laden admitted that he was responsible for 9/11, saying that *"I got this idea"* to attack America, after he saw news reports of office towers falling in Lebanon.

Either showing his ignorance of the American political system, or more likely mocking it, he said: *"Bush Sr. liked the idea of appointing his sons as state governors. Similarly, he did not neglect to import to Florida the expertise in falsifying (elections) from the leaders of this region in order to benefit from it in difficult moments."* Possibly bin Laden's most cryptic statement was: *"Your security is not in the hands of Kerry or Bush or al-Qaeda. Your security is in your own hands, and any U.S. state that does not toy with our security automatically guarantees its own security."* How, exactly, does a state in the United States guarantee its own security by not 'toying' with Islamic security? A very curious statement.

Instead of annihilating America with nuclear weapons, why don't Jihadists just put their efforts and resources into converting Americans to Islam? Radical Jihadists making a reasoned analysis of the possibility of *converting* America to the Muslim faith, would, of course, be more than discouraged. Though there are an estimated 3 to 5 million Muslims in America, there are also 300 million Americans. The *"People of the Book,"* i.e., Christians and Jews, are so numerous that any serious effort to *"revert"* those millions of Christians and Jews to Islam would have to be seen as not doable, certainly not within many decades, if everything went extremely well. Strategically then, there is no reasonable chance that Islam could take over the United States theologically in any short or even medium term. Plus, the American government is too strong to be politically intimidated into accepting Islam as the state religion, unlike Europe where Muslim demographics favor it in the mid term. What does a radical Jihadist do about this problem? Jihadists are faced with a nation that won't, in their lifetimes, become a Muslim nation, and yet, they are also faced with what they perceive as Allah's demand that they conquer the world for Islam. So, what to do?

The options are really only two: 1.) wait and hope that over a hundred years or so America becomes a Muslim state; or 2.) take America out. There are no other options for radical Jihadists. Given the fact that Jihadists apparently have the resources to take America out, option 2 will clearly be most attractive and doable, and much quicker. It would be better for Americans if there were a third option, but that's just not reality. America is in deadly peril from radical Muslim extremists. *Only a fool ignores a credible threat by a committed, strong enemy which swears to destroy his nation, and which enemy swears that the mass murder will all be done in the name of their perceived God.*

WHAT HAVE AMERICAN LEADERS CONCLUDED ABOUT THE JIHADIST THREAT?

Some of America's smartest and most capable public officials were appointed by the United States Congress early in 2008 to a Commission on the Prevention of Weapons of Mass Destruction Proliferation and Terrorism, including former United States Senators Bob Graham (Florida) and Jim Talent (Missouri). The Commission had a staff of 24 experts and professionals in the fields of national security, intelligence and law enforcement. Over 250 government officials and nongovernmental experts were interviewed by the Commission. Members of the Commission traveled across America, visited Moscow and were on their way to Pakistan on September 20, 2008 when the Marriott Hotel in Islamabad was blown up by Jihadists just hours before their arrival. The Commission's Report (*World at Risk*) is quoted at various places in this book, as it reveals the truth of the immanency of a nuclear attack by Jihadists on America, which concluded that *"the risk that radical Islamists-al Qaeda or Taliban–may gain access to nuclear material is real."* The Commission also stated:

"It is our hope to break the all-too-familiar cycle in which disaster strikes and a commission is formed to report to us about what our government should have known and done to keep us safe. This time we do know. We know the threat we face. We know that our margin of safety is shrinking, not growing."

The Commission thoroughly studied the federal government's current organizational structure to deal with the threat of the use of WMDs by terrorists. They found that:

"No single person is in charge of and accountable for preventing WMD proliferation and terrorism";

"Operationally, the U.S. government functions without recognizing a division between national security and homeland security";

"Congress has yet to organize itself to cope with the nuclear age... (which is) deeply troubling and demands action";

"Half of today's (intelligence) analysts entered the intelligence community after 9/11";

"No White House-level coordination position (on WMD proliferation and terrorism) has yet been established."

These findings are the *positive* aspects of the Report by the Commission.

On the other hand, when it came to what the United States should do to *avoid* massive deaths caused by the Jihadists' potential future use of WMDs, the Commission revealed frightening misunderstanding of America's enemies' goals and motivations. The Commission, among many laudable technical recommendations, suggested that the way to avoid future Jihadists' attacks is to 'make nice' with Jihadists and encourage Jihadists to change their opinions of America, so that they give up their warlike demeanor:

"The next administration needs to go much further, using the tools of 'soft power' to communicate effectively about American intentions and to build grassroots social and economic institutions that will discourage radicalism and undercut terrorists in danger spots around the world–especially in Pakistan.

"There are simple steps that most individuals can take to mitigate the consequences of an attack–even a WMD attack. By demonstrating that they could reduce at a national level the potential damage and lasting effects caused by an attack, citizens might convince a terrorist organization that pursuing such an attack was not worth the effort and thus deter it."

What? We can avoid WMD attacks on America by Jihadists if we "communicate effectively...American intentions" or if we demonstrate that we can *bounce back from attacks by terrorists*? Have they read the Quran? Have they reviewed Osama bin Laden's speeches? Do they understand the 1300 plus years of the history of Jihadists' often-stated, and frequently implemented, goal to conquer the world for Allah? Since Jihadists believe their God wants them to conquer and kill unbelievers, what difference do the unbelievers' *"intentions"* make? They know that America's *"intentions"* aren't to *destroy* Islam. Convincing Jihadists that America has good, even sterling, *"intentions"* is a waste of time. Allah, they believe, wants all nations, even America, to become a Muslim, Sharia Law nation, their intentions notwithstanding. Likewise, convincing Jihadists that Americans know how to duct tape their windows and doors in advance of a nuclear attack will not cause Jihadists to give up on acquiring or using nuclear weapons to take down America for Allah.

Until and unless American security officials recognize and understand the ingrained, heart-felt, deeply-believed *spiritual imperative* to conquer the world for Allah that motivates Jihadists every day, these officials will always under-estimate what it takes to protect Americans. It should not be overlooked, though, that the Commission did issue clear and present warnings: *"The risk that radical Islamists-al*

Qaeda or Taliban–may gain access to nuclear material is real." And "*We know the threat we face. We know that our margin of safety is shrinking, not growing.*"

DO AMERICAN LEADERS UNDERSTAND JIHADIST MOTIVATIONS AND GOALS?

As naïve as portions of the Commission's Report may seem, the Report *did* take a clear-eyed view of what nuclear attacks on American cities would look like:

"*New York City–Al Qaeda rents a van, drives a Russian 10-kiloton nuclear bomb into Times Square, and detonates it. Times Square disappears instantly, as the heat from the blast would reach tens of millions of degrees Fahrenheit. The theater district, Grand Central Terminal, Rockefeller Center, Carnegie Hall and Empire State Building would be gone, literally in a flash. Buildings further away, such as the United Nations Headquarters on the East River, the Flatiron Building and the Metropolitan Museum would look like bombed-out shells. Half a million people, who at noontime are in that half-mile radius of the blast site, would be killed. Hundreds of thousands of others would die from collapsing buildings, fire, and fallout.*

San Francisco – A nuclear bomb is detonated in Union Square. Everything to the Museum of Modern Art would be vaporized. Massive destruction would exist from the Transamerica Building to Nob Hill.

Chicago – A nuclear bomb explodes at Sears Tower. Everything from Navy Pier to the Eisenhower Expressway disappears. The United Center and Grant Park are destroyed. A firestorm sweeps from the White Sox's U.S. Cellular Field on the South Side to the Cub's Wrigley Field on the North Side.

Washington, D.C. – A nuclear bomb at the Smithsonian Institution would destroy everything from the White House to the Capitol lawn. The Supreme Court would be rubble. The Pentagon, across the Potomac River, would be engulfed in flames."

(*World at Risk* – "The Report of the Commission on the Prevention of Weapons of Mass Destruction Proliferation and Terrorism" – quote from Commission Member Dr. Graham Allison, Director of the Belfer Center for Science and International Affairs at Harvard University, from his book *Nuclear Terrorism: The Ultimate Preventable Catastrophe* – 2004)

"*Come against her from afar. Break open her granaries;*
pile her up like heaps of grain. Completely destroy
her and leave her no remnant." (Jeremiah 50:26)
"*I will send foreigners to Babylon*
to winnow her and to devastate her land;
they will oppose her on every side
in the day of her disaster." (Jeremiah 51:2)

JIHADISTS HAVE OBTAINED PERMISSION TO USE NUCLEAR WEAPONS AGAINST AMERICANS

In May, 2003, Nasir bin Hamid al-Fahd and other Muslim clerics granted al Qaeda permission to kill ten million Americans with nuclear weapons "*for the sake of parity.*" Their eleven-page "*Nuclear Fatwa*" (see Attachment A) answered a request for a legal ruling on the use of nuclear weapons against American civilians. In al-Fahd's *Nuclear Fatwa*, he referred to American weapons used in Iraq:

"*America's threat to Iraq to use these (nuclear) weapons should Iraq attack Israel is not remote from us. What, then, allows them to America and the infidels and denies them to Muslims? ...If the infidels can be repelled from the Muslims only by using such weapons, their use is permissible, even if you kill them without exception and destroy their pillage and stock. All this has its foundation in the Prophet's biography, the Prophet's sayings about jihad,* and the pronouncements of scholars, may God have mercy on them."

The existence and content of the *Nuclear Fatwah* was confirmed by the *London Daily Telegraph* in 2006 when it reported: *"Iran's hard-line spiritual leaders have issued an unprecedented new fatwah, or holy order, sanctioning the use of atomic weapons against its enemies."* The *Nuclear Fatwah* proclaims that it is permissible to kill women and children as part of the Jihad attacks, and even allows the killing of Muslims if it can't be avoided. It cites the Quran (Koran 2:194) as saying *"Whoso commits aggression against you, do you commit aggression against him like as he has committed against you."* The Fatwah states:

"Anyone who considers America's aggression against Muslims and their lands during the past decades will conclude that striking her is permissible merely on the basis of the rule of treating as one has been treated. No other arguments need be mentioned. Some brothers have totaled the number of Muslims killed directly or indirectly by their weapons and come up with a figure of merely ten million...If a bomb that killed ten million of them and burned as much of their land as they have burned Muslims' land were dropped on them, it would be permissible, with no need to mention any other argument. We might need other arguments if we needed to annihilate more than this number of them."

In November, 2004, CBS News carried an extensive interview on 60 Minutes with Michael Scheuer, who until three days before the interview was the CIA's senior intelligence analyst tracking Osama bin Laden. CBS's Steve Kroft asked Scheuer: *"You've written no one should be surprised when Osama bin Laden and al Qaeda detonate a weapon of mass destruction in the United States. You believe that is going to happen?"*

Scheuer's response: *"I don't believe in inevitability. But I think it's pretty close to being inevitable ...a nuclear weapon of some dimension, whether it's actually a nuclear weapon, or a dirty bomb, or some kind of radiological device. Yes, I think it's probably a near thing."* Kroft asked, *"What evidence is* there that bin Laden's actually working to do this? Scheuer: "He's told us. Bin Laden is remarkably eager for Americans to know why he doesn't like us, what he intends to do about it and then following up and doing something about it in terms of military actions. He's told us that 'We are going to acquire a weapon of mass destruction, and if we acquire it, we will use it'."

CBS Correspondent Kroft continued: "After September 11, Scheuer says bin Laden was criticized by Muslim clerics for launching such a serious attack without sufficient warning. That has now been given. And he says bin Laden has even obtained a fatwa, or Islamic decree, justifying a nuclear attack against the United States on religious grounds. He secured from a Saudi sheik named Hamid bin Fahd a rather long treatise on the possibility of using nuclear weapons against the Americans. Specifically, nuclear weapons," says Scheuer. "And the treatise found that he was perfectly within his rights to use them. Muslims argue that the United States is responsible for millions of dead Muslims around the world, so reciprocity would mean you could kill millions of Americans. Scheuer says the fatwa was issued in May, 2003, "and that's another thing that doesn't come to the attention of the American people."

Because all human beings have at least some innate aversion to the slaughter of other human beings, the Jihadists have obtained the religious permission of a respected Muslim cleric. As they murder for Allah, they have convinced themselves that the slaughter of innocents is not only *for* their perceived God, but actually *pleases* their perceived God, and is *demanded* by their perceived God. As Nasir bin Hamid al-Fahd, the cleric who issued the *Nuclear Fatwah*, has said, "no other arguments need be mentioned," i.e., the matter is settled for radical Islamic terrorists. Raed Said Hussein Saad, the Commander of the Al-Qassam Brigades, summed it up nicely: "We succeed, with Allah's grace, to raise an ideological generation that loves death like our enemies love life." They mass murder with impunity. Specifically, they have clerical permission to use nuclear weapons in America to burn, radiate and kill millions of American men, women and children.

Religious permission having been granted, the remaining question is not, *will they nuke America?* They have quite clearly demonstrated *the will* to do it, and they have openly stated their *full intention* to do it. No, the only remaining question is if they have *the technical ability* to do it?

JIHADISTS HAVE SHOWN THEY HAVE INSCRUTABLE PATIENCE

The *al Qaeda War Manual,* discovered by British police in a raid on an al Qaeda safe house, and translated from Arabic, lists "Patience" as one of the 14 qualifications for membership in the Jihadist organization. *"He should be patient in performing the work, even if it lasts a long time."*

In Osama bin Laden's January 14, 2009 message to the world he provided an insight into Jihadists' patience, saying al Qaeda was prepared to fight in Afghanistan and Iraq *"for seven more years, and seven more after that, then seven more."* In Osama bin Laden's January 14, 2009 videotape he said: *"The Jihad of your sons against the Crusader-Zionist coalition is one of the key reasons for these destructive effects among our enemies. God has bestowed us with the patience to continue the path of Jihad. The question is, can America continue its war with us for several more decades to come? Reports and evidence would suggest otherwise."*

Jihadists trace their struggle to conquer the world for Allah from 632 AD. In light of the many centuries, what's another year, or two, or ten, in the struggle to place Sharia Law in all nations' law books and to place the Muslim flag above every capitol city in the world? The confiscated *War Manual* says the *"main mission of the Islamic movement (is to) overthrow godless regimes"* and replace them with *"an Islamic regime"* for the purpose of *"establishing the religion of majestic Allah on earth."* The *War Manual* states: *"Islamic* governments have never and will never be established through peaceful solutions...*They are established as they always have been...by pen and gun...by word and bullet...by tongue and teeth... Islam does not make a truce with unbelief, but rather confronts it. It knows the dialogue of bullets."*

The same *al Qaeda War Manual* trains members to torture prisoners. *"Information is collected by kidnapping the enemy individual, interrogating him and torturing him... Religious scholars have permitted beating... (and) have also permitted the killing of a hostage if he insists on withholding information from Muslims."* Al Qaeda has never adopted the Geneva Conventions.

On January 19, 2006, bin Laden released a lengthy videotape to al-Jazeera to broadcast. In many ways it was his most threatening speech to date. Bin Laden praised his Mujahedin warriors and proclaimed *"Jihad is continuing."* Even though he suggested a *"long-term truce"* with no specifics given, he made his boldest threats yet to America:

"As for the delay in carrying out similar operations in America, this was not due to failure to breach your security measures. Operations are under preparation, and you will see them on your own ground once they are finished, God willing....Days and nights will not go by until we take revenge as we did on 11 September, God willing, and until your minds are exhausted and your lives become miserable and things turn (for the worse) which you detest. As for us, we do not have anything to lose. The swimmer in the sea does not fear rain. You have occupied our land, defiled our honor, violated our dignity, shed our blood, ransacked our money, demolished our houses, rendered us homeless and tampered with our security. We will treat you in the same way."

Osama bin Laden in his 2006 warning to America reiterated that Islam approves Jihad, the killing of non-Muslims: *"Refraining from performing Jihad, which is sanctioned by our religion, is an appalling sin."* If you're wondering about the timing of the promised attack on America, bin Laden emphasized his patience:

"Do not be deluded by your power and modern weapons. Although they win some battles, they lose the war. Patience and steadfastness are better than them. What is important is the outcome. We have been tolerant for ten years in fighting the Soviet Union with our few weapons and we managed to drain their economy. They became history, with God's help. You should learn lessons from that. We will remain patient in fighting you, God willing, until the one whose time has come dies first. We will not escape the fight as long as we hold our weapons in our hands."

Osama bin Laden teaches his recruits *"let patience outwear patience."* He lives his life around this principle. Would one more year, or two, or three, before a devastating attack on America be 'patience outwearing patience'? Bin Laden waited many years for the 9/11 attacks to be successful. A lack of another American terrorist attack since 2001 may not be encouraging, if during this hiatus, al Qaida says it is acquiring the ability to attack America, in an even more, much more, destructive manner than the 9/11 attacks.

In bin Laden's 2006 attempt to intimidate and to create fear, he makes an important admission–that al Qaida *"hold(s) weapons in our hands."* Remember 9/11 was executed with just box cutters. It doesn't appear likely that bin Laden, in his 2006 speech warning America of future terrorism, is bragging about possessing box cutters. He appears, therefore, to have admitted that in al Qaida's hands are *"weapons"* which it intends to use against America.

But its one thing to claim possession of weapons and quite another to actually *possess* them. National Public Radio carried a segment on its news show *All Things Considered,* on August 6, 2008 ("Evaluating al-Qaida's Nuclear Strategy") that examined this issue. In an interview with Rolf Mowatt-Larssen, the Director of Intelligence and Counterintelligence of the United States Department of Energy, Mowatt-Larssen said: *"(For al Qaida to carry out a nuclear attack) they would have to come to a conclusion, I believe, where they would justify the use of a nuclear or some other weapon of mass destruction in what they would consider rational terms; in other words, how it would help them fulfill specific goals they have, which I think are well established.*" He was referring to the Jihadists' oft-preached command they must conquer the world militarily for Allah.

Tom Gjelten, the NPR reporter, concluded the segment by noting: "*At the Department of Energy, Rolf Mowatt-Larssen says he's operating on the assumption that al Qaida still intends to acquire a nuclear weapon and use it against the United States...He's focusing the energies of the entire U.S. government on the effort to stop al Qaida or another group from acquiring a nuclear weapon or the material to make one.*" The possibility, some would argue the probability, that al Qaida already has nuclear weapons, is being taken more than seriously by the government of the United States of America. Can we do any less?

Thus, Jihadists appear to have the big three:
1.) Desire (to conquer the world for Allah);
2.) Permission (*Nuclear Fatwah*);
3.) Patience (to wait until the time is right).

These aside, have Jihadists *succeeded* in their openly stated goal to actually *acquire* nuclear weapons?

Chapter Nine

THE COMING "GREAT ATTACK ON AMERICA"
JIHADISTS HAVE OBTAINED
SUITCASE NUKES AND NUCLEAR MATERIALS

"Every senior leader, when you're asked what keeps you awake at night, it's the thought of a terrorist ending up with a weapon of mass destruction, especially nuclear." Secretary of Defense Robert Gates

"I'm not an alarmist, but I did spend four years right after 9/11 looking at all this intelligence from violent extremists. They could attack America through biological weapons. God forbid if they get their hands on nuclear materials, they could do it that way as well. And they're ruthless, so we know they'd use them. ...They want to bring down the United States in particular and the West in general." (General Richard Myers, Chairman of the Joint Chiefs of Staff, 2001-2005)

"Terrorists are determined to attack us again–with weapons of mass destruction if they can. Osama bin Laden has said that obtaining these weapons is a 'religious duty' and is reported to have sought to perpetrate another 'Hiroshima" (*World at Risk* – The Report of the Commission on the Prevention of Weapons of Mass Destruction Proliferation and Terrorism, appointed by the United States Congress, December, 2008).

"'You will be victorious' on the face of this planet. You are the masters of the world on the face of this planet. Yes, [the Koran says that] 'you will be victorious,' but only 'if you are believers.' Allah willing, 'you will be victorious,' while America and Israel will be annihilated. I guarantee you that the power of belief and faith is greater than the power of America and Israel. They are cowards who are eager for life,

while we are eager for death for the sake of Allah. (Sheik Ahmad Bahr, Speaker, Palestinian Legislative Council)

'   Jihadists are thoroughly committed, with a burning desire, to make Allah the God, and Sharia Law the law, of every nation on the globe. That religious/political passion might only be academically interesting, if the Jihadists lacked the *ability* to accomplish that which they fervently desire. Harold Stassen, the former Governor of Minnesota, fervently wanted to be President of the United States, running nine times from 1948 to 1992. Unquestionably, though, his zeal wasn't matched with his *ability* to accomplish his goal. It's a legitimate question, therefore, to ask if the Jihadists have the *ability* to acquire or manufacture the weapons required to reach their goal of conquering the world.

WHO IS THE ULTIMATE SOURCE OF ALL WEAPONS?

        Before examining what Jihadists have said about their arsenal of weapons, and what others, in and out of government, have disclosed on the same subject, what does the Bible say?

        "The Lord has opened his arsenal and brought out the weapons of his wrath, for the Sovereign Lord Almighty   has work to do in the land of the Babylonians." (Jeremiah 50:25)

        This verse appears in the lengthy chapters of Jeremiah 50 and 51 in which the Prophet wrote about a future nation, the Daughter of Babylon. Jeremiah 51:33 describes the future nation by name: *"The Daughter of Babylon is like a threshing floor at the time it is trampled; the time to harvest her will soon come."* As we examine how, or even whether, Jihadists can access nuclear weapons, remember that it is the Lord Himself who allows weapons to be acquired, and used:

"See, it is I who created the blacksmith who fans the coals into flame and forges a weapon fit for its work. And it is I who have created the destroyer to work havoc; no weapon forged against you will prevail, and you will refute every tongue that accuses you. This is the heritage of the servants of the Lord, and this is their vindication from me, declares the Lord." (Isaiah 54:16-17)

Therefore, ultimately, weapons forged to be used by the destroyers that the Lord has created, come from His hand. We also know that because God is omnipotent no army may rise, and no weapon may be acquired, *unless* He allows it. Encouraging to God's people, Christians and Jews, is the second part of this verse, i.e., that no weapon that the Lord has allowed to be forged, to be used by a destroyer, can prevail against His people if He chooses to protect and rescue them. This verse is one of many confirming that the Lord desires to protect believers from the wrath of the world, if we'll listen and heed His warnings. Chapter 13 has far more detail about the prophetic verses our loving Father has given us to flee from the end times destroyer which will annihilate the end times Daughter of Babylon/America.

WHAT WEAPONS WILL BE USED TO DESTROY THE DAUGHTER OF BABYLON?

The Lord has given us two similar prophetic verses, by two different Prophets, to confirm the nature of the weapons that will be used to destroy the Daughter of Babylon:

> *"Babylon, the jewel of kingdoms, the glory of the Babylonians' pride, will be overthrown by God like Sodom and Gomorrah."* (Isaiah 13:19)

> *"As God overthrew Sodom and Gomorrah along with their neighboring towns,"* declares the Lord, *"so no one will live there; no man will dwell in it."* (Jeremiah 50:40)

How were Sodom and Gomorrah destroyed? Genesis 19:24: *"Then the Lord rained upon Sodom and upon Gomorrah brimstone and fire from the Lord out of heaven."* What is fire and brimstone? Clues are given in other verses:

"Flee for your lives! Don't look back, and don't stop anywhere in the plain! Flee to the mountains or you will be swept away!" (Genesis 19:17)

The admonition to not look back is the same warning given today–don't look at the flash of a nuclear weapon explosion. Blindness can occur as a result. In addition, the warning to leave the area near Sodom and the three towns near it, is the same as is given today–get away from the area of heavy radiation and fallout.

"Thus he overthrew those cities and the entire plain, including all those living in the cities—and also the vegetation in the land." (Genesis 19:25)

It's interesting that God records for us that His destruction of Sodom and the three towns near it also included the *"vegetation in the land"*. Nuclear radiation destroys vegetation. After the Chernobyl radiation event, it soon was revealed that radioactive caesium was continuously taken up and passed on by organisms in forest ecosystems, and that the animals and vegetation in affected forests and mountains were particularly contaminated. Forest food products such as mushrooms, berries, and game contained the highest recorded levels of caesium-137. (GreenFacts Foundation). If *"fire and brimstone"* were only fire and burning rocks, how could that have destroyed *"vegetation in the land"* surrounding the destroyed cities?

"Early the next morning Abraham got up and returned to the place where he had stood before the LORD. He looked down toward Sodom and Gomorrah, toward all the land of the

plain, and he saw dense smoke rising from the land, like smoke from a furnace." (Genesis 19:27-28)

This verse is a revealing clue of the nature of the destructive force God used at Sodom. A burning city fills the entire sky across the city with smoke from the fires in the city. Pictures of firebombed cities in WWII show the city's horizon filled with billowing, ascending smoke. On the other hand, Genesis 19 records that when He destroyed Sodom, He did it with a force that led to a peculiar shape, like *"smoke from a furnace."* What does that look like? A furnace emits *a column* of smoke, frequently with billowing clouds at the top of the smoke column, formed after the smoke rises and cools, and is swirled by surrounding air. That shape can also be described as a mushroom cloud, which also is atop a column of smoke, *"like smoke from a furnace."* Lest one question whether God could have caused a nuclear reaction millennia ago, suffice it to say that certainly the God of the universe who *created the atom,* (no small feat that) would also be able to *split the atom.*

"The whole land will be a burning waste of salt and sulfur—nothing planted, nothing sprouting, no vegetation growing on it. It will be like the destruction of Sodom and Gomorrah, Admah and Zeboiim, which the LORD overthrew in fierce anger." (Deuteronomy 29:23)

Could this be any more clear? An Academic Survey Team which entered Hiroshima after its nuclear bombing, found radiation damage to the plants that survived, showing chlorophyll deficiency and color variegation. Chernobyl, which was not a nuclear explosion as such, nevertheless, in the early months after the accident, led to levels of radioactivity of agricultural plants and plant-consuming animals dominated by surface deposits of radionuclides. (GreenFacts Foundation)

169

"For the punishment of the iniquity of the daughter of my people is greater than the punishment of the sin of Sodom, that was overthrown as in a moment, and no hands stayed on her....Their visage is blacker than a coal; they are not known in the streets: their skin cleaveth to their bones; it is withered, it is become like a stick." (Lamentations 4:6 & 8)

This section of scripture provides two important facts from which we can determine what force of destruction was used to destroy Sodom, and that which will be employed again to destroy the Daughter of Babylon. First, in the Lamentations verse above Sodom was destroyed *"in a moment."* Isaiah 47:9 tells us that the Daughter of Babylon shall suffer its losses *"in a moment in one day."* A nuclear explosion can destroy in a moment, but a spreading normal fire, or hurricanes, or floods all take much longer than *"a moment"* to fully destroy. The world's richest, most powerful nation will be wiped out, conquered, destroyed in one day, in one hour within that one day, and in one moment within that one hour. How could any large, powerful nation be annihilated today, *except by* coordinated nuclear strikes?

Chillingly, the second clue from this section of scripture is that the radiation effects of the force used to destroy Sodom led to blackened skin and shriveled arms and legs, exactly what was observed in those radiated in Hiroshima and Nagasaki. Doctors in Japan observed that radiation led to skin hemorrhaging due to broken capillary blood vessels. More on this in the next chapter.

"If he condemned the cities of Sodom and Gomorrah by burning them to ashes, and made them an example of what is going to happen to the ungodly." (II Peter 2:6)

This verse confirms that what He did at Sodom and Gomorrah was an *"example of what is going to happen to the ungodly."* In other words, it is implied that the destructive force used to destroy Sodom and Gomorrah and three other nearby cities, will be used again, in the end times, to destroy the ungodly. There have been no other documented instances since Sodom and Gomorrah, of a destructive force, with smoke as from a furnace, destroying vegetation, blackening skin, shriveling arms and legs, with destruction occurring in a moment, with people warned to avoid looking at the event and warned to flee a great distance to avoid harm, except for Hiroshima and Nagasaki. All of these factual descriptions of what took place over 3,000 years ago apply equally to a nuclear event today.

JIHADISTS HAVE SUITCASE NUKES AND NUCLEAR MATERIALS

"The process (of manufacturing nuclear weapons) is intricate, intense and expensive. Indeed, it takes the resources of a state to commence the process of enriching uranium as well as a team of hundreds of highly trained scientists and technicians. There is no way a rogue organization, such as al Qaeda, even with its riches from the drug trade and its support throughout the Muslim world, could embark on such a venture. Al Qaeda has always been dependent upon gaining possession of the raw materials of highly enriched uranium and plutonium from black market sources in order to manufacture its arsenal of small nukes. On occasion, the terrorist organization also purchased ready-made weapons, such as suitcase nukes, from Russia and from the newly created Russian republics." (*The Day of Islam*, Paul L. Williams, Prometheus Books, 2007)

From whom would al Qaeda purchase nuclear materials and nuclear devices? The old statement that if you have enough money you can buy just about anything you want (except love, of course) is true of nuclear material, as currently nine nations of the world possess over 15,000 ready-to-go nuclear weapons. The Federal Bureau of Investigation is charged, along with other federal agencies, with pursuing terrorists who may seek to kill Americans. One of the FBI's Consultants on terrorism is Dr. Paul L.

Williams. In his books he has uncovered and disclosed steps taken by bin Laden to obtain nuclear material and small nuclear devices. Osama bin Laden, Williams believes, has acquired and will continue to acquire the capability of placing small nuclear devices in multiple key American cities, all to be detonated simultaneously, and disastrously for the nation. Dr. Williams disclosed in *Al Qaeda: Brotherhood of Terror* (Prometheus, 2002) that Osama bin Laden purchased twenty, that's *twenty*, RA-115 suitcase nukes from former KGB agents in 1998 for $30 million in cash and heroin (made in Afghanistan by bin Laden) with a street value of $700 million.

How would al Qaeda bring these devices into the United States one might ask? Over 16,000 ships enter U.S. ports every day. Over 21 million tons of freight arrive from the other nations of the world into America on ships, and by air, truck or train, every year. Only 3% of arriving ship containers are ever inspected, including those arriving from the Middle East. The nation is too large, with too many points of generally unsecured entry to effectively screen out small nuclear devices, or large ones for that matter. If al Qaeda wanted to move nukes into America, it could do so. In the next Chapter, we'll look at further confirmation that al Qaeda has obtained fissile material, technical knowledge, and nuclear weapons.

SUITCASE NUKES

For those curious as to what a suitcase nuke looks like, what are the parts and how are they constructed and detonated, just Google 'suitcase nukes.' *Time* magazine looked at the question of whether or not a nuclear device could fit into a case 8 inches by 16 inches by 24 inches. The October 29, 2001 *Time* article quoted Bruce Blair, former U.S. Air Force officer and expert on Soviet nuclear weapons, confirming that such weapons could fit in an area of those dimensions and weigh as little as 60 pounds. The article also reported:

"If terrorists can't buy portable nukes, they would have to make them. And in a frightening study done by the Nuclear Control Institute, a nonproliferation group in Washington, a panel of nuclear-explosives experts concluded that a group of dedicated terrorists without nuclear backgrounds could assemble a bomb if it had the right materials (such as plutonium 239, uranium 235, plutonium oxide and uranium oxide). It would take about a year to complete the job. 'There's little question that the only remaining obstacle is the acquisition of the material,' says Paul Leventhal, the Institute's president. Less than 110 kg of active ingredients could yield 10 kilotons of explosive power – a Hiroshima-size weapon. Even if the terrorists didn't get the recipe quite right, a 1-kiloton yield could still devastate a city. And forget the suitcase: a truck will do, or a container ship to float into an American port.' Where would bin Laden get the material? Again, the most common answer is Russia, with its reputation as a fissile flea market. And a bin Laden associate has told authorities that the mastermind is shopping for nuclear ingredients. Adds Leventhal: 'My feeling is that the prudent assumption is that bin Laden is nuclear capable in some fashion.'"

Suitcase nukes are in the world and may already be in the hands of Jihadists. They claim to have the capability of mass destruction of the world's Kafirs (unbelievers). But, as the *Time* article pointed out, America could suffer nuclear destruction by larger nuclear devices delivered by other means than in a suitcase. These larger nuclear weapons could have been purchased, stolen or donated to the Islamic cause by or from Russia, North Korea or, in the future, Pakistan or Iran. Fiction writers have suggested that a nuclear weapon could be brought into the United States in a canned soda machine taken to a Super Bowl game (*The Sum of All Fears*, Tom Clancy, 1991) or a scud-type nuclear-tipped missile launched from a boat in the Potomac (*Memorial Day*, Vince Flynn, 2004). Over sixty novels have been published and thirty movies produced, all based upon imagining a nuclear holocaust in America.

Two American retired designers of thermonuclear weapons, Thomas C. Reed (Livermore National Laboratory) and Danny B. Stillman (Los Alamos), in a recently published book *The Nuclear Express,* Zenith, 2009) conclude that a *"fierce storm is gathering."* They see the Islamic bomb—whether wielded by Pakistan, Iran, Saudi Arabia, or some unforeseen possessor of the murderous weaponry–bringing about a world in which *"millions will die"* and *"more than one democratic society will be consigned to the dust-heap of history."*

MULTI-DETONATION

The reality is that if al Qaeda obtains nuclear weapons, which appears to be more than probable, it will carefully orchestrate their *multi-detonation.* Exploding only one nuclear device in a country the size of America would insure that the surviving residents of the nation would quickly empty its largest cities to avoid a similar fate. Such a mass exodus would be financially catastrophic to be sure, but over time, the relocated, more widely distributed, nation would eventually come back to some semblance of order and would eventually return to near-normality, even if not at the same status as before the single detonation. Therefore, to destroy, *really destroy,* a nation as large as America, would require multiple detonations of *several* nuclear weapons. Al Qaeda has demonstrated the ability to coordinate its multi-attacks. Al Qaeda seized and crashed four airliners on 9-11 and attempted to coordinate the bringing down of nine airliners heading to the United States in 2006. FBI Director Robert S. Mueller told *Newsmax* magazine in May, 2007 that *"bin Laden and his terrorist group desperately want to obtain nuclear devices and explode them in American cities, especially New York and Washington, D.C."*

Jihadists have historically used multiple weapons, detonated on a coordinated basis, whether in the 9/11 attacks on America, the July 7 and 21, 2005 London subway and bus bombings, the March 11, 2004 Madrid attack (using ten bombs), the series of attacks in Bali or other terrorist incidents. Some novelists who conjecture a nuclear strike against America imagine a *single* nuclear weapon detonated, at ground level, by Islamic terrorists and write about how the nation would then struggle to recover from the attack. These books are interesting fiction, but are largely unrelated to the reality of Jihadists in the world today.

Throughout the history of warfare, no nation has ever been *destroyed in one moment*. The fall of Hiroshima did not destroy Japan, neither did Nagasaki's, though their destruction did, within days, lead to Japan's surrender. It's instructive to study history and the Bible in tandem. In doing so, one would have to conclude that no nation of any significant size, such as the United States, could be destroyed with a single nuclear detonation.

Dr. Williams posits that al Qaeda will target 7 to 10 large American cities in which to detonate nuclear devices. The *New York Daily News* on March 14, 2003 (*"Officials Fear Al-Qaeda Nuclear Attack"*) reported that security officials were concerned by reports that al Qaeda planned simultaneous nuclear attacks on seven U.S. cities: New York, Boston, Miami, Houston, Los Angeles, Las Vegas and Washington, DC.

The destruction of New York, Washington, and Boston would decapitate the nation's government, financial and commercial centers of power. The fall of Los Angeles would not only destroy Hollywood and its cultural influence on the world, but would also wipe out the west coast's biggest center of commerce. Houston would undoubtedly be included by al Qaeda on any list of this nature, as a large percentage of the nation's refining capacity lies within miles of the ports located on the Gulf of Mexico. One may ask why Miami, the only city on the list that brings the credulity of this specific listing into question, though its large number of Jewish residents may explain its inclusion. Why not Chicago, for instance? A final list would undoubtedly also include New Orleans due to the oil refineries located near this important port city. America's economy runs on gasoline.

Interestingly, as this book was in final editing, a novel was published that imagined a single nuclear device exploded over Las Vegas by Jihadists (acting in concert with Russia). *Critical Mass,* Whitley Strieber, Doherty, Tom Publishers, 2009) portrays a Jihadist, calling himself the Mahdi, threatening America, after the atomic explosion in Nevada, with more destruction, unless the President converts to Islam, all churches are closed, etc. Threats of further destruction on other nations after an attack would be inevitable, but what is not at all likely, would be a *single* nuclear detonation, leaving America free to counter-attack known centers of Islamic radicals. The Daughter of Babylon verses prophesy a destroyed nation with an impotent military (Jeremiah 50:23; 30; 36; 51:3), unable to act after its massive national destruction.

DO JIHADISTS HAVE ACCESS TO NUCLEAR WEAPONS?

The initial question is where are the world's 15,700 nuclear weapons located? Here are the estimated number of nuclear weapons (though not all are active warheads) held by the *nine nations* now possessing them:
Russia – 8,800 (not including suitcase nukes);
United States – 5,535;
China – 160-400;
France – 350;
United Kingdom – 200;
Israel – 200;
India – 140;
Pakistan – 60-100; and
North Korea 0-10 (Estimate made before North Korea's recent nuclear tests)
(Source: Natural Resources Defense Council, published in *Bulletin of Atomic Scientists)*
In addition to these nuclear weapons that are assembled and ready for use, forty nations of the world have

176

possession of nuclear material from which nuclear weapons can be manufactured. (*World at Risk,* Report by the Commission on the Prevention of Weapons of Mass Destruction Proliferation and Terrorism, December 3, 2008).

The Commission which was appointed by the United States Congress in 2007, warned that access to nuclear material is not as limited as safety would dictate, noting a South African stockpile of nuclear material was broken into in 2007; a scientific factory worker in Russia stole 1,600 grams of 90 percent enriched uranium one gram at a time; employees at another Russian nuclear facility plotted to steal almost 20 kilograms of nuclear material, enough to assemble a nuclear weapon; and an arrest was made in the Republic of Georgia, Russia, of an operative trying to sell 100 grams of highly enriched uranium. These are incidents which were discovered. How many were not discovered?

Jihadists are not likely to acquire nuclear weapons, no matter how much they would be willing to pay, from either the United States, the United Kingdom, France, China, India or Israel. That won't happen. However, that leaves *North Korea, Pakistan, Russia, and Iran* as potential sources of nuclear weapons. Until recently, most experts thought that North Korea, though it had labored to acquire nuclear weapons, had not yet joined the "Nuclear Club" of nations with such devices. However, three days before the January 20, 2009 U.S. Presidential Inauguration, North Korea announced it had *"weaponized enough plutonium for roughly four to six nuclear bombs."* (*New York Times*, January 18, 2009), and in late May, 2009 successfully tested a nuclear weapon. The Commission on the Prevention of Weapons of Mass Destruction Proliferation and Terrorism, in its December, 2008 Report *(World at Risk),* noted that North Korea had sold ballistic missiles capable of carrying nuclear weapons to *"Pakistan, Iran, and several other states in the Middle East."* Thus, it is possible in our world today, given a sufficient amount of money, to acquire nuclear weapons and missiles to deliver them. Just give Kim Jong-il a call.

177

WILL PAKISTAN BE A SOURCE FOR NUKES
FOR JIHADISTS?

The Commission on the Prevention of Weapons of Mass Destruction Proliferation and Terrorism devoted a section of its December, 2008 Report (*World at Risk*) to threats posed by Pakistan, which it labeled as the "geographic crossroads for terrorism and weapons of mass destruction." The Commission wrote: *"Nevertheless, there is no graver threat to U.S. national security than a WMD in the hands of terrorists. Trends in South Asia, if left unchecked, will increase the odds that al Qaeda will successfully develop and use a nuclear device or biological weapon against the United States or its allies. The reality behind the 9/11 Commission's comment that 'it is hard to overstate the importance of Pakistan in the struggle against Islamist terrorism' is obvious. The difference today is that the situation is urgent."*

Pakistan, officially named The Islamic Republic of Pakistan, is thus, a major problem. Pakistan is the world's sixth most populous nation, with 172,000,000 people, and after Indonesia, the second most populous Muslim nation. Pakistan's nuclear program was developed and is under the direction of Dr. Abdul Q. Khan. In January 2004, Khan confessed to having been involved in transferring nuclear technology to Libya, Iran and North Korea. Khan: *"turned the country (Pakistan) into the biggest source of nuclear weapons proliferation in atomic history"* (*New York Times*, January 11, 2009). Dr. Khan was released from house arrest early in February, 2009, and is free, again, to travel the world to discuss nuclear weapons production. (*Associated Press,* February 7, 2009).

After 9-11, relations between the United States and Pakistan improved as then President Pervez Musharraf ended Pakistan's support of the Taliban regime. As long as Musharraf was President of Pakistan the general belief in the United States was that Pakistan's nuclear weapons were safeguarded from acquisition by Jihadists, who opposed the

Musharraf regime. Musharraf said in 2005, *"There is no doubt in my mind that they can ever fall into the hands of extremists"* (*New York Times,* November 11, 2007). Musharraf assured the world that he and a small group of military officers held the keys to moving or using Pakistan's nuclear weapons. However, President Musharraf resigned under the pressure of impeachment in August, 2008. Nine months before Musharraf resigned, a senior White House official told the *New York Times* that *"The truth is, we don't know how many of the safeguards are institutionalized, and how many are dependent on Musharraf's guys"* (November 11, 2007).

Shortly after this revelation, the *New York Times* front paged a frightening article from Pakistan (*"A Radio-Controlled Reign of Terror for Pakistanis Under Taliban,"* January 25, 2009). The article focused on a central province in Pakistan (Swat District), *not* in the areas of Pakistan where the Taliban has control and launches attacks on American forces in Afghanistan. After about a year, the Taliban forces had gained effective control of the 1.3 million person region in north central Pakistan. How the Taliban did it is the real story.

The Taliban terrorized local residents by broadcasting daily on mobile radio transmitters that residents are forced at the penalty of death to listen to, the names of those who are targeted to be killed, including policemen, local political figures who are suspected as unfriendly to the Taliban, and even women who are dancers. All 169 schools for girls in Swat have been destroyed by the Taliban. On February 16, 2009 the Taliban's terrorism efforts in the SWAT region of Pakistan proved to be very effective indeed. The national government of Pakistan, with 12,000 troops, was persuaded by the Taliban with 3,000 fighters to affirm the imposition of Sharia law on the entire region. In the article announcing the victory for Taliban terrorists, The *New York Times* noted that prior to the capitulation by the Pakistani government, *"Taliban leaders have proscribed what they call un-Islamic activities by residents, including watching television, dancing, and shaving beards, and they have sometimes beheaded*

179

offenders." Emboldened, the Taliban, moved to assume control over the entire province.

Asif Ali Zardari, the civilian President of Pakistan, under U.S. pressure, eventually responded with a military counter-offensive, which when this book went to press was still ongoing. Control over the rest of Pakistan rests in the balance. Pakistan's estimated sixty to one hundred nuclear weapons are the future reward to the Taliban if they take over the Pakistani government.

RUSSIA AS A SOURCE FOR NUKES FOR JIHADISTS

Russia is a likely source of nuclear armaments for Jihadists, by most military experts' projections. When the Soviet Union collapsed in 1991, Belarus had 81 single warhead nuclear armed missiles stationed on its territory; Kazakhstan had 1,400 nuclear weapons; and Ukraine inherited 5,000 nuclear weapons, which at the time made its nuclear arsenal the world's third largest. Purportedly, all three nations returned their nuclear weapons to Russia, completing the transfer by 1996. If only 1% of these devices were diverted by those in charge of the transfer in return for hard currency, drugs, or other consideration, that would be over 60 weapons that never made it back to Mother Russia. How many of the 6,481 devices may have been sold by persons in Russia once they were in the process of being transferred back to Russia?

Russia is the mother lode for acquisition of nuclear weapons:

"Where could they (al Qaeda) get this weapon? Where did they get the material from which it could be made? Well, my list, and I believe anybody at a meeting of the Defense Department or the White House would have a similar list absent specific evidence: Russia, Russia, Russia, Russia, Russia. The first five slots. Maybe they even deserve more, given the amount of material that's there." Dr. Graham Allison, Harvard University's Belfer Center for Science and International Affairs, February 20, 2003.

With the unraveling of the Soviet Union, many have speculated that Soviet suitcase nukes could have easily fallen into the hands of persons with an interest in acquiring them. In the first three years after the fall of the Soviet Union, Germany reported more than seven hundred attempts by Russian citizens to sell nuclear weapons and nuclear materials. (*GAO Report*, "Nuclear Nonproliferation," May 2002)

"We know that bin Laden made strenuous efforts to buy these weapons; we know that security at some Russian nuclear arsenals was terrible; we know that some Russian officials were corrupt. We are told of attempted thefts and of plots that were foiled, but we are never told of the plots that succeeded." Congressman Christopher Shays (R-CT).

Former Russian National Security Advisor General Aleksandr Lebed, appearing on *Sixty Minutes* (September 7, 1997), revealed facts about Russia's lost "suitcase nukes." Lebed said:

"I'm saying that more than a hundred weapons out of the supposed number of 250 are not under the control of the armed forces of Russia. I don't know their location. I don't know whether they have been destroyed or whether they are stored or whether they've been sold or stolen, I don't know."

The threat of nuclear terrorism on our shores has led the U.S. Congress to investigate the spread of nuclear technology and the growth of the global terrorist movement. In May, 1997 a Congressional delegation to Moscow was informed by Russian General and Security Council Secretary Aleksandr Lebed that he could only account for 48 of the 132 small nuclear devices (a/k/a 'suitcase nukes' or RA-115's) that had been produced in Russia. General Lebed confirmed to the delegation what he had said in his interview on *Sixty Minutes* as to the whereabouts of the missing suitcase nukes, that he *"had no idea."* The Russian General said the nuclear weapons were small enough to be carried in a larger suitcase, thus hiding its identity as a weapon; that it could be triggered by just one person; and required no 'secret codes' to detonate. General Lebed's statements were vouched for by Aleksey Yablokov, a former Advisor to Russian President Boris Yeltsin. He told a Congressional subcommittee on October 2, 1997 that he was *"absolutely sure"* suitcase nukes were manufactured upon the orders of the KGB and that he had met with the scientists who designed the devices. The Russian government at first denied any suitcase nukes were missing; then some time later, denied they ever existed, a point apparently not felt to be important enough to mention in the initial denial.

Though the Russian government disputed Lebed's claims, it was later revealed that the suitcase bombs had been under the control of the KGB, and not the Russian military. At first, the Russian government denied that suitcase nukes had been manufactured; then the same government said that the supposedly non-existent weapons had all been destroyed. Later, former intelligence official Stanislav Lunev, who defected, confirmed that such devices were made by the Soviets and do exist. He said they were known as RA-115s and weigh about fifty-five pounds. Lunev said suitcase nukes can last for several years if wired to an electric source. Lunev also said the number of missing nuclear devices *"is almost identical to the number of strategic targets upon which those bombs would be used,"* i.e., a large number.

The highest ranking Russian intelligence officer to defect from Russia, Stanislav Lunev, testified at a Congressional hearing held in California in January, 2000. The former Russian spy official, before his defection, was with the GRU (the Foreign Military Intelligence Directorate of the General Staff of the Armed Forces of the Russian Federation). Hooded while testifying, to protect his identity, as Lunev is in the U.S. Witness Protection Program, he told Congressmen that not only did Russia manufacture the RA-

115 suitcase nukes, but that some were currently planted in the United States.

Within four years of 9-11, Homeland Security Secretary Michael Chertoff warned that the threat of nuclear terrorism on U.S. soil was the emerging top threat to the nation, far in excess of initial concerns over mass-transit systems or similar bombings. In early 2001 the United States Department of Energy created a task force to review and assess the efforts to decrease the amount of nuclear fissile material available from Russia, known as the *Baker-Cutler Report Card on the Department of Energy's Nonproliferation Programs with Russia.* In 2008, the Commission on the Prevention of WMD Proliferation and Terrorism was tasked by the U. S. Congress to "reassess" the Baker-Cutler Report and *"examine how effectively its recommendations have been implemented."*

It would have been significant if the Commission had concluded that the nonproliferation efforts by the U.S. in Russia had been successful. But that's not what happened. The Commission, in its December 2008 Report (*World at Risk*), concluded that *"The report's principal recommendation– that a comprehensive strategic plan be formulated to address concerns over nuclear materials in Russia and stem the flow of expertise –was not implemented,"* noting that *"the program has not had access to all of the sites in Russia where sensitive materials are stored, and it has proved difficult to get a comprehensive accounting from Russia of all its sites and facilities."* The Commission also revealed that even though the United States has provided over $400 million dollars in the last few years to Russia to *"dispose of 34 metric tons of its plutonium,"* no agreement has yet been reached with Russia for the *"establishment of a monitoring and inspection regime,"* even though *"for years efforts have been made to negotiate such a regime."*

Think of these facts tonight as you snuggle in for the evening. Russia, the nation with the world's largest supply of nuclear weapons, and nuclear fissile material produced to be used to manufacture WMDs, *won't cooperate* with U.S.

efforts to *account* for all of those nukes, suitcase and otherwise, even though we are *funding* their purported efforts. *Where* are those nuclear weapons and *where* is Russia's nuclear fissile material? Still in Russia? In Pakistan? In Osama bin Laden's hands? Just as disturbing is the fact that it took several years for a Commission appointed by the U.S. Congress to reveal these disturbing omissions and failures to account for nuclear material.

NUKES FROM IRAN, THE LAND OF THE MEDES

Robert Gallucci, a former United Nations weapons inspector and Dean of Georgetown University's School of Foreign Service, recently said:

"Bad as it is with Iran, North Korea and Libya having nuclear weapons material, the worst part is that they could transfer it to a non-state group. That's the biggest concern and the scariest about all this–that Pakistan could work with the worst terrorist groups on earth to build nuclear weapons. The most dangerous country for the U.S. now is Pakistan, and the second is Iran. We haven't been this vulnerable since the British burned Washington in 1814." The Day of Islam, Paul Williams (Prometheus, 2007).

Iran, the land of the ancient Medes, has been intensively working on building its own nuclear weapons. The International Atomic Energy Agency's Director, General Mohamed El Baradei said in June, 2008 that Iran would have a nuclear weapon within six months. We now are well past that time projection. It was revealed in late 2008 that Iran had significantly more centrifuges carrying our uranium enrichment than earlier believed, now determined to be up to 5,000, enough to produce *"one weapon's worth of enriched uranium every eight months or so."* The IAEA report also estimated that Iran had obtained two tons of enriched uranium within the last two years. Iran's Ayatollah Ali Khamenei's deputy, Mojtaba Zolnour, in mid-2008 warned

Israel and the United States that, if either tried to take out Iran's nuclear facilities, Iran would launch its missiles on Israel and *"32 U.S. military bases."* Newsmax reported *"Even more ominously, Iran has reportedly carried out missile tests for what could be a plan for a nuclear strike on the U.S.."*

Admiral Mike Mullen, Chairman of the Joint Chiefs of Staff, disclosed on March 1, 2009, that Iran *"has sufficient fissile material for a nuclear weapon,"* declaring that it would be *"a very, very bad outcome for the region and for the world should Tehran move forward with a bomb."* Three days later, FOX News reported that Iran has *"enough fissile material to produce up to 50 nuclear weapons, according to a panel of current and former U.S. officials advising the Obama administration"."* The report originated from a "Presidential Task Force" on Iran, issued by the Washington Institute for Near East Policy. The Report may be read at www.washingtoninstitute.org.

Stepping back from previous American diplomatic efforts to halt Iranian nuclear efforts, President Obama in a BBC interview on June 2, 2009 gave approval to Iran's nuclear program, saying, "What I do believe is that Iran has legitimate energy concerns, legitimate aspirations." The President suggested that Iran had until the end of 2009 to "show that it wants to engage" in negotiations over its nuclear program. Iran, one of the world's major sources of oil, has made it clear that it will develop nuclear weapons, a goal which is unrelated to its "energy needs".

WARNINGS FROM AMERICA'S SECURITY EXPERTS

In April 2008, the United States Senate's Committee on Homeland Security and Government Affairs looked at the nuclear weapons issue. One witness, Dr. Cham E. Dallas, Director of the Institute for Health Management and Mass Destruction Defense at the University of Georgia, warned that a ten kiloton nuclear device in a van exploding near the White House would immediately kill 100,000 people, destroy almost all buildings within a half-mile radius and would burn tens of thousands more who survived the initial blast. Dr Dallas told the Senate Committee: *"Burn care is a nightmare, and we're completely unprepared. Ninety five percent of burn victims will not receive care. And most of them will die,"* Dr. Dallas also warned that:

"The impacts of radiation generally occur when people are caught in the open, or, are tied up in traffic jams trying to escape in vehicles, which provide little protection against fallout. Based on evidence from recent natural disasters in Louisiana and Florida it is likely that major exit arteries after a nuclear event will be completely impassable during the time period when fallout is at a maximum, exposing fleeing population to high levels of fallout. It is also expected that due to lack of information getting to the public, many people will try to flee by car or on foot, often in the wrong direction (due to the radioactive plume drifting from the blast site), again exposing themselves to high levels of radiation, as vehicles provide virtually no protection." (Written Testimony to Senate Committee on Homeland Security and Government Affairs, April 15, 2008, and used with permission)

Concern about the future use of nuclear weapons in America is bi-partisan. William J. Perry was the Secretary of Defense and Ashton B. Carter was the Assistant Secretary of Defense, under President William Clinton. Today Perry is a professor at Stanford University and Carter is a professor at Harvard University. They co-authored a jaw-dropping op-ed column in the *New York Times,* published June 12, 2007. In the column, these two former Department of Defense officials acknowledged what many have feared:

"The probability of a nuclear weapon one day going off in an American city cannot be calculated, but it is larger than it was five years ago. Only the federal government could help the country deal rationally with the problem of radiation, which is unique to nuclear terrorism and uniquely frightening to most people. For those within a two-mile-wide circle around

a Hiroshima-sized detonation (in Washington, that diameter is the length of the Mall; in New York, three-fourth's the length of Central Park; in most cities, the downtown area) or just downwind, little could be done. People in this zone who are not killed by the blast itself, perhaps hundreds of thousands of them, would get radiation sickness, and many would die...*"Next is the unpleasant fact that the first nuclear bomb may well not be the last. If terrorists manage to obtain a weapon, or the fissile material to make one (which fits into a small suitcase), who's to say they wouldn't have two or three more?"*

These words were written by two men at the top echelons of the United States Department of Defense, and who were in charge of America's ability to defend itself militarily. These aren't the conclusions of wild-eyed 'Islamaphobics', a label used in Great Britain to marginalize critics of Jihadists, and increasingly heard in the U.S. Instead, these former Department of Defense officials have done their nation a service by warning us, based on what they learned in their years in the Pentagon, what we are facing as a nation.

THE PLANNED 'NUCLEAR FIRE STORM' ON AMERICA

A breakthrough in determining bin Laden's future plans for America came with the capture in March 2003, of al Qaeda's military operations head, Kahlid Shaikh Mohammed, in Pakistan. After several days of intense interrogation involving sleep deprivation, Mohammed admitted to his U.S. interrogators that bin Laden was planning to create a *"nuclear hell storm"* in America. (*New York Daily News*, March 14, 2003, "Officials Fear Al-Qaeda Nuclear Attack"). He said the command structure for the future attack was directly under bin Laden's control, which was coordinating details with Dr. Abdul Qadeer Kahn, the well-known founder of the Pakistani nuclear program. In January 2004, Dr. Khan confessed to having been involved in distributing to Libya, Iran and North Korea secret nuclear weapon technology. In February 2005, *Time magazine* placed Dr. Kahn on its front cover, labeling him *"The Merchant of Menace."* In an August 2005 published interview Pakistani President Mushharraf confirmed that Khan had supplied equipment to enrich uranium and nuclear material to North Korea (*Kyodo News*). Nicholas D. Kristof, Pulitzer Prize winner, was quoted in the *New York Times* on September 27, 2004, as saying *"If a nuclear weapon destroys the U. S. Capitol in coming years, it will probably be based in part on Pakistani technology."*

In the spring of 2004, the FBI arrested Mohammed Junaid Babar, an al Qaeda agent, as he returned to the U.S. from a terrorist planning meeting in Pakistan (*CNN News –* August 11, 2004). Facing the potential of a 70 year federal prison sentence, Babar confessed that al Qaeda *"was planning a spectacular attack on American soil–a nuclear 9/11 that will occur simultaneously in major metropolitan areas throughout the country."* His testimony was confirmed by another al Qaeda participant at the same Pakistani planning session, Sharif al-Masri (*The Day of Islam*).

America's security experts, escaped Russian military leaders, and media investigators have all given ample reason to believe that radical Islamic terrorists *have acquired* nuclear weapons of mass destruction.

Chapter Ten

WHAT WILL 'COMPLETE DESTRUCTION' OF THE DAUGHTER OF BABYLON MEAN?

"For the Lord's purposes against Babylon stand–to lay waste the land of Babylon." (Jeremiah 51:29)

"I will kindle a fire in her towns that will consume all who are around her." (Jeremiah 50:32)

"Daughter of the Babylonians; no more will you be called queen of kingdoms." (Isaiah 47:5)

"Fallen! Fallen is Babylon the Great!" (Revelation 18:2)

"The Commission believes that unless the world community acts decisively and with great urgency, it is more likely than not that a weapon of mass destruction will be used in a terrorist attack somewhere in the world by the end of 2013...in our judgment America's margin of safety is shrinking, not growing." (*World at Risk*–The Report of the Commission on the Prevention of Weapons of Mass Destruction Proliferation and Terrorism, appointed by the United States Congress, December, 2008).

Jihadists, who are sworn and 100% committed to imposing Islam on every nation on earth, are not unknowledgeable of America. They are fully aware that America, as the world's only remaining superpower, is the *"hammer of the whole earth"* and thus, has the ability militarily to attack and destroy any nation on the face of the globe. Thus, being fully knowledgeable of these facts and completely committed to bringing America to its knees, how are Jihadists likely to accomplish such a monumental task?

Just take out:

A.) America's national capital (Washington, DC);
B.) America's financial capital (New York); and
C.) America's major oil refineries.

To sell all of this to other Muslims, who, after all, are going to be adversely financially affected, in different degrees, by America's fall as the world's leading consuming nation–*also* take out:

D.) America's 'cultural pollution capitals' (Hollywood/Los Angeles and/or Las Vegas)

E.) For good measure, and to insure that America does not rise again, at the same time, destroy the nation's major centers of commerce, such as Chicago, Seattle, Houston, Atlanta, Miami, Boston, etc.

When these coordinated nuclear detonations occur, how will that result in the "complete destruction" of America?

ELECTROMAGNETIC PULSE EFFECTS ON AMERICA

There is an exception to the fact that complete destruction of a nation as large as America would require multiple nuclear weapons. EMP enhanced nuclear devices exploded at high altitudes. Former House Speaker Newt Gingrich and William Forstchen have warned of the dangers of electromagnetic pulse (EMP) generated by nuclear devices. They write that nuclear destruction of as few as two U.S. cities, if accomplished by a nuclear device exploded several thousand feet high, will have the effect of shorting out *"all electrical equipment, power grids and delicate electronics"* (*Newsmax*, March, 2009). Without significant delay, any business would cease to have a function and any wealth stored up in investments, housing, or U.S. dollars would vanish. The ability of Americans to buy food and other basic necessities would quickly disappear. Gingrich and Forstchen cite studies estimating that 90% of Americans would die within one year after such an attack, as essential systems upon which life depends eventually collapse.

The Federation of American Scientists reports that a large nuclear device exploded at high altitude over Kansas would affect the continental United States. *"The first recorded EMP incident accompanied a high-altitude nuclear test over the South Pacific and resulted in power system failures as far away as Hawaii".* Gamma rays are released in the blast triggering a massive electrical disturbance. This is not another "Y2K" scare, without a scientific basis, but is instead a well-documented effect of nuclear weapons at high altitudes.

Gingrich and Forstchen warn: *"Those who claim there is little to fear from Iran or North Korea because 'at best' they will only have one or two nuclear weapons, ignore the catastrophic level of threat we now face from just 'a couple' of nuclear weapons. Again: one to three missiles tipped with nuclear weapons and armed to detonate at a high altitude – to achieve the strongest EMP over the greatest area of the United States – would create an EMP 'overlay' that triggers a continental-wide collapse of our entire electrical, transportation and communications infrastructure. Within weeks of such an attack, tens of millions of Americans would perish...Some studies estimate that 90% of all Americans might very well die in the year after such an attack as our transportation, food distribution, communications, public safety, law enforcement and medical infrastructures collapse."*

OIL AND THE LACK THEREOF

Until the beginning of the 20th century, crude oil had negligible importance. Used by some for oil-fired lanterns and similar limited purposes, to replace whale oil, it was largely not essential. Then, Elwood Haynes puttered along

Pumpkinville Pike near Kokomo, Indiana with his gasoline-fired engine hooked up to a formerly horse drawn carriage. The rest is history.

The critical importance of oil was highlighted by British Petroleum (BP) which recently aired television ads in the U.S. proclaiming that *"America's economy is based on transportation, and transportation is based on oil."* It would be an interesting exercise to consider ways al Queda might destroy America. One could discuss our vulnerabilities as a nation and eventually acknowledge the importance of oil. Considering the importance of oil, how can a nation based on transportation, based on oil, be crippled, and even destroyed? America hasn't built a new refinery since 1978, over 30 years. There are only about 60 refineries in the U.S. that refine over 100,000 barrels of crude oil at each refinery per calendar day. Unlike water or food supplies, America's refineries distribute gasoline "just in time" without large surplus stores. That's why gasoline stations run out of supplies quickly, if 'natural disasters' hit.

If an enemy could detonate nuclear weapons in numerous critical locations in the U.S., or a few at high altitude with the accompanying effect of EMP, the available supply of gasoline would drop off precipitously. America's largest refineries are located in Texas (27% of American refined output), Louisiana, Mississippi, (45% of American gasoline is refined in Gulf Coast refineries) Oklahoma, Illinois and California. The largest refinery in the Midwest is within sight (and blast range) of Chicago's skyline. The largest refinery in Pennsylvania is *in* Philadelphia. All that would be necessary to fatally cripple America's economy is to instantaneously cripple its refining of crude oil into gasoline. No gasoline = no commerce = no national economy worth even discussing.

Over half of America's electricity is generated from coal. How does the coal get from the coal mines and fields to the utilities' electric generation plant? Either by semi truck, trains, or barges, generally. What do semis, trains and barges need to haul coal? Yes, they generally operate on petroleum products. How do food products get to local groceries? How will food get to market if the growers can't be paid, and have no way of transporting the food, even if they could get paid? How will America's water supply systems treat and transport water to America's homes without power supplies? How will sewer systems function without electric power? How will our electricity grids function if the electromagnetic pulse effect of nuclear devices exploded at altitude have shorted them out?

If America is devastatingly attacked, how would it ever repay its 14 trillion dollars of debt? Knowing this, America's creditor nations would quickly sell its debt to the highest bidder, thus quickly driving down the offshore value of the dollar. Without a gasoline supply, how long will jobs last, even if the places of work survived the nuclear blasts? How long could anyone count on obtaining food, water and necessary supplies? How will homes be heated in freezing weather? If America has little or no ability to refine crude oil into gasoline, how long can we last as a nation? We currently import a large percentage of all of our gasoline supply from foreign refineries, notably in China, India and Saudi Arabia. But without the ability to pay those foreign national refineries with a currency that has value, and that they will accept, that supply line will quickly dry up.

Overlay on the cessation of transportation the fact that the national government would no longer be in existence, the Federal Reserve and the US Mint, and the Social Security Administration all out of business. In instances of past war and widespread financial crisis, a nation's national currency is usually the first thing that people won't accept. The barter economy quickly takes over, as people will only be willing to part with something of value in exchange for something else of value. Currency of little or no value won't be in that category.

The End of America

'THE DAY'

In *"Alas Babylon,"* Pat Frank's 1959 best seller about a nuclear missile attack on America (republished in 2005), his characters refer to the day of nuclear destruction as *"The Day"*:

"This December Saturday, ever after, was known simply as The Day. That was sufficient. Everybody remembered exactly what they did and saw and said on The Day. People unconsciously were inclined to split time into two new periods, before The Day and after The Day....Most of those who died in North America saw nothing at all, since they died in bed, in a millisecond slipping from sleep into deeper darkness. So the struggle was not against a human enemy, or for victory. The struggle, for those who survived The Day, was to survive the next."

In *Alas Babylon* the author imagines America after nuclear attacks take out the national government and major cities. He pictures a family, and a few of their friends, surviving in a small Florida town (Fort Repose) living on a pecan tree farm, on the banks of a river, surviving on what they are able to raise to eat. In the Foreword to the 2005 republication of *Alas Babylon*, David Brin (author of *The Postman*) is critical of such a peaceful description of the results of a nuclear attack:

"In my opinion, (Frank) downplayed some of the horrors that would have attended any nuclear spasm. Frank's description of the overall death toll feels a bit dry and detached, never going into details. He downplays the inevitable flood of wounded and starving refugees who would have flooded into poor, unprepared Fort Repose."

In *The Postman* (Bantam, 1985) Author, David Brin, concludes that in such a future day, small groups of survivors will erect walls and armed barriers to protect themselves and their supplies of food from marauding

194

hordes, only to be overtaken by the better-armed. He writes that since most people just will not be able to find or erect a suitable fortified and protected safe area, they won't survive, and will die. Brin labeled the post nuclear attack period as *"the great starvation"*:

Consider for the moment the persons who do not live in a target city, and in that moment do not die. But within a few hours they will have realized, based on what they have heard in whatever news may be available, that their food, water and gas supplies will not be sufficient for long term, or even medium term, sufficiency. This frightening thought will not be unique to them, as millions of those who are still alive, will quickly conclude that they had better gas up and obtain more food and water, as soon as possible. The result? Grocery store shelves will quickly empty, very quickly. Gas stations' supply tanks will be drained in mere hours. How many farmers, agricultural growers, orchards, dairies, egg farms, and other growers of food products will want to ship those food products to their traditional wholesalers, distributors and retail markets without assured payment, and knowing their survival may depend on keeping their food for themselves? Jeremiah prophesied that agriculture will effectively cease in the Daughter of Babylon:

"Cut off from Babylon the sower,   and the reaper with his sickle at harvest. (Jeremiah 50:16)

John also prophesied in Revelation 18:8:
"Therefore in one day her plagues will overtake her: death, mourning and famine."

These verses confirm what will happen when the Daughter of Babylon is attacked with weapons that destroy the nation in one day/hour/moment. Agriculture will effectively cease. No sowing or reaping or harvests, which will inevitably lead to *"famine"*. Why? With no gasoline, no electricity, and no acceptable currency, *who will raise food for others*?

Wall Street Journal columnist Peggy Noonan has pondered the question of Americans having enough food to eat in a depression:

"Lately I think the biggest thing Americans fear, deep down–the thing they'd say if you could put the whole nation on the couch and say, 'Just free associate, tell me what you fear'– is, 'I am afraid we will run out of food. And none of us have gardens, and we haven't taught our children how to grow things. Everything is bought in a store. What if the store closes? What if the choke points through which the great trucks travel from farmland to city get cut off? I have two months of canned goods. I'm afraid.' " (January 10, 2009)

If instead of just difficult economic times cutting off food supplies, there is *either* a massive shortage of refined gasoline to move the trucks to move the food to people who want to eat the food, or the trucks' electrical systems have suffered the effects of EMP, or both, the end result will eventually be mass starvation for the many who don't have or who can't find food to eat. A survivor of the sieges and destruction of the Second World War said:

"It got to the point where the only thing we really thought about was food. How to find it. How we were going to survive if we didn't find food. It was terrible, not knowing if we would survive, whether we would starve." (*The World at War*, PBS)

Once the stores are cleaned out, and once it's clear that the trucks will not be rolling into town with the food we were used to consuming, how long will it take for the survivors to realize that without new supplies of food, *and fairly soon*, they may get hungry, and eventually even starve to death. What will be the results of that alarming realization? Two 'd' words– death and destruction.

Initially, in a coordinated nuclear attack, millions of Americans would instantly die, and millions more who are near the blast sites would suffer burn injuries and become violently ill from radiation poisoning, but who don't die as a direct result of the explosions. They will inevitably move away from their local ground zero, and out into the country, mostly on foot, as their cars run out of gas and highways are gridlocked. They will be looking for medical care, which will be in short supply, as surviving hospitals and clinics will quickly be overrun. They will also be looking for food, just simple nourishment. Stores will be empty, stripped clean. That will then only leave fields and barnyards, which will be picked clean in short order. The only remaining source of food, therefore, will be individual homes. Everyone has some food in their homes, right? How long will the average person's food stocks actually last, even if they have stored dried food such as rice and spaghetti? Not long, because they will need to consume it and *others*, who need food, will have the same desire, to consume food belonging to others.

THE NEED FOR FOOD

When the sick and hungry come to your home, farm or apartment what will you do? At first, compassion will lead many to share. But, as supplies dry up, with no replenishment in sight, it will become a matter of personal survival to stave off those begging for food at the door. When the answer is 'no, I can't help you, we have no food,' how many will accept the rejection, and how many will forcefully push in anyway to grab what can be grabbed? When that happens, will anyone let them carry away their sustenance, or will they resist? Will they *shoot* people who want their food?

In 1965 British movie producer Peter Watkins made a controversial mock documentary for the BBC depicting Kent, England after a nuclear attack, entitled *The War Game.* Before it could be released, however, the British government banned it from being shown, and it wasn't shown by the BBC until 1985, twenty years after its production, even though it won an Academy Award in 1967 for Best Documentary Feature. For a glimpse of what life would be like post nuclear attack, one might want to view it, but

197

should be ready to be disturbed. It can be purchased on Amazon. Possibly the most frightening scene in *The War Game* shows a handful of housewives who have broken into 'National Emergency Food Control Centre No. 3,' after killing the policemen who were guarding the door to the food cache. The narrator describes one of those housewives, "*Mrs. Joyce Fischer*," shown grasping a few cans of food in her arms and staring blankly into the camera, with the slain guards behind her. The narrator says:

"In the last war we observed that when people suffer a personal loss, they become indifferent toward the law, even in the decent middle class, engaging in looting and petty theft...behavior becomes more destructive, more a thing of instinct...Would the survivors envy the dead"?

Since electric utilities won't likely be in operation, as it takes petroleum products to either produce electricity or transport the coal that is used to produce electricity, there will be no lights or power to cook food or to heat a home. By the end of the first winter after a coordinated nuclear strike, very few who survived the strikes themselves will also survive *what comes after* the coordinated nuclear strikes. For those who live in southern portions of the United States, in areas that don't require heat to survive the winter's freezing temperatures, they will still face the problem of raising food, as stocks and supplies of food will soon be gone.

For those with emergency generators, they'll also require petroleum products to power the generators, which products won't be available. Natural gas won't be produced or transported, for the same reasons as other petroleum products. Telephone and cell systems that may survive electromagnetic surges from the nuclear strikes won't be in operation, as long as they depend on electricity, which won't be available. No sewage treatment plants or facilities will operate without the availability of electricity. Homeowners and apartment dwellers alike will soon face an unacceptable back up of toilet facilities, which won't function or flush, because drains from sinks, tubs and showers won't drain into non-functioning sewage treatment systems, quickly making life in such homes and apartment buildings unbearable.

RADIATION DEATHS

All of these post-attack problems would be faced by those who *survive* the nuclear weapon detonations. However, the most critical immediate impact of coordinated nuclear strikes, of course, will be those who *die instantly* from the heat (3,600 degrees), bomb blast and concussion of those near the epicenter of the nuclear devices. John Hersey in his epic book *Hiroshima* (Vintage Books, 1946) wrote that *"In a city (Hiroshima, Japan) of 245,000, nearly 100,000 people had been killed or doomed at one blow (8:15 AM with the detonation of America's 13 kiloton atomic bomb over the city on August 6, 1945); a hundred thousand more were hurt. At least ten thousand of the wounded made their way to the best hospital in town, which was altogether unequal to such a trampling, since it had only 600 beds, and they had all been occupied."* Later estimates were that 140,000 died at or soon after the bombing, with 200,000 dead by 1950. Hersey found that *"Of a hundred and fifty doctors in the city, sixty-five were already dead and most of the rest were wounded. Of 1,780 nurses, 1,654 were dead or too badly hurt to work. In the biggest hospital, that of the Red Cross, only six doctors out of thirty were able to function (only one doctor was uninjured), and only ten nurses out of two hundred."*

In Brin's novel his lead character opines that: *"They probably wouldn't have killed so many in America, had the fallout zones not pushed crowds of refugees together, and ruined the delicate network of medical services."* If several nuclear devices are spontaneously set off, which is the only way a nation can be destroyed *in a moment* (Isaiah 47:9), waves of injured refugees fleeing destroyed cities will inevitably present at hospitals in cities and towns not directly hit. They will present with massive, life-threatening injuries. Those medical facilities will quickly be overwhelmed, and as a result, many more will die.

Hersey records that the residents of Hiroshima suffered massive burns, abrasions and lacerations, disfigurement and radiation burns: *"(Every one fleeing the city) seemed to be hurt in some way. The eyebrows of some were burned off and skin hung from their faces and hands...Some were vomiting as they walked. Many were naked or in shreds of clothing. On some undressed bodies, the burns had made patterns –of undershirt straps and suspenders and, on the skin of some women (since white repelled the heat from the bomb and dark clothes absorbed it and conducted it to the skin), the shapes of flowers they had had on their kimonos....(Mr. Tanimoto) remembered uneasily what the great burns he had seen during the day had been like: yellow at first, then red and swollen, with the skin sloughed off (he reached down and took a woman by the hands, but her skin slipped off in huge, glovelike pieces), and finally in the evening, suppurated and smelly."*

Hiroshima's residents who did not die in the initial blast swiftly developed symptoms of radiation disease, a previously largely unknown malady. The disease had three stages. In stage one, people who had absorbed radiation from the nuclear device came down with nausea, headache, diarrhea, malaise and fever. Their bodies had been bombarded with neutrons, beta particles and gamma rays. Apparently uninjured persons, who died seemingly mysteriously within hours or a few days, succumbed in this first stage. 95% of those within a half mile of the detonation center died instantly. Others further away also died, but not immediately.

In stage two, symptoms onset ten to fifteen days after the bombing, persons found their hair falling out, diarrhea and fever, in some cases as high as 106 degrees. Within twenty-five to thirty days blood disorders appeared, gums bled, white blood cell counts dropped (which reduced the ability to resist infection) and skin hemorrhaging due to broken capillary blood vessels appeared. If fever remained high, death was likely.

The third stage was manifested by radiated bodies struggling to compensate for their ills. In this stage, many died of complications, such as chest cavity infections. For those who survived, their symptoms lasted several months in many cases. The lack of medical supplies hampered those treating the survivors, as other communities did not immediately offer to share their medical supplies and personnel. A nation hit by simultaneous nuclear devices in various locations would likely encounter a similar reluctance of surviving communities who may not want to share their precious medical supplies. In *The War Game* a 'physician' notes that *"after four months without orange juice and fresh vegetables, with no vitamin C, the gums hemorrhage, the ankles swell, as the initial stages of scurvy are seen, with bleeding into the joints."*

So where do people who survive coordinated nuclear strikes go to live? They won't stay in the cities destroyed by nuclear devices. In Hiroshima 62,000 of 90,000 buildings were completely destroyed, and 6,000 more buildings damaged beyond repair. In the center of the city, only five modern buildings survived that could be used again without major repairs. Those who would live through an initial nuclear blast, would flee the destroyed city, looking for refuge. Those who are armed, and able to defend a building, or an area behind a defensible barrier of some sort, natural or erected, would stand the best chance to survive against the attacks of other armed people who are desperately seeking food. The desire to eat, and a lack of food to eat, would lead to extreme measures by survivors who seek simply to continue to survive. Many wouldn't choose to survive in a post attack America in conditions such as these.

Can all of this happen to a modern, rich, powerful nation like the United States? These things have happened in other nations in times of war and destruction, so why would America be exempt? Much blood would be shed in such an attack, but actually, much blood has already been shed in America, by Americans.

Chapter Eleven

GOD'S ACCOUNTING FOR THE
SHEDDING OF INNOCENT BLOOD

"God who gave us life gave us liberty. Can the liberties of a nation be secure when we have removed a conviction that these liberties are the gift of God? Indeed I tremble for my country when I reflect that God is just, that his justice cannot sleep forever." (Thomas Jefferson)

" 'Behold I am about to bring a calamity upon this place, at which the ears of everyone that hears of it will tingle. Because they have forsaken Me ... and because they have filled this place with the blood of the innocent and have built the high places of Baal to burn their sons in the fire as burnt offerings to Baal, a thing which I never commanded or spoke of, nor did it ever enter My mind; therefore, behold, days are coming,' declares the LORD, 'when this place will ... be called ... the valley of Slaughter.'" (Jeremiah 19:3-5)

In Chapter 7 several paragraphs are devoted to a short discussion of abortion. This issue has such ominous implications for the nation that allows it that it must be more fully addressed, from God's viewpoint. Men have shed other men's blood since mankind's beginning. One of Adam and Eve's first two sons killed the other son. That's a dysfunctional family. Shortly thereafter, God prescribed the punishment for slaying a fellow human being: *"Whoever sheds the blood of man, by man shall his blood be shed; for in the image of God has God made man."* (Genesis 9:6). After Cain killed Abel, God said that Abel's blood *"cried out from the ground"* (Genesis 4:10). A critical verse is found in Numbers 35:33:

"Do not pollute the land where you are. Bloodshed pollutes the land, and atonement cannot be made for the land

on which blood has been shed, except by the blood of the one
who shed it."

God's Word spells out that the shedding of blood
demands an *accounting*. That is, God has counted and
knows what blood has been shed, and states His view that
the blood calls out to Him for justice from the ground. God
assures us that He will impose vengeance on the
bloodshedders for their criminal acts. In Egypt, when
Joseph's brothers were confronted with their sins toward
their brother Joseph, whom they abandoned in a well to die,
Reuben said: *"Didn't I tell you not to sin against the boy? But
you wouldn't listen! Now we must give an accounting for his
blood."* (Genesis 42:22). In the KJV the phrase 'an
accounting for his blood' is translated *"his blood will I require
at thy hand"* (Ezekiel 33:8).

BRINGING DOOM ON OURSELVES

How do these verses and these divine standards apply
to a community or to a nation which sheds, and allows the
shedding, of innocent human blood? The Prophet Ezekiel
answers: *"Son of man, will you judge her? Will you judge this
city of bloodshed? Then confront her with all her detestable
practices and say: 'This is what the Sovereign Lord says: O
city that brings on herself doom by shedding blood in her
midst ... you have become guilty because of the blood you
have shed ... You have brought your days to a close, and the
end of your years has come. Therefore I will make you an
object of scorn to the nations and a laughingstock to all the
countries."* (Ezekiel 22:2-4). The act which *"brings on herself
doom"* is the act of the shedding of blood in the land.

Numbers 35:33 states that: "Do not pollute the land
where you are. *Bloodshed pollutes the land,* and atonement
cannot be made for the land on which blood has been shed,
except by the blood of the one who shed it." Think about what

God has decreed in His Word. When a nation's land is soaked with innocent blood, the only method of assuaging God's anger is the shedding of the blood *of the bloodshedders.* That's a further extension to a larger community/nation of His requirement early in His Word: *"Whoever sheds the blood of man, by man shall his blood be shed"* (Genesis 9:6a). Isaiah gives us what appears to be an end times prophecy as to how God will deal with all of the blood which has been shed in the world. "See, the LORD is coming out of his dwelling to punish the people of the earth for their sins. *The earth will disclose the blood shed upon her,* she will conceal her slain no longer." (Isaiah 26:21)

What has been the biggest cause of bloodshed? In fact, what has been the leading *cause of death,* in America over the last thirty six years? Murder? Approximately 670,000 persons have died homicidal deaths in that period. That's a tragedy, certainly. Compare, however, the number of Americans who have died at the hands of a murderer, to the number of Americans in the last thirty six years who have died at the hands of abortionists – *fifty million.* One out of every three babies conceived in the wombs of American women have been executed.

URGING OTHERS TO BRING DOOM ON THEMSELVES

Though Finland and England partially legalized abortion, under limited circumstances, before *Roe v. Wade,* almost all nations that passed laws allowing abortion did so *after* America decreed it was legally permissible to abort. It would be accurate to say that America is the nation that culturally led the world into the age of abortion. As in many areas of the popular culture, the United States made the previously unacceptable, acceptable. Jeremiah describes the influence of the Daughter of Babylon on the world: *"She made the whole earth drunk. The nations drank her wine; therefore they have gone mad."* (Jeremiah 51:7) America, through the United Nations Population Division, and other international bodies, has pressured third world nations to change their laws to allow abortion on demand. These efforts have been under the guise of population control. If a nation wants to prohibit abortion, what justifies the world's superpower telling that nation it should be like America, pressuring it to change its laws to legalize the killing of their nation's children in the womb?

The fact that America led in legalizing abortion won't excuse those nations whose land is also soaked with the blood of aborted infants, but it does increase our vulnerability to the punishment decreed in Isaiah 26:21: *"See, the LORD is coming out of his dwelling to punish the people of the earth for their sins. The earth will disclose the blood shed upon her; she will conceal her slain no longer."* For all nations, their time for God's call to an accounting and his exaction of vengeance is surely coming. He said it; He means it.

DO THE MATH

Before *Roe vs. Wade* was decided on January 21, 1973, most states in America had laws prohibiting the aborting of human beings. In 1900, every State had such laws, but in the 1960's some states somewhat liberalized their laws against abortion, while maintaining the criminal provisions of the laws. Only four States had no grounds required for an abortion.

However, on January 22, 1973, the day after *Roe vs. Wade, no states* had valid laws prohibiting or restricting abortion, as the United States Supreme Court struck down *all* state laws protecting children in the womb. *Roe* went so far as to authorize the killing of enwombed children through the entire nine month human gestation period. These are the children that God says are special to Him *"Lo, children are a heritage of the Lord, and the fruit of the womb is His reward."* (Psalm 127:3)

Abortion on demand, since *Roe v. Wade*, has become engrained in American society. Not only have we killed over fifty million Americans in the womb, and emerging from the womb, we also now kill over 90% of all Down Syndrome babies, solely because of their disability. The American College of Obstetricians and Gynecologists actively suggests its members encourage parents who discover in screening tests that they will have a Down child, to kill the child. Republican Vice Presidential candidate Sarah Palin was attacked in the 2008 campaign, not only because of her pro-life views, but specifically because she had declined to abort her son, once she knew he was a Down child. *That* just was not acceptable, the pro abortion forces huffed.

Attempts to protect the lives of those in the womb have met with organized, well-financed opposition. Do the math. America allows one million two hundred thousand abortions per year. According to the Guttmacher Institute, the average cost of an abortion in 2001, the last year for which data is available, was $468.00, so by now the average cost exceeds $600 plus. Multiply the number of abortions times the costs of an abortion. That exercise will yield a total of 'blood money' *every year* in America of close to a billion dollars ($1,000,000,000.00). In addition, American taxpayers send hundreds of millions of dollars to Planned Parenthood and similar groups every year to support "family planning" and "reproductive health." Planned Parenthood is the nation's largest source of abortions. To date, Planned Parenthood has received over two and one half *billion* dollars ($2,500,000,000.00) from the taxpayers of America. The specifics are unknown, because abortion clinics do not openly donate to candidates, but millions of dollars of 'blood money' generated by abortion end up in pro-abortion candidates' campaign coffers.

How does this tie into the Biblical prophecies concerning the Daughter of Babylon? First, the Daughter of Babylon, as was seen in scripture, will fall *because* of its treachery in failing to support Israel, leading to the shedding of blood of many Israelites. Jeremiah says about the Daughter of Babylon in 51:49: *"Babylon must fall because of Israel's slain, just as the slain in all the earth have fallen because of Babylon."* Is the second part of this verse a reference to America's role in leading the world towards acceptable abortion practices? Did the millions, tens of millions, of aborted infants in the world die, in part, because of America's 'leadership' in promoting abortion globally?

Though the Daughter of Babylon will fall *because* of the blood it allows to be shed in its treachery towards Israel, the measure of *the number* of its people who will fall when the Daughter of Babylon falls, must be related to an accounting for the Daughter of Babylon's slain infants. Assume that God *means it* when He says He will avenge the shed blood which cries out to Him from a nation's land, and, assume further He will *take vengeance* on those nations whose land is soaked with innocent blood.

Abraham Lincoln recognized this inescapable principle of scripture. In discussing the still ongoing Civil War, Lincoln, in his Second Inaugural Address said: *"Yet, if God wills that it continue until...every drop of blood drawn with the lash shall be paid by another drawn with the sword, as was said three thousand years ago, so it must be said 'the judgments of the Lord are true and righteous altogether.' "* Lincoln's analysis of God's requirement that spilt innocent blood due to slavery, had to be accounted for, one for one, was certainly fulfilled in the death and disability suffered in our nation's most tragic and deadly war (625,000 total deaths on both sides in the Civil War).

Who has shed the blood of America's fifty million innocent children? Some may say, 'it's those abortionists.' But God says: *"Rescue* the weak and needy; deliver them from the hand of the wicked"* (Psalm 82:4) and *"Rescue* those being led away to death; hold back those staggering toward slaughter."* (Proverbs 24:11). Many have marched against abortion, picketed abortion clinics and participated in rescue efforts of the unborn. If only more American Christians had taken God's Word seriously enough to insure that abortion was banned in our land, as it still is in a handful of nations.

How many should fall in a land which thought so little of its innocent enwombed babies as to allow them to be exterminated? Would the destruction of a *like number* of residents of that land be *just*? If the answer is no, that number would *not* be just, then, *what is the just number*? Would it be the death of one living person for ten babies, or the death of one living person for twenty babies, or one hundred babies? On what basis, would the life of a *born* person be worth more than an *about to be born person* (but for the abortion)? What would be the *just* standard and the *just* number?

In the over 220 Daughter of Babylon verses there are three instances of widespread bloodshed:

1. The shedding of the blood of God's people in religious persecution by the Daughter of Babylon;

2. The shedding of the blood of Israel caused by the betrayal of Israel by the Daughter of Babylon;

After these two events:

3. The shedding of the blood of the residents of the Daughter of Babylon (those who have not fled from the Daughter of Babylon).

It is not unreasonable to assume that the amount of blood shed will be tied to the numbers of the innocent unborn who were aborted in the Daughter of Babylon.

When the Daughter of Babylon is destroyed it will be a sweeping destruction. Fifty million is not an unthinkable number for widespread death by weapons of mass destruction. As stated above, the number who would die after a coordinated nuclear attack increases over time, but the initial level of death could easily be equal to the number of babies aborted, whose blood is on the land, and whose blood cries out for an accounting and for vengeance. Those who may be troubled by that thought, may think about what our country's willing slaughter of fifty million innocent babies must do to their Creator.

Roe vs. Wade was decided in 1973. Most of those Americans who were, say, about fifty years old, in 1973, will not likely be around, due to the sheer passage of time, when the blood of aborted Americans is accounted and avenged. On the other hand, for those of us who were fifty years old or younger when *Roe v. Wade* was handed down, and therefore *Roe v Wade* was allowed by us as Americans to *continue* as the law of the land, though we were of an age and level of influence that we *could have* done something about it, we may likely witness the destruction of the world's leading abortion nation in the end times. *That's justice.* It happened on our watch, during our time of influence, we let it happen, and today we continue to let it happen.

Remember that God says in Numbers 35:33 that *"atonement cannot be made for the land on which blood has been shed, except by the blood of the one who shed it."* When the *accounting* for the blood of the slain innocent fifty million aborted Americans happens, the accounting will likely take at least fifty million non-innocent Americans, who could have stopped the slaughter, but who decided instead to *look the other way*. Is God likely, as we have done, to *look the other way*, and not stop the attack on America? *"'When I called, they did not listen; so when they called, I would not listen', says the Lord Almighty."* (Zechariah 7:13).

It's not necessary to believe America is the Daughter of Babylon to believe that God will keep His word and demand America must make an accounting for the blood of fifty million babies killed by abortion, and that the accounting will be demanded from those who shed/allowed the shedding of the blood. God either means what He said, or He doesn't.

God decries the shedding of innocent blood. He requires an accounting as a result. Therefore, those who saved lives by rescuing babies from abortions, in reality rescued *two people, the baby* who was allowed to be born, and *the living person* who would not lose their life as divine vengeance for the baby. These are deadly serious thoughts, just as aborting babies is a deadly serious national sin.

God is deadly serious about His word. He is deadly serious when He tells us in His Word that; a.) He will bless those who bless Israel and curse those who curse Israel; and b.) He demands an accounting for spilt innocent blood. He said it, He meant it and He *will* enforce His Word.

THE SIN OF THE AMORITES/AMERICANS

Consider this Biblical narration of historical facts. God made a covenant with Abram to give him the land that would become Israel. He eventually took Abram and his small family out of Canaan down to Egypt. He told Abram they would be in Egypt for four hundred years. One could conclude the purpose of that long sojourn in a foreign land was to increase the numbers of Abram's descendants so that, when they entered the land, they would have enough population to conquer and occupy the land. That was a benefit of the four century side trip, but God tells why Abram had to wait: *"In the fourth generation your descendants will come back here, for the sin of the Amorites has not yet reached its full measure."* (Genesis 15:16)

What was *"the sin of the Amorites"* which had not reached its full measure until after 400 years? In Leviticus 18, God lists certain sins of the Amorites, mostly of a sexual nature, but a predominant sin in the list involved the shedding of innocent human blood: *" 'Do not give any of your children to be sacrificed to Molech, for you must not profane the name of your God. I am the Lord."* (Leviticus 18:21) The Amorites believed if they sacrificed their children in sacrificial fires to the false God they called Molech, they would have a good life. To re-phrase that belief in contemporary terms: The Americans believed if they sacrificed their children in abortion clinics to the false God called convenience or prosperity, they would have a good life. Doesn't sound too good, does it?

God warned the descendants of Abraham:

"'Do not defile yourselves in any of these ways, because this is how the nations that I am going to drive out before you became defiled. Even the land was defiled; so I punished it for its sin, and the land vomited out its inhabitants. But you must keep my decrees and my laws....for all these things were done by the people who lived in the land before you, and the land became defiled. And if you defile the land, it will vomit you out as it vomited out the nations that were before you. Even the land was defiled; so I punished it for its sin, and the land vomited out its inhabitants." (Ezekiel 18:24-28)

Did Israel listen? For a while it did, but over time, as faith in Jehovah, and fear of His power to enforce His word waned, Israel began to imitate its predecessors in the land, and started killing its own children, as did the Amorites. Manasseh, the King of Judah, sacrificed his own children to pagan false gods and caused the slaughter of others: *"Moreover, Manasseh also shed so much innocent blood that he filled Jerusalem from end to end—besides the sin that he had caused Judah to commit, so that they did evil in the eyes of the Lord."* (II Kings 21:16) Seeing their King kill his children meant it was not against the laws of Judah to sacrifice the young. (Compare with *Roe v. Wade* by which our Supreme Court told Americans it's not against the law to sacrifice our young). The residents of Judah now had a kingdom standard set by King Manasseh for his followers. *"Manasseh led them astray, so that they did more evil than the nations the Lord had destroyed before the Israelites."* (II Kings 21:9)

Just as the Amorites were vomited out of the land for their sin, God eventually demanded an accounting and He avenged the slain blood of innocent children. How did He do it? He sent the Babylonians to conquer Jerusalem and Judah. The Prophet Ezekiel was a resident of Jerusalem at that time. He had been warning his fellow Israelites of what

212

would come, which led them to want to kill Ezekiel, in that his warning was not a popular message. Ezekiel was specific in telling Judah why judgment was coming: *"they caused to pass through the fire all that open the womb, that I might make them desolate, to the end that they might know that I am the Lord."* (Ezekiel 20:26). Judah was throwing its first born children–who were supposed to be dedicated to the Lord for service to Him–instead into fires lit for pagan gods. Ezekiel bluntly told Judah that because of this sin–the same sin as the Amorites–they would lose their homes and be taken into slavery in Babylon. *"So I poured out my wrath on them because they had shed blood in the land."* (Ezekiel 36:18a)

This can be a cosmic test for the ages–will God keep His recorded Word and require an atoning, an accounting, and avenge fifty million slain American babies? Or, do those scriptural promises not apply to America? God didn't give His chosen people, the Israelites, the apple of His eye, a pass when they killed their young, but will he overlook America's slaughter of its infants? Some may ask, 'but which nations can legitimately say they don't deserve judgment for killing their young'? It's a simple answer: *Those nations that don't kill their young.* Doesn't it sound like such nations might be safer, saner, more Godly places to live? The countries that still *forbid abortion* on demand, in spite of U.S. and U.N. pressure, are listed in Chapter 13.

I'll never forget an incident a few years ago when I was in a deposition, half-listening, frankly, to another attorney's droning interrogation of a witness. I was seated facing an American flag on a stanchion. As I studied the flag I didn't actually see the blood dripping down from the red stripes onto the white stripes, but I saw it in my mind's eye, and I wondered if that was how our Lord viewed our nation's national standard. We've had a third of a century to stop the slaughter of Americans killed in the safety of their mothers' wombs. We didn't do it. So, is it time for an accounting? It is time for us to *repent* for all of the blood shed by fifty million American babies. That's a good reason to cry, in repentance for ourselves and our blood-soaked land, but those tears will soon be too late.

Chapter Twelve

THE WORLD WILL CHANGE AFTER THE FALL OF THE DAUGHTER OF BABYLON

"The extremes of 20 years ago are no longer extreme, and we must guard against any conventional thinking that places limits on the art of the possible for terrorist action. It is precisely the potential to surprise, along with the asymmetric impact of weapons of mass destruction that makes them appealing to the desperate designs of terrorists. Thus, it is not difficult in today's world to imagine an escalation of stakes to the ultra-violence represented by unleashing a nuclear attack on the world." (Rolf Mowatt-Larssen, Director, Department of Energy Office of Intelligence and Counterintelligence)

POLITICAL AND FINANCIAL RESULTS OF THE FALL OF THE DAUGHTER OF BABYLON

Major societal changes generally follow a crisis. When America encounters a significant economic downturn or recession, all of the world's financial markets are affected. "When America catches a cold, the world sneezes," as we have witnessed dramatically in the recent economic crisis.

Imagine again, the impact on the world of numerous nuclear devices triggered at the same time in America's largest metropolitan areas, or a smaller number of EMP emitting nuclear weapons detonated at high altitudes. No more United States Treasury; no seat of the national government in the District of Columbia; no Congress; no Supreme Court; no White House; no Federal Reserve; no World Bank; no United States Mint; no more functioning American stock exchanges; no more operating commodity exchanges; no method of making transfer payments to foreign banks; no Pentagon nor unified command of the armed forces; no operating broadcasting or cable networks; and no more nation of consumers buying the world's goods.

The traditional interpretation of end times prophecy has been that the Antichrist will be a European leader who seizes power over a nation, then three, then ten, and then moves on to try and conquer the world. Actually, that view of prophecy is correct, except the Antichrist will not be your standard run-of-the-mill European despot, such as Hitler or Mussolini. True, they were over-ambitious tyrants who wanted to conquer the world for their nations' proposed empires, but they had no perceived religious or philosophical platform upon which they based their fight to conquer other nations. Any European leader today who began to imitate, militarily, what Hitler and Mussolini did, would quickly be repelled by other European nations, certainly by the United States, and most likely Russia and China.

But in the world today, how could the Antichrist ever possibly come to power? A European leader can't today lead the European Union into a war of conquest. The EU nations combined only spend about half of what America spends for military purposes. So, how could the Euro-based Antichrist come to power and make a credible attempt to conquer the nations of the world for a united Europe?

Once the initial shock of the loss of America hits the inhabitants of the world; once the weeping (in some nations) stops, and once people adjust to a new world without its only superpower; it won't take long before Muslim leaders living in the nations of Europe seize power. How? The process of Jihadists gaining power isn't too hard to imagine. The Muslims then holding office (Muslims hold seats in the British Parliament, the United States Congress, and other legislative bodies in non-Muslim countries), and those who aspire to office, in various European nations, may not so subtlety proclaim that what happened to America will soon happen next in _____. Just fill in the blank–France, Italy, Great Britain, Spain, Sweden, Greece, etc. France may be first on Jihadists' list, as its President recently spoke against women wearing *burqas* in public.

It shouldn't take long for Europe to become the *European Islamic Union.* The star and crescent, then will fly over Number 10 Downing Street and the British Parliament in London; the National Assembly in the Palais Bourbon and the Palais Royal in Paris; the Reichstag and Chancellery in Berlin; the Italian Parliament; and every European capitol. As night follows day, a leader of the European Islamic Union will inevitably arise from the newly proclaimed Muslim European nations, after the Islamification of the individual governments of the nations of Europe.

Once America is destroyed in the *"Great Attack on America,"* the Jihadists will be in a position to make credible threats of similar destruction to the other non-European nations that may refuse to install Muslim leaders and adopt Sharia Law. Faced with the potential for national destruction at the hand of radical Jihadists, what nations would refuse to bow to these demands?

The newly powerful governmental CEO of the *European Islamic Union* will be in a position to promise the 245 nations and territories of the world he can protect them from annihilation, assuming, of course, they submit to his leadership, and agree to regime changes accommodating the Muslims in their borders. How long will the process of worldwide domination by the Muslim Leader of the *European Islamic Union* take? Not long, for those nations with significant Muslim populations. Longer, for those without resident Muslims bent on pushing their nation into the emerging worldwide Muslim confederation. Which national leader, given the recent destruction of the world's only superpower, would seriously suggest that his or her nation stand up to the new Leader of the world, a Leader backed by the ability of Jihadists to nuke any unyielding country?

The founder of Pakistan's fundamentalist Muslim movement (Mawlana Abul Ala Mawdudi) has succinctly stated the ultimate goal of Islam:

"Islam is not a normal religion like the other religions in the world, and Muslim nations are not like normal nations. Muslim nations are very special because they have a

command from Allah to rule the entire world and to be over every nation in the world....Islam is a revolutionary faith that comes to destroy any government made by man....The goal of Islam is to rule the entire world and submit all of mankind to the faith of Islam. Any nation or power in this world that tries to get in the way of that goal, Islam will fight and destroy."

In the 1970's, virtually every Bible commentator wrote that the Antichrist prophesied in the Bible would be the consensus leader of the revived Roman Empire, i.e., Europe. At that time there were no serious efforts to unite Europe. It had been posited decades before, but with no real potential to happen. By 1982, one could buy a symbolic coin, then called the ECU (European Currency Unit), but the ECU was not yet used as coinage in any nation. The unification of Europe accelerated, though, and in 1999 many European nations were using the newly named *Euro* as their currency. In those years three decades ago, certainly no one suggested that a Muslim would or could become the leader of a united Europe. A *Muslim?* Couldn't happen At least that's the way it appeared a few decades ago.

CONQUERING BY BIRTHING

In 1973, with America leading the way with *Roe vs. Wade,* the world began to view birthing a conceived baby in a different way. The world demographic changes resulting from the aborting of unwanted children have been nothing short of astounding, though you won't hear or read about these trends in the mainstream media. In the '70's, the '80's, the '90's and into this millennium, tens of millions of European couples, and single moms, made the conscious, deliberate decision to end the life of the baby that had been conceived in the womb. What has been the societal impact in Europe of these several tens of millions of decisions to abort? Europe, in a word, is dying.

In order to just sustain a nation's population, with no growth in numbers of residents, the reproduction rate must equal or exceed *2.11 children per couple.* Why is that true? It took two couples (that's four people) to produce the two members of a couple. If they only have one child (the current culturally acceptable reproduction rate), that simply means in two generations, the numbers have gone from four grandparents to two parents to one child. Ominous numbers indeed. Herewith are the reproduction rates of leading European nations:

Spain – 1.1; Russia 1.14; Italy – 1.2; Greece – 1.3; Great Britain – 1.6; France – 1.89; and Ireland -1.9.

The European Union Average – 1.38

What do these numbers mean? Simply that the populations of European nations are not self-sustaining, and that these nations are declining in numbers of citizens and will ultimately die off.

The more critical number is the reproduction rate of the average Muslim family living in a European nation. What's a good guess? . . . 3, 5? Way off. The average is a documented 8-10 children per Muslim family. Muslim men are allowed to marry up to four women (Quran 4:3). Marriage of pre-pubescent girls was a practice of Muhammad and widely practiced in many Muslim nations (Quran 65:4) Abortion is seen as against the will of Allah, and having all of the children that Allah sends is considered a religious duty. Ironically, radical Muslims, though they may have many children and ban all abortions, are not what we in the west would call "pro-life". Jihadists specifically disclaim the value of life, and admire death, honoring those who bring death to innocent unbelievers.

> *"Allah bears witness that the love of jihad and death in the cause of Allah has dominated my life and the verses of the sword permeated every cell in my heart..."*
> (Osama bin Laden, October, 2002)

Immigration officials in the various nations of Europe in the '70s, ''80s, '90s and into this millennium, lowered the bars to immigration by Muslims, rapidly filling the void left by aborted descendants of nationals. The results:

Country	Percentage Muslim Population	Muslim Population
Russia	19%	27,040,000
France	10%	6,120,000
Germany	3.7%	3,050,000
United Kingdom	2.5%	1,151,000
Italy	2.4%	1,420,000
Netherlands	5.4%	890,000

One of every two births in Belgium and the Netherlands today is a Muslim child; half of the students in French kindergartens are Muslim; in 15 years, half of the population of the Netherlands will be Muslim.

Libya's leader Colonel Muammar al-Gaddafi, the world's longest serving head of government, has said it succinctly:

"There are signs that Allah will grant Islam victory in Europe–without swords, without guns, without conquests... The fifty million Muslims in Europe will turn it into a Muslim continent within a few decades."

If radical Islam leaders were willing to wait those fifty years, Islam would eventually, by sheer growth of numbers, take over Europe. But Jihadists don't see their role in conquering the world for Allah in such a benign manner, preferring instead the sword over demographic conquest.

Once America is removed from the global geopolitical scene, Osama bin Laden's goal, which he has promised for decades–a Muslim world–would be close to accomplishment.

WHAT ABOUT ISRAEL?

But, not so fast, some may say. The world's only superpower may be destroyed in the future, and Europe may become Muslim, but the world would still not be a Muslim world, because of *Israel*. Oh, that pesky Israel. That stumbling block of a nation. In the end times Israel will fall for *two* treaties of peace, the second one signed with the Antichrist. The first peace treaty, which may have already

220

been signed by this reading, will cause Israel to be in a *false sense of peace* and security at the time the Russian-Muslim invasion we have previously examined takes place:

"*"This is what the Sovereign Lord says: On that day thoughts will come into your mind and you will devise an evil scheme. You will say, "I will invade a land of unwalled villages; I will attack a peaceful and unsuspecting people—all of them living without walls and without gates and bars. I will plunder and loot and turn my hand against the resettled ruins and the people gathered from the nations, rich in livestock and goods, living at the center of the land." "Therefore, son of man, prophesy and say to Gog: 'this is what the Sovereign LORD says: In that day, when my people Israel are living in safety, will you not take notice of it? You will come from your place in the far north, you and many nations with you..."* (Ezekiel 38: 10-14)

Only God knew when He led Ezekiel to write these words that He would *"resettle"* Israel back in their land and that He would lead them to officially become a nation again, and that He would do it in 1948. Since 1948, and at the time this book was written, Israel has not been living in peace or safety. The world wants Israel to give up its land for peace, which it will eventually agree to do. God's view? In Joel 3:2 He says He will enter into judgment against the nations of the world because *"they divided up my land."* Chapter 14 includes more about America's past pressure on Israel to give up its land.

As we have seen from scripture, once Israel is at peace, Russia and Iran, and their Muslim allies, will try to wipe out Israel, but God will miraculously intervene, with no help from Israel's military treaty partner, the Daughter of Babylon. The invaders will be destroyed, with destruction back in the homelands of Russia and Iran. Israel, though bloodied, will still stand (Ezekiel 38 and 39). So much for the *first* peace treaty.

After the Daughter of Babylon betrays Israel during the Russian-Muslim invasion, and is itself destroyed as a result, the new Muslim head of the *European Islamic Union,* a/k/a Revived Roman Empire (Daniel 2), will take power. The newly selected Leader of the European Islamic Union (a/k/a the Antichrist), will be sworn to conquer the world for Allah, but he also will be confronted by the tiny nation of Israel. A nation itself armed with several nuclear weapons, with the ability to deliver them by air. What will the Antichrist do? Scripture says the leader of Europe will enter into a solemn peace treaty with Israel. Will Israel fall, again, for the peace treaty scam? Yes, she certainly will. Knowing that it was only God, *not* the Daughter of Babylon, its military defense treaty partner, that saved her in the Russian-Muslim invasion, Israel will nevertheless, choose again to rely *on man.* Israel will *again* lean on promises of peace, all the while the European Muslim Antichrist prepares to exterminate Israel, once and for all.

What does the rest of the world do during this period after the fall of the Daughter of Babylon, and during which the new Antichrist makes peace with Israel? It appears from prophecy the world's nations will submit to the Antichrist, his control of the world's finances and to his religion.

THE SPIRITUAL RESULTS OF THE FALL OF THE DAUGHTER OF BABYLON

In telling His disciples about conditions in the last days, Jesus said *"at that time many will turn away from the faith and will betray and hate each other"* (Matthew 24:10). Paul wrote that end times Christians should not be deceived into thinking that Jesus had returned until *"the great apostasy"* or the *"great falling away"* had *first* taken place:

"Let no man deceive you by any means: for that day shall not come, except there come a falling away first, and that man of sin be revealed, the son of perdition." (II Thessalonians 2:3) The New American Standard translates the phrase *"falling away"* in this verse as the *"apostasy."*

Paul reiterated his warning in I Timothy 1:4:

"The Spirit clearly says that in later times some will abandon the faith and follow deceiving spirits and things taught by demons."

In the end times many will *'fall away'* from their 'faith' in Him. Scripture confirms such a major theological event in the three above quoted verses. Why will the great apostasy Jesus warned will happen come to pass? It should be noted that our Savior prophesied that at the end, many of those who had expressed faith in Him will *turn away* from their faith. Who or what will they turn to, instead?

To answer this question, consider a future world in which the world's only superpower, the world's leading military, financial, and entertainment power, is destroyed in one day. Imagine further, that it soon becomes obvious to the remaining 95% of the world's inhabitants, that the superpower was destroyed by leaders of a *militant religion* representing one out of five of the population of the world, the followers of which religion previously had very little worldly success. As author Joel Richardson puts it:

"Because one of Islam's core doctrines is faith in Allah's absolute and complete sovereignty, many Muslims have had a hard time psychologically with the idea that Islam has had to play second fiddle to Christianity for such a long time. If Allah is all powerful and Islam is his only religion, then why does Islam play such a secondary role to Christianity throughout the world?" ("Antichrist –Islam's Awaited Messiah")

Nations which win major wars soon find they have many friends, just as winners of elections are besieged with friends and patrons, while losers of elections are soon left alone. That's human nature. We all like winners. Again, imagine a world in which the world's leading nation, seen, inaccurately, by many as a "Christian nation," is no more, and *Islam* widely seen as being responsible for its destruction. Governmental leaders across the globe will quickly seek closer ties with Jihadists, not at first aware that they *themselves* will soon be replaced by Muslim leaders, as Jihadists threaten to destroy nations *without* Islamic governments, governed by Sharia law.

Applying Jesus' parable of the seed, those who do not have spiritual roots, will, when the pressure of such events increases, soon fall away from their faith: *"The one who received the seed that fell on rocky places is the man who hears the word and at once receives it with joy. But since he has no root, he lasts only a short time. When trouble or persecution comes because of the word, he quickly falls away."* (Matthew 13:20-21) Jesus thus warns that when trouble or persecution comes, a "Christian" who is not rooted will *"fall away."* The phrase to *"fall away"* is the same as in II Thessalonians 2:3, that there will *"come a falling away first."* Most commentators write that this refers only to those superficially interested in following Christ, but who never truly place their faith in Him.

It would be hard to think of a larger source of trouble or persecution for non-American Christians, in a post-America world, than the fall of the nation seen by most as the world's leading Christian nation. Many Christians are alive in the world today because their martyrdom has been stayed due to fear of what the United States might do if wholesale slaughter were to take place. The *Voices of Martyrs* organization reports, in spite of this, many Christians still are martyred every day. However, in a post-America world it will be much easier to kill Christians. Many believers who refuse to renounce their faith will be killed. Those who are nominal Christians, not rooted in Christ, as their *'troubles and persecutions'* increase, and they're faced with a competing world religion of increasing strength and power, will be likely to *"fall away,"* just as Jesus and Paul warned they would.

Thus, much of the *'great apostasy'* or *'great falling away'* will arise from fear. Richardson notes that the "Stockholm Syndrome" could cause many to fall away as

224

they see Islam becoming the world's largest religion, due to population increases by Muslims worldwide. Stockholm Syndrome is a response sometimes seen in an abducted hostage, in which the hostage shows signs of loyalty to the hostage-taker. The syndrome is named after a bank robbery in 1973 in Norway, in which the abductees, held for five days, became attached to their captors, not having killed them during their captivity; they then defended their captors when finally released unharmed.

Many who don't face martyrdom for their faith will likely turn from their faith because they want to 'join the winning team.' The conversion to Islam by westerners following the 9/11 attacks has been documented. (*Islam Attracts Converts by the Thousands, New York Times,* October 22, 2001). This phenomenon would only increase if an entire nation falls, instead of just falling buildings. There will be millions of believers in the world after America falls. Many of these will have heeded God's several warnings in the Bible to flee from the Daughter of Babylon to save their lives. But there will also be many nominal "Christians" in the world in the end times who will fall away from their faith, just as Jesus and Paul said they will. The future Jihadist destruction of the Daughter of Babylon is a more than plausible explanation for why so many will depart the faith, and fall away, in the end times.

Chapter Thirteen

GOD'S WARNINGS TO LEAVE THE DAUGHTER OF BABYLON

"Wise people see danger and go to a safe place. But childish people keep going and suffer for it." (Proverbs 22:3 and 27:12)

"The word of the Lord came to me: "Son of man, speak to your countrymen and say to them: 'When I bring the sword against a land, and the people of the land choose one of their men and make him their watchman, and he sees the sword coming against the land and blows the trumpet to warn the people, then if anyone hears the trumpet but does not take warning and the sword comes and takes his life, his blood will be on his own head. Since he heard the sound of the trumpet but did not take warning, his blood will be on his own head. If he had taken warning, he would have saved himself. But if the watchman sees the sword coming and does not blow the trumpet to warn the people and the sword comes and takes the life of one of them, that man will be taken away because of his sin, but I will hold the watchman accountable for his blood.'

"Son of man, I have made you a watchman for the house of Israel; so hear the word I speak and give them warning from me." (Ezekiel 33:2-7)

If God states *once* in his Word to take an action, that obviously has great importance. How much more so if He says *two or three times* to do the same thing? Because God loves His people He has graciously provided through *four different writers* of the Bible the same identical message, stating it *nine times*.

227

NINE SEPARATE WARNINGS TO FLEE

The prophet Jeremiah, along with Zechariah, Isaiah, and the apostle John gave these nine specific warnings to God's people to flee the Daughter of Babylon. The first seven of the nine warnings are:

"Flee out of Babylon; leave the land of the Babylonians, and be like the goats that lead the flock." (Jeremiah 50:8)

"Let everyone flee to his own land." (Jeremiah 50: 16)

"Flee from Babylon! Run for your lives! Do not be destroyed because of her sins. It is time for the Lord's vengeance; he will pay her what she deserves." (Jeremiah 51:6)

"We would have healed Babylon, but she cannot be healed; let us leave her and each go to his own land, for her judgment reaches to the skies, it rises as high as the clouds." (Jeremiah 51:9)

"Come out of her, my people! Run for your lives! Run from the fierce anger of the Lord." (Jeremiah 51:45)

"You who have escaped the sword, leave and do not linger! Remember the Lord in a distant land, and think on Jerusalem." (Jeremiah 51:50)

"Then I heard another voice from heaven say: "Come out of her, my people, so that you will not share in her sins, so you will not receive any of her plagues." (Revelation 18:14)

These seven specific warnings all appear to be addressed to God's people-the Church, made up of believers in the Lord Jesus Christ. God also warns His Jewish people through the prophet Zechariah:

228

"Oh Zion! Escape, you who live in the Daughter of Babylon." (Zechariah 2:7)

God likewise, through Isaiah, warns the Jewish residents of the Daughter of Babylon to flee:

"Leave Babylon, flee from the Babylonians! Announce this with shouts of joy and proclaim it. Send it out to the ends of the earth; say, 'The Lord has redeemed his servant Jacob.'"(Isaiah 48:20)

The Lord, a total of *seven times,* tells His Church, believers in the Lord Jesus Christ, and *twice warns* Jewish residents of the Daughter of Babylon to FLEE from this great end times nation. No other warning in scripture is recorded *nine separate times.* S*even warnings* to Christians and *two warnings* to Jewish residents of the Daughter of Babylon should dramatically, and decisively, confirm that He has repeatedly and emphatically warned His people to flee the coming disaster that He knew from the beginning of time would occur.

God doesn't waste His words. So why does He tell Christians seven times and Jews twice to flee from the Daughter of Babylon? Most Jewish people know they are Jewish, some are Orthodox, and some adhere to more liberal branches of Judaism. But they know who they are. In these verses they are warned not to continue residing in the Daughter of Babylon. Moving to Israel is, of course, an option, but one to be seriously studied before such a move, in light of the coming Russian-Muslim invasion, and accompanying blood shed in Israel.

[Author's Note] *We've just read that Christians are warned seven times to flee. God evidently wants to be sure that His people get the message, which leads to an obvious question:* Are you one of God's people? *For the first few years of my life I thought I was a Christian. I was active in our church's youth group–I bought the cider and donuts every* *other week. If someone had asked me in high school if I was a Christian (which no one ever did) I would have said, 'sure, I'm not a Buddist or a Hindu.' Then in college, I married a girl, my dear wife now of 48 years, who knew exactly what she believed–she was an avowed agnostic. We had some interesting discussions in those early married years. I remember driving back to college late one evening and I was listening to Billy Graham on the car radio. My wife soon tired of the message and told me to* "turn that stuff off." *I said,* "hey, do you want lightning to strike this car?" *So you can see we had an elevated theological tone to our discussions.*

After law school, we moved to a traditional suburb of Indianapolis to raise our children. After we were in our neighborhood for a short time I came home one night and my wife asked me "guess what I did today?" *I didn't have a clue, but she soon told me that she had been invited to attend a neighborhood women's Bible study. I admitted that I was surprised, but after I thought about it I thought it was a good idea, so she could* "meet our neighbors." *I didn't hear any more about the Bible Study for a few weeks, then one night she asked the same question again,* "guess what I did today?" *Before I could guess, she told me that she heard a speaker at the Bible Study that she had been attending every week (I didn't know she had become a regular). She said the speaker, the wife of a dentist,* "told us that to know God personally we need to accept His Son, Jesus Christ, as our own personal Lord and Savior. So, I did it."

My reply? "You did what?" *She said,* "I accepted Jesus as my Lord and Savior." *My response–not so good– particularly since before this time I was the 'religious one' in the family. I said,* "that sounds like something you hear on your car radio driving through the Bible Belt."

Needless to say, that comment, and my increasing resistance to my wife's continued use of her growing knowledge of scripture, led to a running, and not always harmonious debate. Even though I had been on my college debate team, I was soon losing the debate, because my wife was acquiring her debate points from scripture and the

230

Christian books that soon began to fill our house. After several months of the ongoing debate, I was leaving for a business trip to California and, on the way out the door, not having a book to read on the long flights, I picked up a book my wife had (conveniently) left lying around for me to notice. It was Hal Lindsey's "The Late Great Planet Earth", which eventually became the 1970's biggest seller.

On the red eye coming back from California I couldn't sleep, so I decided to see what my wife had been reading. Lindsey focused on Israel, in which I had some interest as a political science major. Lindsey wrote that God had written in the Bible, through the prophets, that the people of Israel would go into dispersion around the world, for centuries, but would in some future day be re-gathered back in the nation of Israel, in the same location of its original home. I knew, of course, that no nation in the history of the world had gone out of existence, been scattered widely into other nations, and then 2,000 or so years later, been re-gathered into the same location. I can take a Jewish person to lunch, but I can't take a Chaldean or an Assyrian to lunch, as they've been dispersed and disappeared over time. There is neither Chaldea nor Assyria in the world today.

Lindsey then said that the Bible contains hundreds of prophecies about a coming Messiah, all of which were fulfilled in the life of one man, Jesus of Nazareth. He said that the mathematical chances of that just happening were so high that it would be the equivalent of tossing a marked silver dollar into the State of Texas, filled with four feet of silver dollars, stirring them up, and then finding the marked silver dollar on the first try. I was convinced. Lindsey also said what my wife's Bible Study speaker had said–that I needed to get to know Jesus personally as my own Lord and Savior. Because Jesus was resurrected after His death on the cross, if I know Him, I could be sure of life after the death of my earthly body. He gave a simple prayer to start the process of knowing Jesus.

When I came to the prayer I thought, briefly, ' hmm, my wife's going to win our argument,' *but I went ahead anyway, bowed my head on the airplane, and prayed a prayer like this:* "Jesus, I don't really know you. But I want to, so I'm asking you to come into my heart as my Lord and Savior. Help me in the days ahead to understand what this is all about and what you want me to learn from the Bible. Amen." *I didn't see any fireworks, but within a short time I knew things had changed. I had changed. Over time, I lost interest in things I used to pursue, and I developed an interest in things I didn't previously care about. I soon developed a peace about why I was on the earth and what God expected me to do while I was here. And, losing that debate to my wife was the best thing I ever did.*

If you are pondering the content of this admittedly frightening book, you may wonder if you are a Christian or not. If you can't say that a point in your life came, in which you placed your faith and trust in Jesus and came to know that He is the Lord of your life, you may wish to pray a similar prayer. If you draw near to Him, He will draw near to you. Once that issue is settled, you can move on to other warnings God has given to His people in His Word.

WHO BEHEADS TODAY?

God's warning to his people to flee from the Daughter of Babylon must be seen in the context in which the warnings are given. In Jeremiah 51:50 the prophet includes these words in his warning to flee the Daughter of Babylon: *"You who have escaped the sword, leave and do not linger!"* Thus, Jeremiah in the Old Testament warns God's people to flee the world's richest, most powerful nation in the end times, noting they will escape *from the sword.* In the New Testament, the apostle John has a similar warning as to how Christians will be executed in the last days:

"I saw thrones on which were seated those who had been given authority to judge. And I saw the souls of those who had been beheaded because of their testimony for Jesus and because of the word of God. They had not worshiped the

232

beast or his image and had not received his mark on their foreheads or their hands." (Revelation 20:4).

Scripture is specific in warning that in the end times, Christians and Jews will be martyred for their faith. Jesus warned in Matthew 24 and again in John 16, of the martyrdom of the church in the end. He even said that *"a time is coming when anyone who kills you will think he is offering a service to God. They will do such things because they have not known the Father or me. I have told you this, so that when the time comes you will remember that I warned you"* (John 16:2-4).

Jesus has thus given us the keys to determine who will martyr His people. These future murderers have two critical characteristics: a.) they will think they are beheading Christians and Jews *for God*, but, b.) they won't know God, or His son. Who in this world make a mandated five times a day effort in regimented prayer to please "god"? Who else but Muslims regularly proclaim "Allahu Akbar, Allahu Akbar" (Allah is Great). Pursuing Jesus' prophecy, do these people know the God of the Bible, or His Son? No, but they will kill, thinking they are doing a service to Allah, just as John said (Surah 9:5).

Beheading one's opponents is not an historical oddity as we know from English history (and particularly Henry VIII) and the history of the church in the reformation period. *Fox's Book of Martyrs* dramatically records the stories of Christians who believed they were doing God's will by killing other Christians. Those deaths, though reprehensible, are to be distinguished from Jesus' warning that a time will come when people, who *are not themselves Christians,* will martyr Christians, thinking they please Allah. Such prophecy foretells Jihadists' efforts in the world today.

The world has been exposed to Jihadists' favorite method of killing, as websites and other media sickeningly show on video, American reporters and others being beheaded. Some in the media have tried to distinguish these gruesome videos by saying beheadings aren't truly "Islamic." Minimum research reveals that beheadings of one's enemies are called for in the Quran, and was the preferred method of killing by Muhammad and those who came after him. At the Battle of Badr, Muhammad rejoiced at the beheading of Abba Hakam, of the enemy tribe of Quyraysh, proclaiming upon seeing his severed head: *It is more acceptable to me than the choicest camel in all Arabia"* (*Antichrist, Islam's Awaited Messiah*, Richardson, Winepress Publishing).

In 627 A.D. Muhammad led the beheading of several hundred men in trenches, which became mass graves, at the Jewish village of Quyrayzah (*Sirat Rasul,* Ibn Ishaq). The beheadings continued and became common in Muhammad's battles. When he entered Mecca with an army of ten thousand, he told his soldiers to *"Go and slaughter them."* Dr. Gabriel gives us the meaning of slaughter:

"The Arabic word for slaughter presents the picture of a farmer harvesting his crop with a scythe. In other words, Muhammad was telling them, 'Cut their heads from their bodies as you would cut fruit from the branch of a tree" (*Jesus and Muhammad,* Dr. Mark Gabriel, 2004, Charisma House).

History records that Muslims have beheaded their enemies in the intervening centuries *since* Muhammad. Joel Richardson notes that over 2,000 at the Battle of Kabul in 1842 and 3,000 Soviet troops in Afghanistan in the 1980's were beheaded by Muslim warriors. Under Sharia law, beheading is also the method of executing those found guilty of capital crimes. *The Voices of the Martyrs* has confirmed and regularly posts on its website (www.persecution.org) details of Christians around the world who have been beheaded by Muslims. Christians and Jews are likely to continue to face martyrdom by beheading at the hands of Jihadists? Muslims are permitted to do so:

"If you encounter (in war) those who disbelieve, you may strike the necks" (Surah 47:4).

Joel Richardson states that those who will someday dispute the authority of the Antichrist, the ruling Caliph, seen as the successor of Muhammad, will face beheading:

"If a man comes forward, disputing his (the Caliph's) authority, they (the Muslims) should behead the latter." (Hadith, Sahih Muslim Book 20, Number 4546)

Christians and Jews who recognize they have an implacable enemy sworn to removing their heads may conclude that leaving one's homeland a bit more acceptable. Other Christians in centuries past have had to face the same issue; flee or die.

THOSE WHO FLED THEIR HOMELAND BEFORE US

The thought of leaving America to live in a foreign land, at first, naturally seems unthinkable. But, it should be seen in an historical context, a Christian and Biblical historical context. The history of Christians and Jews fleeing from persecution is well documented. The Bible contains many instances of God taking an action in the Old Testament He mirrors in the New Testament. For example, the sacrifice of a spotless innocent lamb was a picture or foreshadow of the physical sacrificial death of Christ. Similarly, we find in this section of Jeremiah, God's warnings to His people at the time of Jeremiah to *leave* their home city and nation of Jerusalem in Judah. When they obeyed His warnings to leave, given through Jeremiah, *they lived*, they *"escape(d) with (their) life, (they) will live"* (Jeremiah 42). The warnings also given to Jeremiah (chapters 50 and 51) and to the Apostle John (Revelation 18) to flee from the Daughter of Babylon have the same result–*if we flee-we live, if we don't-we die.* It's a simple concept. It's doing it that's tough.

The Lord warned the Jewish inhabitants of Jerusalem and the cities of Judah well before Nebuchadnezzar's invasion, that they should flee from Jerusalem and not try to remain as residents. Jeremiah warned Jewish residents that the Lord had told him Jerusalem and the cities of Judah would become a *"desolation without an inhabitant."* (Jeremiah 34:22) Those who heeded His words were safely secured in Babylonian captivity for seventy years. *"This is what the LORD says: 'Whoever stays in this city will die by the sword, famine or plague, but whoever goes over to the Babylonians will live. He will escape with his life; he will live.'"* (Jeremiah 38:2) *"Do not be afraid of the king of Babylon, whom you now fear. Do not be afraid of him, declares the Lord, for I am with you and will save you and deliver you from his hands. I will show you compassion so that he will have compassion on you and restore you to your land."* (Jeremiah 42:11-12)

Our nation was settled and populated by Christians who could not abide persecution. Shipload after shipload of our Christian ancestors, for decade after decade, chose to move from their homeland in Europe immigrating to a land known for its religious freedom. Their decision to leave their own nation, leaving most of their family members and lifelong friends, in almost all cases to never see them in this world again, had to be gut-wrenching and tearful. They left their nation because the level of religious persecution they were experiencing was not tolerable. .

In the last century, in the 1930's and 1940's, Jewish residents of central and eastern Europe were increasingly alarmed that they were being targeted for extinction by the growing Fascist movement. Russia's Czar instituted pogroms to exterminate Jews in Russia. As a consequence, many Russian Jews moved to Germany, only to be confronted not long after with Adolph Hitler's "Final Solution." Those who moved to Poland, and Austria had similar problems, as Hitler expanded the reach of the Third Reich.

As more Jews were taken into captivity and their assets seized, increasing numbers began to realize that fleeing Europe was a rational, life-saving option. France rounded up and deported 76,000 Jews (including 11,000 children) to concentration camps. Only 3,000 returned alive. Prior to deportation, across Europe, tens of thousands fled to freedom, most with only the clothes on their back and a suitcase. Millions who chose not to flee were killed in Hitler's Holocaust, *"Hitler's Final Solution."* Nazi Germany, purposefully and deliberately, slaughtered millions of men, women, and children, with bullets and nerve gas, solely because they were of Jewish descent. (A&E series – *The World at War*). By the time they had been rounded up and detained, it was *too late* to flee. 25% died within ten days of being taken captive. Almost all eventually died, a total of Jewish deaths of almost six million. Confirming God's demand for an accounting of shed blood, Germany, which led the slaughter throughout conquered Europe, suffered over seven million deaths. One million Jewish residents of the Soviet Union died, but over time one million Jewish residents of Russia immigrated to Israel. Those who saw the danger and fled from it lived; many still alive even today. It is estimated that about 50,000 Jewish émigrés left Germany fleeing to freedom.

A common denominator of the Christians and Jews fleeing for their lives over the last two hundred years was they trusted God to provide for their needs, as He promised, and as He did. We find no reports of emigrants who fled to America dying from lack of food. The oft times quoted phrase is true: *"Where He guides, He provides."* But what of those Christians and Jews who didn't flee Europe when life was threatened? Jeremiah told his fellow countrymen: *"Whoever stays in this city will die by the sword, famine or plague."* (Jeremiah 38:2[a]).

In the same sections of scripture which contain the prophecies warning of what will happen to the Daughter of Babylon, it is also stated that *in the Daughter of Babylon* will be found *"the blood of the...saints."* If people in churches or Bible studies because of their faith, have been arrested and hauled off to jail or prison or worse, God's warnings to flee will become a lot more urgent.

BUT WHERE SHOULD WE FLEE?

God has warned the residents of the Daughter of Babylon to flee their native land before its destruction, but *where should we go*? Jeremiah suggests that the residents of the Daughter of Babylon may want to go to their own land (50:16). That observation fits a 'melting pot' nation of mixed peoples described in Jeremiah 50:37. For many people that will mean moving to countries in which they have relatives. For those who don't have any known relatives in foreign nations, they may be surprised how many people they know who do have family in other nations. For others it may mean immigrating to other parts of the world in which they may have some connection. Fortunately, God's people who have been engaged in missionary activities, even short term, will have contacts in other nations who will facilitate emigrating. For many, however, it will mean locating in a new land, with little or no prior connections.

No one, least of all our Lord, would suggest that leaving the land of one's birth is an easy task. When Jeremiah warned the residents of Jerusalem to leave Judah going into captivity in Babylon their first reaction was to accuse Jeremiah of *treason*: *"But when he reached the Benjamin Gate, the captain of the guard...arrested him and said, "You are deserting to the Babylonians!"*– Jeremiah 37:13. The leaders of Judah then had Jeremiah *flogged* and thrown into a prison dungeon, where he *"remained there many days"* (Jeremiah 37:16). Shortly after, *"Then the officials said to the king, 'This man should be put to death. He is discouraging the soldiers who are left in this city, as well as all the people, by the things he is saying to them. This man is not seeking the good of these people but their ruin"* (Jeremiah 38:4).

What happened to the warned residents of Jerusalem? Many listened to God's warnings, given through Jeremiah, fled Jerusalem and then lived relatively comfortably in ancient Babylon. They wept for home *"by the rivers of Babylon"*–Psalm 137, but they were alive to weep. After their time in Babylon, along with their families that grew during their time in relative safety, they returned to Jerusalem, following the prophesied period of seventy years. Those who refused to heed God's warnings were either slain in Jerusalem, or died after fleeing to Egypt, a nation that God specifically warned them against. (Jeremiah 42:13-22)

There is a distinguishing characteristic between Jeremiah's warnings to the residents of Jerusalem of his time to flee, and his warnings to the future residents of the Daughter of Babylon to flee. God told the residents of Jerusalem at the time of Jeremiah they would *come back home* after seventy years (Jeremiah 25:11; 29:10). That promise was fulfilled. Jeremiah's warnings to God's people who will live in the nation called the Daughter of Babylon never, not once, are told they will *return home* after the destruction of their home nation. On the contrary, Jeremiah, Isaiah, Psalm 137, and John all specifically, and unequivocally, say that the Daughter of Babylon will be destroyed and desecrated. *"The land trembles and writhes, for the Lord's purposes against Babylon stand—to lay waste the land of Babylon so that no one will live there"* (Jeremiah 51:29). Thus, there will be no return of those who flee, back to the Daughter of Babylon, unlike the residents of Jerusalem at the time of Jeremiah who did return home after seventy years, as He said they would.

As God's people examine the difficult decision as to where they should emigrate, it will be evident that European nations will not offer an acceptable relocation venue. As previously noted, the nations of the European Union, after the fall of the worlds only superpower, will most likely be re-named the *European Muslim Union,* or a similar name will be chosen conveying the new Muslim identity of the continent. Muslims tried over the centuries, unsuccessfully, to conquer. Therefore, moving to a European nation before the Daughter of Babylon falls would result in living in the "belly of the beast" and will be highly dangerous for a Christian or a Jewish immigrant. Recall that Daniel warned the Antichrist will be *"a king of fierce countenance"* (Daniel 8:11) and *"He will cause astounding devastation...He will destroy ...the holy people"* (Daniel 8:24). The prophesied Antichrist will emerge from the European nations and will rule that continent of the world with an iron fist, with his power expanding to other nations of the world. So, fleeing *to* Europe would be an unwise move.

239

Likewise, most of the Middle Eastern, and many African nations, let alone many Asian nations, would be poor relocation choices due to current significant Muslim domination of the government and population. They also have high levels of abortion, inviting God's justice. Australia and New Zealand also allow abortion on demand. Australia's Muslim population is growing rapidly. Islands of the world aren't ideal as potential places to move, due to the potential of being 'trapped' on an island, with no escape, if things go bad politically or in any other way. Riots over food prices and against *"elites"* broke out on two Caribbean islands in February, 2009, with tens of thousands in the streets.

So where does one move? This clearly is a matter for much prayer and seeking God's face. In doing so, two factors should be taken into account: a.) does the potential location for emigration allow abortion; and b.) what is the level of Muslim? The remaining nations of the world that today prohibit or severely restrict abortion and that have low levels of Muslim population are mostly in Central and South American, nations that, therefore, may offer an appropriate refuge.

AVOIDING NATIONS ALLOWING ABORTION

Since God says in His Word that He demands an accounting for the blood of innocents spilled in a nation, moving to a nation which has *legalized abortion* would be foolish. Why choose to move to a nation where the shed blood of innocents cries out from the ground for God's accounting and justice? What Central and South American countries don't allow *any* abortions? Specific abortion statistics are readily available:

I. NO ABORTIONS – These nations *prohibit all abortions* by law and enforce the law (Source: Johnston's Archives, United Nations Population Division, Center for Reproductive Rights): Chile
El Salvador

II. LIMITED ABORTIONS – These Central/South American nations have laws/legal controls that *strictly limit* abortions, but do allow abortions under *highly rigid rules* and approval requirements: (Source: Johnston's Archives, United Nations Population Division, Center for Reproductive Rights):

Belize	Honduras
Brazil	Nicaragua
Bolivia	Panama
Columbia	Peru
Ecuador	Uruguay
Guatemala	Venezuela

III. ALLOW ABORTION – These Central/South American nations have laws that allow abortion, usually to *"prevent danger to the life or health of the pregnant woman."* Abortion rates as a percentage of pregnancy are listed for each. (Source: Johnston's Archives, United Nations Population Division, Center for Reproductive Rights; Guttmacher Institute):

Costa Rica (10%)
Guatemala (16%)
Guyana (10% +)
Mexico *(Allows abortions by law only in Mexico City and in Yucatan, if the mother has three children.)*

The following Central/South American nations have laws against abortion, but allow it in practice, in many cases in *large* numbers. (Source: Johnston's Archives, United Nations Population Division, Center for Reproductive Rights; Guttmacher Institute):

Argentina *(A bill to allow abortion by law has been under consideration in Argentina's Chamber of Deputies).*
Paraguay

AVOIDING HIGH MUSLIM POPULATION NATIONS

There are fifty nations in the world with 50% or more Muslim population, ranging from 100% of the Saudi Arabian population to 91% in Egypt, to 50% in Ethiopia. These nations are largely located in the Middle East, East and Southeast Asia. It would be dangerous to immigrate to a nation already Muslim, for quite obvious reasons. Likewise, moving to a nation with a large number of Muslims, such as the nations of Europe, and others, would be dangerous. After the fall of the Daughter of Babylon and threats by Jihadists that the threatened nations accede to a Muslim government and adopt Sharia law, the number of available nations will be limited. Therefore, moving to a nation that today has a resident Muslim population will most likely result in living in a fully Muslim nation, soon after the fall of the Daughter of Babylon, along with Jihadists who believe that Christians and Jews must "revert" to Islam, or be decapitated. Not a good choice.

This is not to say that Christians should presently ignore Muslim nations. Currently, only a small percentage of mission funding goes towards reaching the Muslim world. Efforts to reach Muslims for Christ, in the last few years, have become increasingly successful, with many testifying that they came to faith in Christ after heaven-sent dreams of the Messiah. This is not to suggest that living in a nation with Muslims is, by itself, dangerous. The vast majority of Muslims are not violent. Jihadists, under their Wahabist extremist training, however, have intimidated their fellow Muslims into neutrality, by creating fear of the fanatics who resort to violence. Living in a nation in which Jihadists have little or no Muslim contacts or influence would appear to be the most prudent course of action.

So what would be a good move? Pick a nation with: a.) no or extremely low abortions and also b.) a nation with no or extremely low numbers of resident Muslims. Here are those nations with no or extremely low numbers of resident Muslims, listed by category of level of abortions:

242

MUSLIM POPULATION IN NATIONS WITH *NO ABORTIONS*

Nation In 2006	% Muslim	Muslim Population
Chile	0	0
El Salvador	0	0

MUSLIM POPULATION IN NATIONS WITH *LIMITED ABORTIONS*

Belize	0	0
Brazil	0.9	1,590,000
Bolivia	0	0
Columbia	0.024	10,651
Ecuador	0	0
Guatemala	0	0
Honduras	2	140,000
Nicaragua	0	0
Panama	5	150,000
Peru	0	0
Uruguay	0	0
Venezuela	0.035	90,000

MUSLIM POPULATION IN NATIONS THAT *ALLOW ABORTION*

(Lower levels of abortion)

Costa Rica (10%)	0	0
Guatemala (16%)	0	0
Guyana (10%)	13	100,000
Mexico (2 areas)	0.26	260,000

(Higher levels of abortion)

Argentina	1.33	50,000
Paraguay	0	0

(CIA World Factbook, the United States State Department International Religious Freedom Report and www.islamaicpopulation.com, Islamic population websites claim significantly more Muslim residents of Brazil than do non-Muslim sources.)

Based on a cross indexing of *abortion free/limited abortion nations* alongside nations with *no Muslim population* yields these eleven nations in our hemisphere as potential future homes for emigrating American Christians and Jews:

Central America

Belize
El Salvador
Guatemala
Honduras
Nicaragua

South America

Bolivia
Brazil
Chile
Ecuador
Peru
Uruguay

Which of the foregoing eleven nations offers the best potential for an expatriated American family to move and live? Though these nations all appear to be good locations, thorough research is required. Bolivia, for example, is headed by President Evo Morales, who is a socialist and a close ally of Venezuelan President Hugo Chavez. Nicaragua is headed by a former Communist leader and Argentina's socialist economy is in shambles. Some Central and South American nations have high crime levels, though America has no bragging rights in this regard. There is no perfect location in this world in which to live, this side of heaven, but the goal is to find a nation which is safe, abortion free, low in Muslim population and influence, not expensive and is receptive to emigration by Americans.

LIVING CHEAPER

Living in Central and South American countries is generally cheaper than a comparable lifestyle in America. Food, housing, entertainment, medical care, utilities and taxes are generally lower, but of course, vary nation-by-nation, and region-by- region within the nation. Some Americans living abroad write that two people can live quite comfortably on $1,000 to $1,500 per month, though expenses related to automobile transportation tend to be higher. This fact of economic life has attracted many American "expats," purely on financial grounds.

Good resources for more research include *International Living,* www.InternationalLiving.com, which publishes guidebooks on individual countries and sends daily e-mail detailing life abroad. *Getting Out–Your Guide to Leaving America,* (Mark Ehrman, Process Media, 2006) provides details on 50 nations which American expatriates have favored as they emigrate, the emigration rules, suggestions on what to do in a new home nation, and provides an exhaustive list of resources by website, that's worth the price of the book ($17 on Amazon). Full disclosure, not everything in the book will be attractive to religious readers. Ehrman claims that over 300,000 Americans emigrate from America every year. That's a sizeable number, which goes against the conventional wisdom that the entire world wants to immigrate to the U.S. Apparently, for many reasons, large numbers of Americans have decided to live in a nation other than their native land.

If you know someone in one of the above ten nations, you have a built-in advantage. Apart from that, the internet provides tens of thousands of pages of information about any nation, and allows one to engage in e-chats about specific overseas locations. Let what you learn help guide your decision, after much prayer and fasting.

FORSAKE NOT THE ASSEMBLY OF BELIEVERS

In planning to emigrate, God's people should remember the importance of assembling together with other believers. *"Not forsaking the assembling of ourselves together, as the manner of some is."*(Hebrews 10:25). Not only are we commanded to associate with, and pray and worship with, fellow believers, it's medically indicated. After 20 years of research, Neuroscientist John Cacioppo has concluded that people who don't associate regularly with other people are more prone to illness, obesity and feelings of helplessness. *(Loneliness: Human Nature and the Need for Social Connection)*.

Those who decide to emigrate will find that the many tasks involved in doing so are best accomplished when shared with others, such as those in one's Small Group, Sunday School, Bible Study or church. The Pilgrims who immigrated to America didn't arrange their moving plans separately, but as a group of believers, committed to a common goal. Think of it as an adventure, a Godly venture into the next chapter of our walk with Him, as He leads us to step out in faith, in obedience to His Word.

As a future safety consideration, arranging housing in locations not clustered together could be advisable. Networking in common church activities could still be easily arranged, just without the obvious "American Christian Compound" potential as a target. That's how we live today, scattered in various neighborhoods and gathering to meet, worship and fellowship as the body of Christ. For more specifics, plans and immigration rules, detailed by nation, see *FLEEING AMERICA*, now being written, for publication in 2010.

Chapter Fourteen

IRREFUTABLE PROOF THAT GOD HAS BEEN WARNING AMERICA NOT TO CURSE ISRAEL

"I really wish the Jews again in Judea an independent nation." (President John Adams, 1798)

"It remained for Richard Nixon to create the now familiar U.S.- Israel alliance...It was Nixon who made Israel the largest single recipient of U.S. foreign aid; Nixon who initiated the policy of virtually limitless U.S. weapons sales to Israel. The notion of Israel as a strategic asset to the United States, not just a moral commitment, was Nixon's innovation." (J.J. Goldberg, *Jewish Power*)

Christian believers likely understand the basic message of this book, how America matches, like fingers in a glove, each of the clues disclosed in the several *"mystery"* prophetic verses describing the Daughter of Babylon. However, belief in this message and then applying these verses to *our* country leads to a natural level of *doubt*. What if the Daughter of Babylon is some other nation, *instead* of America, though in light of God's clues, that appears to be a remote possibility? Or what if the Daughter of Babylon *is* America, but these prophetic verses are for America in *another time*, for *another generation*? All of which would be legitimate questions.

After re-studying these verses for several months in 2008, I was convinced that only America could be the Bible's prophesied Daughter of Babylon, but maybe for another day, later than our times. It was then that I was shaken out of my wavering ambivalence. A brother in Christ sent me an e-link to a web-available sermon by a Pastor. As I started listening to the sermon, which began with a review of the verses in

247

which God informed Israel that He was giving them the land on which they would dwell, I initially thought, 'yeah, I know all that.' But as the message continued, I was shaken to my core. My view of God's current relationship with America hasn't been the same since.

The Pastor's message was largely based on a book by William Koenig, who is a White House correspondent and author. His recent book, Eye to Eye: Facing the Consequences of Dividing Israel (About Him Publishing, 2007) is in its tenth printing. Koenig's book was the inspiration for the concept of this chapter. I've highlighted certain concepts in Koenig's book, researched further, and added more current evaluations of events not covered in the book. If you want to read further into the matters covered in this chapter, I recommend Koenig's book.

The Pastor's message disclosed that in the last few years, God has caused/allowed "natural disasters" to occur in the United States, *immediately after* the United States violated His prohibition against forcing Israel to *give up the land* that God had given to Israel. God has been warning America, in these "natural" events, against forcing Israel to give up its land, and we have been ignoring His warnings. For example, Hurricane Katrina, and the loss of thousands of *homes* in New Orleans, came the very next day after the US pressured Israel to push the residents of Gaza out of hundreds of their *homes*, in which they had dwelt for decades? (More detail below).

Why is that important? God is also warning His people in America, Christians and Jews, through His Daughter of Babylon prophecies that the time will come when His people are to flee out of the Daughter of Babylon. What God has already done to get our attention, which we have largely ignored, is Exhibit A proving that we need to take His warnings to flee seriously, and then actually FLEE. Read on, and see that God is quite serious about what He says in His Word, which we ignore at our own peril.

GOD'S PROMISE TO BLESS THOSE WHO BLESS ISRAEL

In Genesis 12:2-3 God delivers a promise to Israel that He has never repealed and has always fulfilled:

"I will make you into a great nation and I will bless you; I will make your name great, and you will be a blessing. I will bless those who bless you, and whoever curses you I will curse; and all peoples on earth will be blessed through you."

America has been *greatly blessed as it has blessed Israel*, beginning with Israel's founding in May, 1948. On October, 28, 1946 President Truman wrote to King Saud of Saudi Arabia, informing the king he believed *"that a national home for the Jewish people should be established in Palestine."* The next year, 1947, President Truman instructed the State Department to support the U.N. plan for partition, and reluctantly, it did so. There was a significant question though, as to whether Israel would ever be (re)born. In March, 1948 President Truman's friend, and former business partner in a Missouri haberdashery, Eddie Jacobson, walked into the White House without an appointment, and pleaded with Truman to meet with Chaim Weizmann, the president of the Jewish Agency for Palestine and the World Zionist Organization. Truman responded: *"You win, you baldheaded (expletive deleted). I will see him."* Five days later President Truman met with Weizmann. Truman said he wished to see justice done in Palestine without bloodshed, and that if the Jewish state were declared, and the United Nations remained stalled in its attempt to establish a temporary trusteeship over Palestine, the United States would recognize the new state immediately.

At midnight on May 14, 1948, the Provisional Government of Israel proclaimed the new State of Israel.

That was 6:00 PM EST in Washington, D.C. At 6:11 P.M., in the same day, the United States, in the person of President Harry S Truman, recognized the provisional Jewish

249

government as the *de facto* authority of the new Jewish state. Truman crossed out *"Jewish State"* in his recognition document and inserted *"State of Israel."* The U.S. delegates to the U.N. and top ranking State Department officials were angered that Truman released his recognition statement to the press without first notifying them. On May 15, 1948, the Arab states issued their response statement- Arab armies invaded Israel and the first Arab-Israeli war began.

Has the United States been blessed for its critical role in Israel's re-birth? Financially, America has certainly prospered. In the intervening 60 plus years since 1948, America has grown by 1,400%. In 1948 the gross domestic product (GDP) of the United States was just over $1 trillion dollars. In 2008 America's GDP had grown to about $14 trillion per year. In the same period, the nation also enjoyed a time of great freedom, though what Americans have done with that freedom is another issue.

Under Presidents Eisenhower, Kennedy, Johnson, Nixon, Ford, Carter and Reagan, the United States proved to be a reliable and generally trustworthy friend of Israel. See the Nixon quote at the beginning of this Chapter. The Nixon tapes, released as a part of the Watergate investigation, revealed ethnically unfriendly words by Nixon for certain individual Jewish Americans who opposed him, but he was a consistent friend of Israel. Nixon's Secretary of State, William P. Rogers, pushed an early land-for-peace-plan, but Nixon sided with Henry Kissinger, his National Security Advisor, in killing Roger's plan. Jimmy Carter signed a military defense treaty with Israel. God has blessed America when America has blessed Israel, just as He promised He would.

GOD GAVE ISRAEL THE LAND

In Genesis 15:18 God told Israel: *"To your descendants I give this land, from the river of Egypt to the great river, the Euphrates."* In Genesis 17:8, God confirms that the land given to Israel was *"an everlasting possession."* Here's what God calls the land he gave to Israel:

1. THE LAND OF ISRAEL (I Samuel 13:19)
2. THE LAND OF THE HEBREWS (Genesis 40:15)
3. THE LAND OF THE JEWS (Acts 10:39)
4. THE LAND OF PROMISE (Hebrews 11:9)
5. THE HOLY LAND (Zechariah 2:12)
6. THE LORD'S LAND (Hosea 9:3)
7. IMMANUEL'S LAND (Isaiah 8:8)

These names are familiar to many, but it may not be well known that God told Israel *not* to make peace treaties with other nations.

"Do not make a covenant with them or with their gods." (Exodus 23:32)

God told Israel that if it made a treaty with Egypt, Israel would be injured like one leaning on a broken reed. Israel was to look *to God* for its protection, *not* to the nations of the world. Israel's current military defense treaties with America will be worthless, as we have seen in prophecy, when the Russian bear (Gog) and the Kings of the Medes (Iran and Muslim allies) invade Israel, and Israel is betrayed.

God also told Israel *not* to give up or *exchange* any of Israel's land with other nations.

God provides only one way that Israel is to divide the land that He gave to Israel: *"So you shall divide this land among yourselves according to the tribes of Israel"* (Ezekiel 47:21). But, what about dividing the land or *exchanging* the land with others:

"They must not sell or exchange any of it. This is the best of the land and must not pass into other hands, because it is holy to the Lord." (Ezekiel 48:14).

These verses are relevant because for much of the last twenty years, America has been trying to force Israel to divide its land and to give some of its God-given land to its neighbors in a *"land for peace"* treaty exchange, contrary to scripture. From these verses, we know the U.S.-led effort to literally make Israel give up its land is an invitation to disaster. God says that He blesses those who bless Israel.

251

Trying to pressure Israel into giving up the land that God said not to give up, is not a blessing to Israel, but is instead, a curse. According to Genesis 12:3, as we curse Israel, we are cursed. Has God indicated and confirmed His Genesis 12:3 statements in scripture in any other demonstrable, observable, current-day way? *Yes, He certainly has.*

PRESIDENT JIMMY CARTER

The Israeli-Egyptian Camp David Accords were reached under President Jimmy Carter in 1978. The Camp David peace agreement between Israel and Egypt included a military defense agreement between the United States and Israel. Egyptians, of course, are a people separate from those who call themselves Palestinians. The written and signed agreement provided that America would come to Israel's defense, militarily, if Israel were ever invaded. Israel required this commitment, understandably, before it would sign the larger treaty with Egypt. This is the primary treaty that the Daughter of Babylon will break when Israel is invaded by Russia, Iran, and their allies. (The *"Memorandum of Agreement between the Governments of the United States of America and the State of Israel,* signed March 26, 1979, is included at Attachment B.) The Camp David Accords are a fulfillment of the end times prophecies which *do not list Egypt* as one of the nations invading Israel. This is relevant because prior to Camp David, Egypt invaded Israel, and was part of invading forces from other nations, numerous times, including its May, 1948 attack on Tel Aviv by the Egyptian air force, and its ground invasion in 1967 with 1,000 tanks and 100,000 soldiers.

America does not appear to have suffered any major climatological, financial, or other catastrophic harm as a result of the Camp David Accords; but they did not require Israel to give up any of its God-given land in order to obtain peace with Egypt. The area in the Sinai Peninsula that Israel had briefly occupied, and then vacated, as part of the Camp David agreements, was never Israel's land, and is not in the area God described in Genesis 15 as the legal description of the land given to Israel. Though Jimmy Carter later in his life abruptly turned against Israel, and in support of the Palestinians, the Camp David peace and military defense agreements between Egypt, Israel, and the United States appear to have been blessed by God.

PRESIDENT GEORGE HERBERT WALKER BUSH

President George Herbert Walker Bush (the 41st President of the U.S.) and his Secretary of State James A. Baker, III, decided at some point in 1991 that the United States should seek to make peace in the Middle East by causing Israel to *exchange some of its land,* its real estate, its territory, to its Muslim neighbors, in return for *"peace."* Secretary of State Baker made several trips to the Middle East between March and October of 1991, working out the details of what the U.S. was proposing–a first ever peace conference with bi-lateral talks between Israel and its Palestinian neighbors.

ANNOUNCEMENT OF ISRAELI-PALESTINIAN PEACE CONFERENCE & THE OAKLAND FIRESTORM

The Carter initiated Camp David Accords did not require Israel to give up any of its land. However, 13 years after Carter's Camp David Accords, President George Bush and Secretary Baker took a new and different approach to Israel's God-given land. Bush and Baker initiated not only the first ever bi-lateral peace conference between Israel and its Arab neighbors (attended by Syria, Lebanon, and Jordan, with the PLO as part of the Jordanian delegation), but also launched a *new* American-initiated proposal for peace. The peace conference was announced by Baker on October 18, 1991. The public announcement of this groundbreaking effort to force Israel to give up its land was quickly followed by a firestorm in Oakland, California which resulted in over $3.5 billion dollars in damages, and was the worst California fire since the San Francisco earthquake and Fire of 1906. The fire was fed by unusual 65 mph winds from the *east*. Why is this significant? California always has fires–right? Yes, with winds normally blowing from the west. The highly destructive Oakland Firestorm was just the *warm-up* for what was to come.

MADRID CONFERENCE OF 1991 & 'THE PERFECT STORM'

The Bush/Baker initiated peace conference, labeled the *"Madrid Conference,"* convened on October 30, 1991 and lasted for three days. What President Bush announced in Madrid continues to affect the world today. President Bush told the delegations from Israel, Syria, Lebanon and Jordan that:

"Our objective must be clear and straightforward. It is not simply to end the state of war in the Middle East and replace it with a state of non-belligerency. This is not enough, this would not last. Rather, we seek peace, real peace. And by real peace I mean treaties. ...Israel now has an opportunity to demonstrate that it is willing to enter into a new relationship with its Palestinian neighbors; one predicated upon mutual respect and cooperation. Throughout the Middle East, we seek a stable and enduring settlement. We've not defined what this means; indeed I make these points with no map showing where the final borders are to be drawn. Nevertheless, we believe territorial compromise is essential for peace. Boundaries should reflect the quality of both security and political arrangements."

There it was-openly stated by the President of the world's only superpower, and the nation that the world sees as Israel's main ally and primary protector. The United States wanted Israel to give up its land–*"territorial compromise"*–in exchange for *"peace,"* even unsubtly assuming the power for the U.S. *to help draw the new "borders"* and *"boundaries"* at some future unspecified date. Did the Muslim world get it? Of course they did. They immediately knew that America had launched a geopolitical effort to get them that which they could not obtain on their own, try as they had on several bloody occasions, control of *the land of Israel* in their own hands. Who else got it? The German Foreign Minister, Joschka Fischer, later said *"The idea is not to go backwards, but to return to the basic formula that was established in Madrid: the exchange of land for peace."* Israel got it, certainly, and to this date large numbers of Israelis in public opinion polls favor the idea of giving up their land in exchange for what they hope will be peace. One analyst put the seismic change initiated by Bush and Baker this way:

"The emergence of an American-Palestinian axis broke the familiar mold of Middle Eastern politics...This reversal of the Palestinian and Israeli positions in relation to American policy in the Middle East marked a watershed in the history of the Arab-Israeli conflict...After Madrid the Administration kept up the pressure on Israel to negotiate on the central issue of land for peace." (The Iron Wall: Israel and the Arab World, Avi Shlaim, W.W. Norton)

From God's perspective, what could be a more dramatic way to express displeasure than to do what no human, nor any group of humans, could ever do–stir up a Perfect Storm and send it into the President's living room, covering his three story house with unprecedented waves and extensive damage? And, of course, for maximum impact, precisely *time* the Perfect Storm following the offending words by the owner of that home in which he called on Israel to do what God had said *not* to do–enter into treaties to give up Israel's land?

On the same day as the speech by President Bush, October 30, 1991, an *"enormous extra tropical low,"* combined with a tropical cyclone, which then became a hurricane, centered on the northeastern coast of the United States. The storm was so massive in scope, and so unusual in its components, that it was quickly labeled *"The Perfect Storm,"* and designated by the National Weather Service as a *'once in a century storm.'* The rare combination of weather factors led to waves ten stories high and winds of 120 mph. A book about The Perfect Storm was made into a movie, featuring waves that *"few people on earth had ever witnessed,"* and was based on the loss of the Andrea Gail, a commercial fishing boat that tried unsuccessfully to survive the mammoth storm.

The *New York Times* reported that *"President Bush's home and vacation compound were severely damaged by the North Atlantic storm that struck the Northeast on Wednesday. Waves as high as his three-story house filled the house with sea water and caused extensive damage to the retreat on Walker's Point in southern Maine."* (November 1, 1991, "Three Story Waves Heavily Damage Bush Vacation Compound in Southern Maine") One report said that a several hundred pound rock had been thrown into the Bush living room. *USA Today* on November 1st front-paged two adjoining articles, both concerning the President: *"One-on-One Peace Talks Next"* and *"East Coast Hit Hard by Rare Storm."* The *Times* article quoted Kennebunkport, Maine police as saying the storm struck their town at about 2 PM, which would have been within just hours of the President's speech at the Madrid Conference on October 30, 1991.

A coincidence? No, but it was a 'Perfect Storm,' created *to send a perfect message.*

ROUND SIX OF BILATERAL PEACE TALKS & HURRICANE ANDREW

Immediately following the Madrid Conference, the Bush Administration swiftly pushed for *"Bilateral Talks"* between Israel and Palestinian representatives. Israel was reluctant to participate, for obvious reasons. Just 40 days after the October 30th Madrid Conference, President Bush and Secretary Baker pushed anyway, convening the first Bilateral Talks conference, on December 9, 1991, in Washington D.C. Israel didn't show up. Prime Minister Yitzhak Shamir, instead, gave a speech in Israel in which he said, *"Israel's leaders cannot conceive of considering ideas aimed at concessions on Jerusalem, the West Bank, Gaza and the Golan Heights."* President Bush was not amused.

The U.S. pressured Israel into attending the next four Bilateral Talks, all in Washington D.C. At all four, Israel ruled out swapping their God-given land for purported 'peace' with the Palestinians, who didn't even have a nation. Shamir wouldn't budge, so the U.S. turned up the pressure:

"Bush and Baker concluded that Shamir would not alter his policy. So they took the bold step of indicating to the Israeli electorate that, if they wanted American financial support to continue (including a US $10 billion loan guarantee), they should change their government." (*The Iron Wall: Israel and the Arab World*, Avi Shlaim, W.W. Norton)

American threats were effective, as Israeli voters on June 23, 1992 turned out of office the Likud Party, which had been in power for fifteen years, and its leader Yitzhak Shamir, one of Israel's most hawkish leaders, replacing him with one of its most dovish leaders, Yitzhak Rabin. Rabin quickly came to Washington, D.C. to attend the Sixth Round of the Bilateral Talks initiated by the Bush Administration, which commenced on August 24, 1992 and lasted for several days. Remember that date–*August 24, 1992.* At the newly convened Sixth Round of Bilateral Talks, Prime Minister Rabin reversed the past course set by Prime Minister Shamir, offered to create a 15 member Palestinian Administrative Council and made other concessions. President Bush and Secretary Baker were pleased by these trend-setting actions of the Israeli leader whom they had just helped to elect by direct U.S. threats to the voters of Israel.

Ten months and five rounds of unfruitful Bilateral Talks had taken place between the Madrid Conference and the critical Sixth Round. During that period, frustrated with Israel's refusal to cave in to American demands to give up its land, American pressure resulted in a new Israeli government, which on August 24, 1992, performed as the Bush Administration expected. But, something else, besides the U.S. pressured-Israeli capitulation, also happened in the United States on August 24, 1992.

Hurricane Andrew smashed into the U.S.– *as the most destructive 'natural disaster' to hit America* up to that time. Hurricane Andrew was a category five, 177 mph storm (officially corrected from a recorded wind gust of 212 mph), with a seventeen foot storm surge. Andrew left over 200,000 people homeless, killed 65, caused damages in excess of $38 billion (in current dollars), disconnected electrical power for 152,000 customers, and destroyed 25% of the trees in the Florida Everglades. In Dade County, 90% of homes had major roof damage. One hundred seventeen thousand homes were either destroyed or had major damage. The Turkey Point Nuclear Generating Station, built to withstand 235 mph winds, suffered $90 million in damages. The city of Homestead was virtually destroyed. Homestead Air Force Base was closed as a full active duty base due to damage caused by Andrew.

When did Andrew hit the United States? *Not* during the first five rounds of Bilateral Talks, during which Israel either didn't show up, refused to grant concessions or even discuss giving up its land. No, Andrew hit America on August 24, 1992, *the very day* of the opening day of the Sixth Round of the Bilateral Talks, the day Israel's new government capitulated to American pressure to talk about giving up its land.

"A National Weather Service-Miami Radar image recorded on August 24, 1992 at 4:35 PM (EDT) superimposed on a street map by the Hurricane Research Division of NOAA clearly indicates the most powerful winds within the northern eyewall ... made landfall between SW 152 St. (Coral Reef Drive) and SW 184 St. (Eureka Drive)." (National Hurricane Center)

Within hours after the Sixth Round of the Bilateral Talks had convened in Washington, D.C. on August 24, 1992, Hurricane Andrew plowed across Florida and into Louisiana, causing more damage than *any* previous U.S. 'natural disaster.' A coincidental event-that just happened to hit America on *the very day* of the U.S.-convened and election result-manipulated Sixth Round of Bilateral Talks, called to force Israel to give up its land?

CLINTON'S PRESSURE ON ISRAEL TO GIVE UP LAND

In Koenig's book (*Eye to Eye: Facing the Consequences of Dividing Israel*) he documents *twenty five instances* in which President William J. Clinton pressured Israel in various ways to give up its land in exchange for promised peace from the Palestinians. Obviously, space does not permit covering each of President Clinton's efforts to make Israel give up its land, and then the 'natural disaster' that accompanied and followed *each* attempt. Following are three striking expanded examples of God's irrefutable response to President Clinton's efforts to strip Israel of the land that He gave to Israel:

CLINTON'S SECRETARY OF STATE'S TRIP TO JERUSALEM/WORLD TRADE CENTER BOMBING

On January 20, 1993 William J. Clinton was sworn in as President of the United States. Shortly thereafter, career diplomat Warren M. Christopher was sworn in as the nations' 63rd Secretary of State. Within three weeks, Clinton dispatched Christopher to the Middle East to visit eight nations, including Israel. On February 24, 1993 Christopher and Prime Minister Yitzhak Rabin held a joint news conference. Neither 'land for peace' nor 'territorial compromise' were specifically mentioned by either Christopher or Rabin, but Christopher's closing words clearly show where he wanted Israel to move in the peace process: *"I leave the Middle East hopeful but cognizant that there still are obstacles...The parties are at a historic crossroad. This is an opportunity which I hope all the parties will embrace, and we'll do our part to help them in that regard."* (U.S. Department of State, Secretary of State's Speeches, 1993)

Based on what President Clinton and Secretary of State Christopher did in the next eight years to push Israel into abdicating control of much of its land, there is little doubt that Christopher's February 24, 1993 meetings with Israel's leaders were part of that effort, the *'historic crossroad'* and *'opportunity'* that Christopher referred to in his *public* remarks. What Christopher said to Israeli officials in private talks is not yet known, but can be conjectured. Following the private talks with Rabin, which undoubtedly included U.S. demands on Israel to give up its land, while Secretary Christopher was still over the Atlantic Ocean, returning to Washington, D.C., a car bomb exploded in the underground parking garage of the World Trade Center in New York City.

The bomb, contained in a yellow Ryder van opened up a 98 foot wide hole through four sublevels of concrete. The van, which was parked under the North Tower, and was intended to knock the North Tower into the South Tower, to take both towers down. Fortunately, the plan failed, but six people were killed and over 1,000 were injured. The bomb knocked out the World Trade Center's electrical system and thus cut off most of the City's radio and television stations. The blast filled the North Tower with smoke to the 93rd floor. Telephone service for much of Lower Manhattan was also disrupted. Previously seemingly immune from terrorist acts, America quickly came into the real world with the February 26, 1993 World Trade Center bombing that took place as Secretary of State Christopher was returning from his *'land for peace'* diplomatic visit to Jerusalem.

THE OSLO ACCORDS & THE GREAT MIDWEST FLOODS OF 1993

Under President Clinton's direction, the United States continued to push Israel to arrive at an agreement to eventually lead Israel to trade its land for peace with its neighbors. A secret series of negotiations took place in Oslo, Norway from late April, 1993 to August 20, 1993. As a result of the ongoing negotiations, in which America continued to pressure Israel, an agreement was reached between Israel and the Palestine Liberation Organization (PLO). The *"Oslo Accords"* were then officially signed on September 13, 1993 on the White House Lawn with President Clinton presiding, and drawing Yitzhak Rabin and Yasser Arafat together in an historic handshake. The Oslo Accords led to the creation of the Palestinian Authority, which was given control over specified territory. Israel agreed to withdraw its military forces from parts of the Gaza Strip and the West Bank, contrary to Prime Minister Shamir's promise in 1992 to never do so. *'Permanent issues'* such as Jerusalem and *'borders'* were put off until after the five year agreement had expired. The Israeli Knesset on September 23, 1993 approved the Accords by a vote of 61 in favor, 50 against and 8 abstained. After the signing and approval of the Oslo Accords, Palestinian attacks against Israel intensified, with 15 Israeli soldiers dead.

Thus, under *U.S. pressure,* Israel agreed to the Oslo Accords, negotiated from April 27 to August 20, 1993, and signed at the White House on September 13, 1993. Did anything else happen of note during that same period?

Here is a portion of a presentation by Lee Larson, Chief of the Hydrologic Research Laboratory of the Office of Hydrology, of the NOAA/National Weather Service presented at an IAHS Conference in Anaheim, California in June, 1996, entitled: *Destructive Water: Water-Caused Natural Disasters – Their Abatement and Control.*

The Great USA Flood of 1993

Abstract. The 1993 midwest flood was one of the most significant and damaging natural disasters ever to hit the United States. Damages totaled $15 billion, 50 people died, hundreds of levees failed, and thousands of people were evacuated, some for months. The flood was unusual in the magnitude of the crests, the number of record crests, the large area impacted, and the length of the time the flood was an issue.

261

From May through September of 1993, major and/or record flooding occurred across North Dakota, South Dakota, Nebraska, Kansas, Minnesota, Iowa, Missouri, Wisconsin, and Illinois. Fifty flood deaths occurred, and damages approached $15 billion. Hundreds of levees failed along the Mississippi and Missouri Rivers.

The magnitude and severity of this flood event was simply over-whelming, and it ranks as one of the greatest natural disasters ever to hit the United States. Approximately 600 river forecast points in the Midwestern United States were above flood stage at the same time. Nearly 150 major rivers and tributaries were affected. It was certainly the largest and most significant flood event ever to occur in the U. S . Area Impacted by the 1993 Midwest Flood

Tens of thousands of people were evacuated, some never to return to their homes. At least 10,000 homes were totally destroyed, hundreds of towns were impacted with at least 75 towns totally and completely under flood waters. At least 15 million acres of farmland were inundated, some of which may not be useable for years to come.

Transportation was severely impacted. Barge traffic on the Missouri and Mississippi Rivers was stopped for nearly 2 months. Bridges were out or not accessible on the Mississippi River from Davenport, Iowa, downstream to St. Louis, Missouri. On the Missouri River, bridges were out from Kansas City, downstream to St. Charles, Missouri. Numerous interstate highways and other roads were closed. Ten commercial airports were flooded. All railroad traffic in the Midwest was halted. Numerous sewage treatment and water treatment plants were destroyed.

During June through August 1993, rainfall totals surpassed 12 inches across the eastern Dakotas, southern Minnesota, eastern Nebraska, Wisconsin, Kansas, Iowa Missouri, Illinois and Indiana. More than 24 inches of rain fell on central and northeastern Kansas, northern and central Missouri, most of Iowa, southern Minnesota and southeastern Nebraska, with up to 38.4 inches in east-central Iowa. These amounts were approximately 200-350 percent of normal...A critical factor affecting the record flooding was the near continuous nature of the rainfall...The persistent, rain-producing weather pattern in the Upper Midwest often typical in the spring, but not the summer, sustained the almost daily development of rainfall during much of the summer."

Was it a 'natural disaster'? Who else, but God, can change the weather patterns so that it rains virtually every day for week after week? All of that rain, up to three and a half times normal rain patterns with over 38 inches of rain in some areas, *just happened* to fall for a time period starting *right after* the Oslo Accord negotiations were called to order for the purpose of making Israel give up military control of part of its land? And *just happened* to *end* when the Oslo Accords were finally signed and sealed at the White House?

CLINTON PRESSURES NETANYAHU & THE LEWINSKY SCANDAL

Moving forward five years to 1998, we'll not address the 1994 treaty brokered by President Clinton between Israel and Jordan, and what followed the treaty signing-the worst flooding in Texas history with 17 dead and $1 billion in damages. We'll also skip the 1995 signing of a treaty brokered by the Clinton Administration between Israel and the PLO over the West Bank and Gaza, which was accompanied by Hurricane Opal, the strongest to ever hit Pensacola, Florida, with 27 dead and losses of over $3 billion. Probably just *coincidences*, anyway.

By 1998, the leadership of Israel had changed. Prime Minister Yitzhak Rabin had been assassinated in November, 1995 by an Israeli who opposed giving up Israel's land. After Shimon Peres served seven months in office (also of Israel's Labour Party, as was Rabin) Benjamin Netanyahu from the Likud Party, was elected Prime Minister in June, 1996. To say that Netanyahu and Clinton did not get along well would be a gross understatement, as both publicly admitted they did not see eye-to-eye on matters involving Israel, primarily, of course, Netanyahu's reluctance to give into Clinton's demands that Israel give its 'land for peace.'

In January, 1998 President Clinton invited Netanyahu and Yasser Arafat to two separate meetings at the White House to *"jump-start the stalled Israeli-Palestinian peace process,"* in the words of Wolf Blitzer of CNN News (January

19, 1998). Blitzer told CNN viewers in his report on the meeting between Clinton and Netanyahu that *"The pressure begins this morning when Clinton sits down with Netanyahu...The bottom line for Clinton and his advisers includes another significant Israeli withdrawal from the West Bank...Sources say he will spell out his views in detail. Without U.S. pressure, Clinton fears the stalled peace process will completely collapse...If there were ever a U.S. President well-positioned to pressure an Israeli leader, it is Clinton, who in his final term has a solid reservoir of support both in Israel and within the American Jewish community."*

It was revealed a few months later in 1998 that Clinton was pushing Israel at the January, 1998 meeting with Netanyahu to *"surrender 13 percent of the West Bank territory that it now controls."* Imagine for a moment that some major world power was "pressuring" America to "surrender 13 percent of the continental United States territory that it now controls"–say give up New Mexico or New Jersey. We might legitimately take exception to such a proposal. So did Netanyahu, evidently. A further indication of President Clinton's views and tactics may be gleaned from his comments made in a televised media interview after meeting with Netanyahu:

"We worked on Mr. Netanyahu yesterday exhaustively to try and narrow the differences, but we made some headway and we're going to work with Mr. Arafat tomorrow and then we're going to see if there's some way we can put them together."

What's in a preposition? Several commentators noted that Clinton may have revealed his differing proposals and pressure tactics in his statement that he was working *"on"* Netanyahu, but he was working *"with"* Arafat. The Clinton family appears to have been in agreement as to Israel, as Hillary Clinton later, in May, 1998, told the media that eventually Israel would have to agree to a separate Palestinian state, with land ceded by Israel. Mrs. Clinton is now the Secretary of State of the United States and has called on Israel to give up its land, under the leadership of

President Obama. (More on the current Administration's pressure on Israel below.)

President Clinton met with Netanyahu on January 20, 1998. President Clinton *"worked on"* Netanyahu, in his own words, but to no avail. Though no source materials are currently available to confirm what the President said to 'pressure' Prime Minister Netanyahu, Clinton undoubtedly refreshed his guest's memory that Mr. Clinton in 1992 had intervened in the politics of Israel by threatening Israeli voters with the loss of U.S. support and loan guarantees, leading to the replacement of the Likud Party's Shamir with the Labour Party's Rabin. But, whatever was said, whatever was threatened, Netanyahu wouldn't bend, nor would he agree, at that time, to any give away of the land of the sovereign nation of Israel. President Clinton was not amused. Secretary of State Madeleine Albright, who was present in the Oval Office while Clinton *"worked on"* Netanyahu, was scheduled, along with the President, to have lunch with the Israeli Prime Minister during his White House visit on January 20, 1998. When it became more than apparent that Netanyahu would not 'surrender',' the President abruptly terminated the meeting, sending Netanyahu out of the Executive Mansion unfed, and diplomatically insulted.

The very next day, on January 21, 1998, President Clinton had something else to think about besides *"working on"* Israel's leader to give up Israel's land. *The Washington Post* broke the news that Independent Counsel Kenneth Starr (who had been appointed by a three judge panel to investigate 'Whitewater' scandal allegations concerning First Lady Hillary Clinton and to look into the suicide of White House Aide Vince Foster) had been authorized by the judicial panel to expand his investigation into whether Clinton had encouraged a White House intern to lie to lawyers for Paula Jones about an affair with the President.

The obvious irony is that within 24 hours of undoubtedly suggesting to the Prime Minister of Israel that he could lose his job as the leader of Israel, the leader of the

United States stood on the brink of his own political oblivion, with over one hundred American newspapers eventually editorially calling for him to resign.

But, President Clinton wasn't done with Israel, and God wasn't done with President Clinton. On December 12, 1998 President Clinton flew to Israel under an "impeachment cloud." As the House Judiciary Committee had just approved three Articles of Impeachment, literally as the President was packing to go to Israel. In Israel, President Clinton again pressured Netanyahu to withdraw from Israeli territory, which Netanyahu refused to do.

The President failed to head off an impeachment vote by the full House of Representatives with his diplomatic efforts in Israel. Shortly thereafter, the President ordered a military strike against Iraq, using cruise missiles and 300 air sorties. The House delayed the impeachment vote because of the military action, that is, until December 19, 1998. On that date, William Jefferson Clinton became the first elected United States President and the second United States President in history to be impeached by the U.S. House of Representatives.

PRESIDENT GEORGE W. BUSH'S PLAN FOR A PALESTINIAN STATE BY 2005 & 9/11

On June 1, 2001 a suicide bomber killed 21 Israelis in a Tel Aviv nightclub. President George W. Bush ("43", son of George H.W. Bush, "41"), in office less than five months, was critical of the attack as *"heinous"* and unjustifiable. Two nights later, President Bush dined at the White House with his Secretary of State, Colin Powell, and his National Security Adviser, Condoleezza Rice. Their guest was Saudi Arabian Ambassador to the United States, Ambassador Bandar bin Sultan. According to Washington Post reporter Bob Woodward, Bandar was a longtime friend and ally of President Bush's father, George H.W. Bush, and had given campaign advice to the new President, on the suggestion of his father. The dinner lasted five hours, until midnight, during which Bandar complained that the United States raised objections when terrorists killed Israelis, but was generally silent when Palestinians were killed. Bush responded that Arafat was a liar and that he wouldn't have any dealings with Arafat. According to Woodard, Bandar conceded that Arafat was a liar, and *"a schmuck,"* but he was *"the only schmuck we have to deal with."* Bandar pleaded with Bush: *"Mr. President, you've got to do something. I mean you're killing us basically. We are being slaughtered left and right, and you're not doing anything."* (*The Sunday Times* (London), June 10, 2007). Woodward's article about this incident was published in London six years after it happened.

Two months later, Bandar returned to Washington with a message from Saudi Arabia's then Crown Prince Abdullah bin Abdul Aziz Al Saud (who in 2005 became King). Abdullah was then, and had been since 1996, the *de facto* ruler of Saudi Arabia due to the stroke of his half brother. The royal message to President Bush from the leader of Saudi Arabia was that he was going to *"cut off communications with the White House and that Saudi Arabia would pursue its own interests without taking America's into account."* President Bush reacted, it's fair to say, in a state of panic. Secretary Powell cornered Bandar and said, according to Woodward, *"You're putting the fear of God in everybody around here. You scared the **** out of everybody."* Woodward wrote that *"The Saudi threat worked. Two days later, August 29 (2001), Bush sent the Crown Prince a two-page letter stating: 'I firmly believe the Palestinian people have a right to self-determination and to live peacefully and securely in their own state, in their own homeland, just as the Israelis have the right to live peacefully and safely in their own state.' It was a much bigger step than Clinton had taken. At Saudi prompting, Bush agreed to come out publicly for a Palestinian state. A big roll-out was planned for the week beginning Monday, September 10. That Tuesday, September 11, Al-Qaeda attacked America."*

267

Notice that President Bush in his letter to Crown Prince Abdullah, agreed to take land that was within the borders of Israel, Israeli owned and possessed land, and cause it to be the Palestinian's *"own state...their own homeland."* Just like that. The President's statement is jaw-dropping in its scope and audacity. But his words were soon followed by concrete steps to make it happen.

On September 7, 2001 Bandar returned again to the U.S. and met with Bush, Rice, Powell, and Vice President Cheney to hammer out the details of the history-making announcement which would be made by the Presidential son of the President who had first launched the *"land for peace"* plan in Madrid nine years earlier, in 1992. The negotiations continued through the week-end. On Monday, September 10, 2001 Vice President Cheney, Secretary Powell and National Security Advisor Rice, meeting with Ambassador Bandar at the White House, completed the Bush plan *to create a Palestinian state in Israel* by 2005. It was decided that Secretary Powell would present the plan at a General Assembly meeting of the assembled nations of the world at the United Nations two weeks later. Look at the date of the decision meeting again – 9/10/2001.

The very next day, 9/11/2001, while President Bush was in Florida, 3,000 Americans were killed in the World Trade Center, the Pentagon, and a field in Pennsylvania, at the hands of radical Muslin Jihadists, most from Saudi Arabia. Bandar was quoted later as saying that he went from being *"the happiest man in the world"* on the evening of September 10, 2001 to experiencing the worst crisis of his career on September 11th, as the attacks decidedly took off the table American plans to force Israel to give up its land for a Palestinian state. More Americans died at the hands of the Jihadists on 9/11 than at Pearl Harbor in 1941 (2,350) or the D-Day Invasion in 1944 (1,465). Estimates of the financial costs of 9/11 vary widely. The owner of the World Trade Center sued for $12.3 billion. Victim compensation, costs of re-building the Pentagon, the creation of the Office of Homeland Security, and the invasion of Afghanistan were all directly attributable to 9/11. The airlines lost billions in revenues from Americans hesitant to fly. The stock markets dove, the economy sharply slowed, and in some sectors never recovered. According to the Institute for Analysis of Global Security, 9/11 cost over *two trillion dollars* in total economic impact. Coincidental timing?

U.S. BACKED EVICTION OF WEST BANK SETTLERS – KATRINA FORCED EVICTION OF U.S. RESIDENTS

To those who doubt that God is a God of justice–and of linkage–world events in late August, 2005 may give pause. During the years following President George H.W. Bush's (41) Madrid Conference's *'land for peace'* program, the United States on a bipartisan basis, under both Republican and Democrat Presidents, pressured Israel to give up its land, specifically focusing on the Gaza Strip and the West Bank. During the same period, Israelis continued to live in those areas of Israel and raised their families. Israelis lived in Gaza and the West Bank for decades. In late May, 2005 Palestinian leader Mahmoud Abbas flew to Washington to *"seek a commitment from George Bush to a swift revival of peace talks,"* stating that *"the only partner that matters in the peace process is Washington."*

Under U.S. pressure, the Israeli government, led by Prime Minister Ariel Sharon, on August 15, 2005, sent its Israeli Defense Force soldiers throughout the Israeli settlements in Gaza (also known as northern Samaria) to serve eviction notices on the Jewish residents of Gaza, many of whom had lived there for 35 years. How long were these settlers given before they were to be forcefully removed from their homes? All of forty eight hours. Settlers in Gaza and Northern Samaria were notified they could leave their homes voluntarily or they could be *forcefully removed*. Over 55,000 Israeli soldiers and 8,000 police officers were called in to enforce the eviction. On August 17, 2005 U.S. Secretary of State Condoleezza Rice said that Gaza was just the beginning, *"Everyone empathizes with what the Israelis are facing, but it can't stop with the Gaza Strip,"* further showing the Bush Administration's continuing political pressure on Israel to abdicate its acres.

On August 17, 2005 Prime Minister Sharon gave final authorization to evict settlers from the Gaza Strip and parts of the West Bank. Twenty one settlements in Gaza were planned to be completely evacuated, by force, if necessary. The forced evacuation of settlers, as part of the disengagement, commenced with approximately 14,000 Israeli soldiers and police prepared to forcibly evict settlers. There were scenes of troops dragging screaming settlers from houses and synagogues. Some settlers left their homes with their hands up or wearing a Star of David badge, to associate their forced eviction with the actions of Nazi Germany during the Holocaust. Many chanted *"Jews don't evict Jews."* Parents and children were in tears as they were torn from their homes, which were soon bulldozed on orders by the government. Though Sharon said that only homes would be bulldozed, leaving the synagogues, after the eviction, Palestinians destroyed the synagogues.

On August 22, the city of Netzarim's inhabitants were expelled by the Israeli military. The eviction officially marked the end of the 38-year-long Israeli presence on the Gaza Strip. The next day, on August 23rd the evacuation of the four West Bank settlements was completed, with many tears and anguish as human beings were thrown out of their homes located on land that they believed God had given to them to inhabit. Over 2,700 homes were bulldozed in Gaza and 300 in northern Samaria (West Bank). Over 9,000 Israelis, who did not want to leave their homes, were forcibly *removed from their homes.*

On August 22, 2005, President Bush in a speech to the Veterans of Foreign Wars in Utah, congratulated Sharon for his *"bold leadership"* in removing Israeli residents from Gaza and claimed that *"peace is within reach in the Holy Land."* Bush also pledged to *"continue working for the day when the map of the Middle East shows two democratic states, Israel and Palestine, living side-by-side in peace and security."* The President of the United States thus confirmed U.S. involvement in the forced eviction of Israelis from Gaza and Samaria and the dismantling of their homes. Secretary Rice told BBC News that *"Jewish homes in the Gaza Strip will be destroyed when Israel pulls out its troops and settlers...The view is that there are better land uses for the Palestinians to better address their housing needs."* Palestinians taking over the settlement areas shouted *"Death to Israel! Death to Israel!"* After seizing Gaza, Palestinians, eventually led by Hamas, launched literally hundreds of missiles against Israel. Giving up the land, contrary to God's directives, did not prove to be a formula for peace, but instead death and destruction.

The United States of America was complicit in late August, 2005, *more than complicit,* we were the moving force, pressuring the Israeli government to move thousands of people from their houses, which were then bulldozed, turning the land over to others. Why? Because the Palestinians *wanted* the land. They *demanded* the land. Imagine for a moment that the U.S. was in a dispute with Mexico, and Mexico wanted San Diego back. Also imagine that a world superpower, say Russia, intervened and *forced* the U.S. to remove San Diegans from their homes, bulldozing their homes, because the superpower said the land could have a *"better use"* for *"the housing needs"* of Mexicans, rather than San Diegans' use of the land for their own housing needs. The reality of what happened right after the late August, 2005 evictions in Israel won't be too difficult to believe.

On August 23, 2005, *the very same day* as the completion of the forced eviction of Israelis from Gaza and Samaria, a tropical depression formed near the Bahamas. Note the date: *August* 23, 2005–not July–not September– not the 10th, not the 18th, but *August 23rd*. Just a coincidence? Soon the tropical depression was upgraded to a Tropical Storm named Katrina. The initial National Weather Service–Hurricane Center forecasts stated that Katrina was not expected to become a meteorological force. By the 25th of

August the tropical depression that became a tropical storm had become a full-fledged hurricane. The next day, Hurricane Katrina came ashore on Southeast Florida as a relatively mild Category One hurricane. But, by the time Katrina had moved into the Gulf of Mexico, it had grown in strength into a Category Three hurricane that pounded Louisiana, Mississippi and Alabama. Katrina quickly grew in strength after entering the Gulf, growing from a Category Three hurricane into a Category Five hurricane in only nine hours, with maximum sustained winds of 175 mph.

Katrina would begin turning northward after landfall, eventually to hit the Florida panhandle approximately three to four days later. Katrina, however, defied these computer projections and continued a westerly and west-southwesterly track, which eventually shifted the forecast track westward to New Orleans, the most vulnerable area at which it could come ashore. Storm surges in Mississippi peaked at 28 feet, with Mobile, Alabama seeing its highest storm surge since 1917. Nine Mississippi coastal towns were decimated. High winds coming across Mississippi affected virtually the whole state. After slamming the Louisiana, Mississippi and Alabama coasts, Katrina moved north, and didn't dissipate until hitting the Great Lakes and eastern Canada. One meteorologist called Katrina *"one of history's most bizarre hurricanes."* *The New York Times* later described Katrina as *"a hurricane of biblical proportions"* (1/11/09). True.

How were people affected by Katrina? How were their homes affected? Hurricane Katrina forced one million Americans from their homes. Over 225,000 homes in the three states were destroyed, rendered uninhabitable. Many have never returned to their homes. Hmm. Let's see, thousands of Israelis were evicted from their homes and their homes destroyed. Sharon used force to evict them. New Orleans Mayor Ray Nagin used force, including military force, to evict those who did not want to leave New Orleans. Human beings in *both* Gaza and New Orleans shed tears as they left their homes, *involuntarily.*

Jewish commentators said that Israel's forced eviction would be seen as *Israel's worst abandonment of its own people.* American commentators said that Washington's response, or lack thereof, to Katrina would be seen as *America's worst abandonment of its own people.* More Americans were forced from their homes into a mass evacuation than at any time in U. S. history. The federal government sought $105 billion for reconstruction. One economic impact projection calculated a loss for Louisiana and Mississippi of over $150 billion. *Katrina was the worst, most expensive, most damaging 'natural disaster' in American history.*

The following should evoke thought and prayer:

Since God kept his Genesis 12:3 promise to curse those who curse Israel, and did so with Katrina, formed as the Gaza/Samaria evictions were being concluded, then what will be the result if America breaks its military defense agreements with Israel? These are serious times and, as God's people, we need to think and pray seriously about our future, and what God is telling us in His Word about the end times, and what we are to do in the final days.

"Come, O Zion! Escape, you who live in the Daughter of Babylon!" For this is what the LORD Almighty says: "After he has honored me and has sent me against the nations that have plundered you—for whoever touches you touches the apple of his eye-I will surely raise my hand against them ... Then you will know that the LORD Almighty has sent me." (Zechariah 2:7-9).

2005-2007 U.S. ACTIONS AGAINST ISRAEL

After Gaza/Katrina, the Bush Administration continued to push for Israel to give its land to Palestinians for a *"two state solution."* On October 20, *2005* President Bush met with Palestinian Authority President Mahmoud Abbas. The President publicly reaffirmed his support for a Palestinian state, to be carved out of Israel: *"I appreciate your service, Mr. President. I assured him that the United States will use our influence to help realize a shared vision of two democratic states, Israel and Palestine, living side-by-side in peace and security."* Did anything unusual happen at the same time? It did, only the most intense hurricane in Atlantic basin history–Hurricane Wilma-with over 60 deaths and costs near $30 billion dollars, the 3rd costliest in US History.

In the next year, *2006*, for whatever reason, *no* public efforts were obvious under which the U.S. pressured Israel to abandon its real estate. As a result, in 2006, only two storms made landfall with the mainland U.S., Tropical Storm Alberto in Florida and Hurricane Ernesto, which had become a tropical storm by the time it arrived in Florida and North Carolina. No Hurricane hit the United States in 2006, no deaths and no floods occurred, also no raging U. S. wildfires. Probably just a coincidence.

That changed early in 2007. Secretary of State Condoleezza Rice flew to Israel on January 12th for four days of meetings with Israeli, Saudi Arabia, and Palestinian officials to discuss the *"peace process,"* and to gather support for President Bush's vision for a *"two state solution"* in Israel. While there, a massive ice storm hit the U.S., with 500,000 people without electricity in New York. The ice storm was described as *"one of the worst the region has ever seen in breadth of coverage in so many states,"* laying down ice from Maine to Texas. The State of Oklahoma was declared in a state of emergency. By the fourth day of Rice's trip to Israel the storm had arrived in California, with icicles hanging from oranges, and destroying 75% of the state's citrus crop, for a billion dollar loss.

Rice left Israel and met in Germany with German Foreign Minister Frank-Walter Steinmeier, to solicit Euro-support for America's plans for Israel. While there, Germany was hit with a winter storm, which included unusual winds up to 118 mph. The weather was so severe the German long-distance train service was shut down, with the director of the national railroad declaring *"we have never yet had such a situation in Germany."* Europe was pounded by the storm, leaving 41 dead.

On February 2, 2007 the "Diplomatic Quartet" met to discuss Israel's future. The Quartet, also referred to as the "Madrid Quartet," consists of the United States, Russia, the European Union, and the United Nations. The former Prime Minister of the United Kingdom, Tony Blair, is its special envoy. Blair is paid $1 million per year by J. P. Morgan Chase, a U.S. bank. The unabashed purpose of the Quartet is to add further pressure to Israel to give in to U.S. and Palestinian demands to give up its land. The afternoon of the meeting of the Quartet, Florida was hit with the second deadliest series of tornadoes in its history.

But all these divine responses pale in comparison to what started on November 27, 2007.

ANNAPOLIS AND THE SOCIALIZATION OF AMERICA'S ECONOMY

In late 2007 Secretary of State Condoleezza Rice and President George W. Bush decided to prioritize a land-for-peace agreement by Israel, to be completed before the President left office at the end of his second term on January 20, 2009. The media described the plan as 'legacy building' by Bush and Rice. The Bush Administration proposed a "peace conference" to be held in Annapolis, Maryland in late November, 2007. In mid-October, 2007, Secretary Rice made a four day "shuttle diplomacy" trip to the Middle East to "shore up support" for the upcoming Annapolis Conference. Two weeks before the Annapolis Conference, Secretary Rice, in a speech to the United Jewish Communities, hinted that Israel was prepared at the upcoming Conference to give up *all of the West Bank, including parts of Jerusalem,* in return for "peace."

Palestinian President Mahmoud Abbas announced before the Annapolis Conference that only a Palestinian state comprising the West Bank and the Gaza Strip *"in their entirety would be acceptable."* At about the same time, Israeli

275

Prime Minister Ehud Olmert indicated that he would be willing to give up parts of the West Bank and East Jerusalem to the Palestinians at Annapolis. On the day of the Annapolis Conference, the leader of the Shas Party in Israel threatened to leave the government coalition if Olmert agreed to divide Jerusalem, which would have brought down the Israeli government.

The November 27, 2007 Annapolis Conference, hosted by President Bush, was the first time Israel and Palestinian leaders met in a conference with a common understanding that the final state of Israeli-Palestinian *"peace"* would be a *"two state solution,"* with Israel giving up its land to form a Palestinian state. Fifty nations had representatives present at Annapolis for the Conference, including Saudi Arabia and Syria. After what was described as a contentious negotiation, Israel and the Palestinian Authority issued the *"Annapolis Joint Declaration,"* which stated that *"implementation of the future peace treaty will be...judged by the United States."* President Bush released the *Joint Declaration* in a news conference late in the day, telling the media: *"We agreed to immediately launch good faith, bilateral negotiations in order to conclude a peace treaty resolving all outstanding issues, including core issues, without exception... The final peace settlement will establish Palestine as a homeland for the Palestinian people just as Israel is the homeland for the Jewish people."* (*Haaretz,* November 28, 2007)

In response to Israel signing the *Annapolis Joint Declaration,* Rabbi Dov Lior of the Yesha Rabbis Council, in an emergency meeting of the Council said *"No leader, in any generation, has the right to give away Eretz Israel (Land of Israel)...we will save the people of Israel from the government's terrible plan."* Many Jewish and Christian groups spoke out against the U.S. developed and crafted plan to give Israeli land up to others.

Bi-weekly negotiation meetings started in December, 2007, but in the first several months of 2008, nothing emerged from the talks. Seeing an opportunity to force Israel to agree to abandon part of its land, the Bush

Administration planned to announce in Israel in May, 2008, on the occasion of Israel's 60th anniversary, that an agreement for a peace treaty had been reached, to be implemented by November 12, 2008.

The *Jerusalem Newswire* on May 9, 2008, revealed America's pressure tactics on Israel: *Both sides 'need to draw a map (showing their agreed-upon borders of Israel and Palestine) and get it done,' (Secretary of State Rice) said tersely." Rice was on her way back to Washington from a two-day visit to Israel when she let her irritation show. She appears to have failed in her quest on that visit, where her brief was supposedly to try and get something substantial for President George W. Bush to work with when he arrives in Jerusalem next week. Instead, after meeting with a newly-scandal-plagued Israeli Prime Minister Ehud Olmert and ineffectual PLO terror chief, Mahmoud Abbas, Rice was forced to leave empty-handed."*

President Bush also left Israel empty-handed, not marring Israel's 60th Anniversary with an announcement that Israel would capitulate. He went on to Saudi Arabia to celebrate the 75th anniversary of Saudi-American diplomatic relations. Secretary Rice continued to push for a new, more important deadline to announce a completed 'peace treaty.' *"U.S. Secretary of State Condoleezza Rice is pressuring Israel and the Palestinian Authority to try and agree on a document of understandings by September, ahead of the United Nations General Assembly, according to Palestinian sources. The sources said Rice wants to be able to present the document during the General Assembly to show progress in the talks. The document would include agreed-on points particularly on borders, an issue where, according to an American diplomat, the gap is not significant...A senior government official in Jerusalem confirmed that Rice wants to use the UN General Assembly to present a document summarizing the progress of the last nine months...According to (an) Israeli official, the main issue the American will bring up in the meeting is the document they hope to present at the General Assembly."* (*Haaretz*, July 28, 2008)

277

Secretary Rice greatly increased American pressure to get an agreement to be announced at the September, 2008, convening session of the UN General Assembly: *"Israeli and Palestinian officials have confirmed that US Secretary of State Condoleezza Rice is putting heavy pressure on both sides to hammer out a 'document of understandings' detailing progress in the peace process before the UN General Assembly convenes in September...Some fear it may be used to ram through a hasty final status peace agreement before the end of President George W. Bush's second term."* (*Israel Today*, July 28, 2008)

Time for the divine shoe to drop. A familiar pattern has emerged since the original 'land for peace' proposal at the Madrid Conference in 1991. America's elected and appointed leaders, acting on behalf of Americans, exerted *"heavy pressure"* on Israel to force to Israel give up her God-given land. Followed by God's reaction. What happened at the time the United Nations General Assembly convened, during which the final two state land swap deal was supposed to be announced? Well, first, *when* did the UN General Assembly convene in 2008? September 16, 2008. Any relevance to that timing? The Bush Administration planned to announce its *"Two State Solution"* in New York City on that date, calculated to make major headlines around the world. The Administration placed enormous diplomatic and political pressure on Israel to bow to America's demands to give up Israel's land. Turns out that major headlines *were* made, from *New York City*, at about *the same time* the UN General Assembly convened, just not the news from New York in mid-September, 2008 that had been planned.

On September 15, 2008 stocks on "Wall Street" in New York City tumbled, following weekend news that Lehman Brothers had declared bankruptcy, Merrill Lynch was bought out and AIG Insurance was seeking an $85 billion 'bailout' rescue package. On September 19th the President proposed a $700 billion 'bailout' package, initially to buy troubled assets all planned to prevent "an economic crisis." The House of Representatives initially rejected the plan and on September

29, 2008, the Dow fell an additional 777 points in one day, the biggest one day point decline since the great depression. By mid-November it was estimated that new loans, purchases and liabilities of the U.S. Treasury, the Federal Reserve and the FDIC, arising from the financial crisis, would total over $5 *trillion dollars.* Within hours of the headlines from New York City, which were *not,* incidentally, that Israel had caved in to U.S. pressure and agreed to give up its land, markets and governments all over the world were in financial crisis. There is obvious irony in what the nations of the world were preparing to celebrate in mid-September, 2008, the capitulation of Israel, and what they actually suffered, the significant collapse of their equity markets.

Since the world planned to announce in mid-September, 2008, that Israel was giving up its God-given land, the nations of the world have experienced the worst economic meltdown since the 1930's.

IV. PRESIDENT BARACK H. OBAMA

Three weeks before the November 4, 2008 Presidential election the Rev. Jesse Jackson was quoted in an interview in the *New York Post:*

"Prepare for a new America. That's the message that the Rev. Jesse Jackson conveyed to participants in the first World Policy Forum, held at this French lakeside resort (Evian, France) last week. He promised 'fundamental changes' in US foreign policy...The most important change would occur in the Middle East, where "decades of putting Israel's interests first" would end. Jackson believes that although 'Zionists who have controlled American policy for decades' remain strong, they'll lose a great deal of their clout when Barack Obama enters the White House... 'Barack will change that, because as long as the Palestinians haven't seen justice, the Middle East will remain a source of danger to all of us. Barack is determined to repair our relations with the world of Islam and Muslims ,' Jackson says, 'Thanks to his background and ecumenical

approach, he knows how Muslims feel while remaining committed to his own faith'."

This is a revelatory insight into President Obama from Rev. Jackson, who stated that *"We helped him start his career. And then we were always there to help him move ahead."* President Obama's close friend's statement could prove to be the most revealing quote in this book. The first television interview that President Obama gave after he became President was given to Al-Arabiya. He said in the interview:

"THE PRESIDENT: I think it is possible for us to see a Palestinian state – I'm not going to put a time frame on it – that is contiguous, that allows freedom of movement for its people, that allows for trade with other countries, that allows the creation of businesses and commerce so that people have a better life.... I think that you're making a very important point. And that is that the language we use matters. And what we need to understand is, is that there are extremist organizations – whether Muslim or any other faith in the past – that will use faith as a justification for violence. We cannot paint with a broad brush a faith as a consequence of the violence that is done in that faith's name."

Thus, in one interview the President endorsed the *"two state solution"* for Israel that will require Israel to give up part of the *land* that God gave to Israel, contrary to God's warning not to divide the Land. He also disregarded the 1500 year history of Islamic violence, openly committed to conquering the world for Allah, including the killing of non-Muslims. President Bush (41) initiated the 'two state solution.' President Bush (43) backed up on assurances given to Israel in a 2004 letter. Not supporting Israel appears to be a bipartisan movement.

At the end of President Bush's (43) term in 2008, Secretary of State Condoleezza Rice made it known that Israel and the Palestinian Authority were very close to a 'peace' treaty. The issues of the return of Palestinians to the land, and the division of Jerusalem, were still not then resolved, but apparently, an agreement was near, to give back most of the land acquired by Israel in 1967 when it was attacked. Thus, the incoming Obama Administration had a 'road map' for a peace treaty. Officials in President Obama's State Department confirmed in February, 2009, that the Obama administration backed a *"two state solution." "That is the end of the issue. There is no official support for anything other than the two-state solution,"* U.S. Ambassador to Jordan Robert Beecroft told the media. In March, 2009 Secretary of State Hillary Clinton, during a visit to Israel, publicly called on Israel to turn over part of its *land* for the creation of a new Palestinian state.

President Obama met with Israeli Prime Minister Benjamin Netanyahu for two hours on May 18, 2009. Media reports highlighted the President's pressure on the Prime Minister to agree to a 'two state solution'. Netanyahu was later quoted as saying at one point in the White House meeting *"Nobody can say you're not focused and determined to get what you want. I hear you, Mr. President."* (*Wall Street Journal,* May 26, 2009).

It will be more than interesting to watch the political dynamics of Israel if it surrenders more of its *land* for purported 'peace'. In the late 2008 Israeli elections, Benjamin Netanyahu was selected as Prime Minister, again running on a platform against giving up land under a 'two state solution.' One of Netanyahu's opponents in the elections, Avigdor Lieberman, who also opposed the 'two state solution' in the campaign, became Israel's Foreign Minister in the Netanyahu cabinet, and stunned the international community soon after assuming his office. He announced that Israel would *not* abide by commitments made by the prior Israeli leadership at the Annapolis peace summit that Israel backed a 'two state solution,' thus closing the door on Palestinian statehood. Others in the ruling Israeli coalition strongly back giving up the *land,* in exchange for what they hope will be 'peace'. President Obama, Vice President Biden and Secretary of State Clinton issued public calls on Israel to agree to a 'two state solution', with the President pressuring Netanyahu in a several hour

White House meeting. Pope Benedict XVI visited Israel to call on it to give up its *land* for 'peace'. Egypt, Jordan, Germany, Great Britain and the leaders of the G20 Summit all called for Israel to give its land to a new state of Palestine.

Netanyahu, faced with Washington's and the international community's strong pressure to give up its *land* for peace, changed his campaign position against the 'two state solution', in a major policy speech on June 14, 2009. The Associated Press, in reporting that Netanyahu *"dramatically reversed himself in the face of U.S. Pressure"*, also concluded that Netanyahu *"appeared to favor Israel's all-important relationship with the U.S. at the risk of destabilizing his government."* For the first time, Netanyahu agreed to a "Palestinian State", though he demanded that it have no military, Israel's right to exist would be acknowledged and recognize Israel as the Jewish State, thus giving up any demand for return to the land by refugees. The conditions were initially rejected by Palestinian leaders, but we should expect that in the next few months/years, under increasingly intense U. S. and global pressure, Israel will be forced to, and will eventually agree to, sign a treaty, with or without acceptable conditions, imprudently giving up much of its *land*, in exchange for a 'recognition of its right to exist' by its enemies. Israel will then dwell 'safely'–that is, until it doesn't.

On June 4, 2009 President Obama gave an hour long speech in Cairo, Egypt. The overseas trip was the second to the Middle East, and in neither visit did the President land in Israel, or meet with Israeli officials. In his speech the President referred to the "Holy Quran" and quoted from the Hadith, referring to the *"story of Isra, when Moses, Jesus and Mohammed (peace be upon them) joined in prayer."* It's safe to say that these three persons have never been in prayer, though the President gave his approval to the mythological Muslim story. He also said that *"Islam has a proud tradition of tolerance"*, not mentioning that there is not a single Christian church or Jewish synagogue in Saudi Arabia or in many other Muslim nations. The Zionist Organization of

America called the Presidents' speech *"strongly biased against Israel"*. The organization's President, Morton A. Klein, said Obama's remarks *"may well signal the beginning of a renunciation of America's strategic alliance with Israel."*

On September 17, 2009 President Obama announced that he was reversing previous U. S. plans to place American missiles in Poland and the Czech Republic. The American missile shield was designed to defend Israel and other nations against Iranian missiles. The cancellation disappointed America's allies, worried about the re-emerging Russian Bear. It also emboldened Russian leaders and worried Israel. John Bolton, former US Ambassador to the United Nations described the decision as *"Just an unambiguously bad decision. Russia and Iran are the big winners. I just think it's a bad day for American national security."* Scripture prophesies that Russia and Iran will invade Israel. Thus, strengthening Russia and Iran's military standing in the region advances the fulfillment of Ezekiel's prophecies (Ezekiel 38 and 39). The decision, which does not favor Israel's security, must be seen as another indication of an emerging anti-Israeli American foreign policy.

What has been God's response to the strongest pressure yet on Israel, by Presidents Bush (43) and Obama, to force Israel to give up His land? America, having ignored His past warnings, mostly "natural disasters" from President Bush (41) forward, He allowed what has been happening since September 15, 2008, events quite dear to the hearts, and wallets, of Americans:

Taxpayer bailouts in the trillions, threatening future hyper-inflation and possible future default.
General Motors and Chrysler both file bankruptcy.
Unemployment levels not seen in decades.
Most States and local governments in financial crisis.
The value of personal retirement accounts slashed.
Income and wages decline.
Home values dive by large percentages.

Personal bankruptcies and home foreclosures skyrocket.

Ironically, in the months following the emerging financial crisis, several media outlets used *meteorological terms* to describe the financial crisis the world was experiencing:

> *"Into the Storm–How the Emerging World Copes With the Tempest Will Affect the World Economy"* (The Economist)
> *"The Financial Tsunami"* (Fox News)
> *"It's a financial hurricane."* (Richard Yarmaron, Argus Research)
> *"Foreclosure Storm Hit U.S. in 2009"* (Bloomberg News Service)

Whether it is unremitting rain, historic storms, or financial collapse, the sovereign God of the universe has everything under His control. Those who think He really doesn't mean what He says in His word should rethink their position.

Chapter Fifteen

GOOD REASONS TO EMIGRATE FROM AMERICA, APART FROM PROPHECY

"I thought I would never be able to experience what the ordinary, moral German felt in the mid-1930's... Don't forget that Germany was the most educated, cultured country in Europe. It was full of music, art, museums, hospitals, laboratories and universities. And in less than six years – a shorter time span than just two terms of the U. S. Presidency – it was rounding up its own citizens, killing others, abrogating its laws, turning children against parents, and neighbors against neighbors. All with the best of intentions, of course. The road to Hell is paved with them." (Pam Geller, former Associate Publisher, *The New York Observer*, at AtlasShrugged.com)

"Leaving the country sounds like a radical solution, but history has shown us that at times it's the most rational one you can make. Whatever your motivation, you're not the first and you're not alone. In 2004, the State Department released estimates that over seven million Americans live abroad...So seize the opportunity and let no one question your patriotism. If you've had enough of what they're selling here and want to take your business (that is, your life) elsewhere, well, isn't that the American way? At any rate, it's not illegal. Not yet, anyway." (*Getting Out – Your Guide to Leaving America*, Mark Ehrman, Process Media)

In addition to God's prophetic warnings to His people who are inhabitants of the Daughter of Babylon/America to flee, in order to live, are there *other* reasons that are helpful in deciding to emigrate? This chapter is for those who would like to emigrate, who believe that God's Word warns His people in America to "flee," but who would feel a lot better about it if they had what they feel is a "practical" reason to leave. This chapter is for those who would rather base their decision to emigrate from the United States to another nation on some reason rather than an interpretation of prophecy from the Bible. Fair enough. What are the good, very good, non-Biblical reasons to leave?

AMERICA IS TARGET ONE FOR JIHADISTS

In this book we have looked in some detail at what Jihadists believe-that Allah has told them to conquer the world for him, including the slaughter of those who won't convert to Islam, and other Muslims with whom they don't agree. We've studied what Jihadists are doing to conquer the world (killing innocents, terrorizing governments and accumulating fissile material and nuclear devices) and we've learned that al Qaeda has been granted theological permission from Muslim religious leaders to kill millions of Americans ('*Nuclear Fatwa*', issued by Nasir bin Hamid al-Fahd, May, 2003, CBS News November 14, 2004, Appendix C).

One doesn't have to believe in Biblical prophecy, believe in the Bible, or even believe there is a God, to believe that America is 'target one' for Jihadists. Why? Because *they have told us*, repeatedly, *that we are*. Only two choices: a.) Jihadists are just trying to scare us–they aren't really serious; or, b.) they are serious as a heart attack, and fully committed to bringing down America, on the theory that if Islam can overthrow the world's only superpower, the rest of the nations of the world will fall like ripe plums into their blood-stained hands.

The nature of the spreading threat of terror was recently well stated by Jeffrey T. Kuhner in the *Washington Times*:

"*Islamic extremism is on the march. Nuclear-armed Pakistan has become a hot-bed of fundamentalism. The Taliban and al Qaeda have established a vital sanctuary within its borders. NATO troops are in a bloody quagmire in Afghanistan. Hezbollah has set up a theocratic statelet within*

Lebanon. North Korea continues to sell missile technology to Syria (which, in turn, supports Hamas and Hezbollah). Somalia is teetering on the brink of an Islamist revolution. Saudi Arabia continues to fund radical madrassas around the world. Sudan is recruiting jihadists in its genocidal campaign against Darfur. The biggest threat, however, comes from revolutionary Iran: 2008 was when Tehran reached the point of no return in its quest for the bomb. Iran's mullahs are now within reach of possessing the capability for a nuclear weapons program." (January 12, 2009)

Pretend that you aren't an American, don't live in America and are not related to any Americans. Say you are an observer of world events with no particular bias. The question is this: Which nation in the world is most likely to be hit with an attack of nuclear devices? There is no advantage for al Qaeda to nuke any country in Africa, Asia, South America, or even Europe. It would invite a nuclear response, even if the response attack was centered on just the mountains between Pakistan and Afghanistan. But destruction by Jihadists of such a single nation would not fundamentally alter the world balance of power, nor guarantee future success for Jihadists' plans to conquer the world for Allah. There is only one nation which Jihadists, and their allies, many with nuclear devices, instinctively understand *they must bring down.* That is Target America. (Because of sites holy to Islam, Jihadists won't use nukes on Jerusalem.) With the carefully timed simultaneous destruction of key American centers of political, financial and commercial power, Jihadists would not only destroy the world's only remaining superpower, it would also prove to every other nation in the world that each remaining nation should give in to Muslim demands, or else face a similar deadly fate.

A sound mind analysis of the world of today, not as it was as recently as ten years ago, should lead one to conclude that *'getting out of Dodge'* is a reasonable conclusion based on the available evidence. For those living in Dresden before its carpet bombing, or Jews living in Poland before Hitler's invasion, or the residents of Hiroshima before it was nuked, *as all of the people living in these areas were warned*, and yet they still didn't depart in the face of impending danger, whose fault was it? A decision to leave a dangerous area can be reached totally apart from any belief in Biblical prophecy, but when it's overlaid with what the Bible says about the *"hammer of the whole world"* which will be destroyed *"in one moment,"* the ultimate difficult decision is easier to make.

THIS ISN'T YOUR GRANDPARENTS' COUNTRY (IT'S NOT EVEN OUR PARENTS' COUNTRY)

"Oh, posterity, you will never know how much it cost us to preserve your freedom. I hope that you will make a good use of it. If you do not, I shall repent in heaven that I ever took half the pains to preserve it." (President John Adams)

As we look at non-prophetic reasons to emigrate, it's important to realize that *America today is not the same nation as when you were born.* Depending on your age, if you were born in America, your home nation was a significantly different land than it is today:

- America didn't allow aborting babies in the womb;
- Same sex marriage was not only illegal, no one ever talked about it, or even seriously considered the possibility; *("The speed and breadth of change (in the gay movement) has just been breathtaking.", New York Times,* June 21, 2009)
- Mass media was relatively clean and non-offensive. Think of *The I Love Lucy Show* or *The Walton Family,* contrasted with material aired today;
- The United States government did not take $300 million dollars every year from the taxpayers and

give it to Planned Parenthood, the nation's largest abortion provider.

- Videogames that glorify violence, cop killing and allow gamesters, who have bought millions of copies, to have virtual sex with women before killing them, did not exist.

- Americans' tax dollars did not fund Title X grants to Planned Parenthood who fund a website which features videos that show a "creepy guidance counselor who gives advice to teens on how to have (safe) sex and depict teens engaged in sex."

- Americans didn't owe $483,000 per household for unfunded retirement and health care obligations (Peter G. Peterson Foundation).

American Christian missionaries who have been abroad for relatively short times say they find it hard to believe how far this nation has declined morally since they were last in the country. Recently, in just a two week period, these events all occurred: the Iowa Supreme Court declared that same sex marriage was legal in the State; the President on a foreign tour declared that *"we do not consider ourselves a Christian nation..."* and a day later bowed before the King of the nation that supplied most of the 9/11 terrorists; Vermont became the first State to authorize same sex marriage by legislative action, as opposed to judicial dictate; the CEO of General Motors was fired by the federal government; an American ship was boarded and its crew captured by pirates for the first time in over 200 years; and a major Christian leader/author apologized on *Larry King Live* for supporting California's Proposition 8 in defense of traditional marriage, reversing his earlier position. The pace of societal change is rapidly accelerating.

AMERICA'S CONVERSION TO SOCIALISM

There is a bountiful supply of material demonstrating America's turn to socialism. Former Clinton Political Advisor, Dick Morris, made the following prognostications in an inaugural day column *("Here Comes Socialism")*, which was published on January 20, 2009:

"2009-2010 will rank with 1913-14, 1933-36, 1964-65 and 1981-82 as years that will permanently change our government, politics and lives...Simply put, we enter his administration as free-enterprise, market-dominated, laissez-faire America. We will shortly become like Germany, France, the United Kingdom, or Sweden – a socialist democracy in which the government dominates the economy...In the name of stabilizing the banking system, Obama will nationalize it... But it is the healthcare system that will experience the most dramatic and traumatic of changes...as government imposes ever more Draconian price controls and income limits on doctors, the supply of practitioners and equipment will decline as the demand escalates. Price increases will be out of the question, so the government will impose healthcare rationing, denying the older and sicker among us the care they need and even barring them from paying for it themselves."

What are the future prospects for a country that turns from the economic and political principles that made it the world's economic giant, and towards the European socialist state philosophy? Who would have ever thought that the world's leading free enterprise, free market nation would: a.) nationalize its banks; b.) replace the CEO of the nation's largest industrial corporation by demand of the White House; c.) force itself into a position of majority ownership of that corporation and force bondholders and shareholders into a minority position; d.) force the CEO of the nation's largest bank to buy a company that could destroy the bank and then force the CEO to lie to shareholders about the transaction, at the demand of the Secretary of the Treasury and the Chairman of the Federal Reserve?

Can we really feel comfortable with trusting our financial future, our grand childrens' financial future, to a government that is today transferring trillions of dollars *from future* generations *into* the hands of *our* generation. It's called debt. Someday it has to be paid, either directly or through inflating the currency. And, sadly, the younger generations, and their children, will be paying the bill. America used to shun nations that nationalized their banks or businesses, blacklisting them as, anti-democratic and socialist. Today, our government is doing it, and only a handful of members of the Congress have stood up in protest against the nationalization of American commerce. Billions of dollars have been disbursed from the federal government, not based on approval by Congress as required by the Constitution, but at late night meetings at the U.S. Treasury or White House. Secured creditors have been pushed to the end of the line behind others who made no investment, let alone a secured investment. Even a non- student of economic history can read about nations that turned to the socialist model, as we are surely doing in our time, and the end results for those nations.

The first draft of this paragraph asked these three questions: *Is living in a socialist America appealing ? Is socialized health care appealing, with age-testing to decide who should receive medical care, and who is too old to be treated? For someone who's lost half of their assets recently, how long might it take to lose the other half?* But in editing, reality hit. It quickly became apparent that whether America turns back to free enterprise or free markets, or continues nationalizing and socializing its economy, either one is *essentially irrelevant* to a person's decision to move or not to move from America. A socialist America won't be as wealthy or comfortable or powerful, but one *could* survive in it. Esther told King Xerxes that if slavery had been the future lot of the Jewish people, she would not have bothered the King with her plea to save Israeli lives. It was only their threatened death and destruction that caused her to act. (Esther 7:4) Similarly, if only tough economic times, or irrational, even harmful, laws from Washington, DC, were the only problems ahead for America, those things by themselves, might not be enough of an incentive to emigrate.

On the other hand, whether America in the future is free enterprise, socialist, or a combination, if it stabs Israel in the back at its hour of greatest need, as a betraying nation *it will be destroyed.* The nature and form of its *financial system* won't be a determining factor in its survival.

Thus, the significant, critical question is not the current or future financial condition of America. That's simply because those who manage to survive the initial devastating attack on the Daughter of Babylon will soon find that their money, that their nation's money, will be worth *nothing, zero, nada.* What about those who emigrate out of the Daughter of Babylon, before its destruction, but still hold onto its money? Same result–from plenty to poverty *"in one moment"*-certificates of deposit, mutual funds, bank accounts will, one hour after the detonations, be worth *nothing, zero, nada.* If a nation is nuked, its money will be not acceptable to other nations. A nation that owes trillions in debt, and which then suffers the loss of its governmental, financial, and commercial capitals, will not survive in world markets. Which nations would advance more credit, which corporations in the world would ship goods to a nation with no viable method of payment?

If one believes that America is the nation the Prophets of the Bible described as "The Daughter of Babylon," and does not want to keep living in America, how to best protect financial assets when moving to a safer land? Go to www.endofamericabook.com or www.americanexodus.org for more information on this topic. It's considerably cheaper to live in most Central and South American countries, which can also be an incentive to Americans pummeled by the economy. God's promise that His children will not have to beg for bread applies even if His children have changed their locations on the globe.

Any thinking Christian since September, 2008's collapse of the credit system, has had to wonder why God allowed it. We saw one possible reason in Chapter 14, that is, the collapse coincided with America's major push on Israel to give up its land, and to announce it at the United Nations in New York, just up the island from Wall Street. Only God knows, of course, why He has allowed the economy at this time in human history to decline so dramatically, but another potential reason (there are undoubtedly many) could be to change the *focus* of His people who dwell in the world's richest nation. If we aren't so caught up in the things of the world, if we aren't so rich anymore, or even employed, emigrating is not such a dubious option, and may increasingly be the *preferred option.*

Chapter Sixteen

WHEN Do We Leave?

"As Jesus was sitting on the Mount of Olives, the disciples came to him privately." Tell us," they said, "when will this happen..." (Matthew 24:3)

"A prudent man sees danger and takes refuge, but the simple keep going and suffer for it." (Proverbs 22:3)

In discussing over the last few months what the Bible reveals to us about the Daughter of Babylon/America the most common reactions have been: *'Where* do we go?' *'When* do we go?' Those are quite appropriate questions once one concludes that staying in a potentially dangerous location isn't wise.

Leaving one's homeland is never easy, no matter the nation being left behind. Christians who left England for America, the Jewish Russians who moved to Israel and all persons emigrating from their homes had to face similar challenges. Moving to another country involves significant family, financial and other practical considerations. Once the decision is made to depart, the first and foremost next decision is *when* to leave, for from this timing determination arise all of the other choices. For those who conclude that our loving Father has told us ahead of time what will happen to our nation, and who have determined to flee America, a sound mind analysis of *when* to leave is the next step. Here are the choices:

a.) LEAVE NOW – This can be a logical and appropriate timing choice, as it *guarantees* a safe escape *before* the destruction of the Daughter of Babylon/America. The downside, if one thinks in this way, is that the flight from America could be 'too early,' that is, several months or years before escape is required;

b.) LEAVE ONCE ISRAEL IS 'AT PEACE' – This is probably the most prudent timing when one is concerned about leaving family, job, home and friends. The 'timing of fleeing' would then be of importance, as many will not want to flee their homeland until they decide that the destruction of America could be imminent. Scripture confirms that Russia, Iran, Libya and the other nations named by Ezekiel won't invade Israel *until Israel is at peace.* Once Israel *is* 'at peace,' the time to pack up and move out will have arrived.

c.) LEAVE ONCE AMERICA STABS ISRAEL IN THE BACK– Prophetic verses tell us that the Daughter of Babylon/America will allow many Israelites to fall and die in the Russian/Muslim invasion of Israel, which invasion will come when Israel is *'at peace.'* As a consequence of the refusal to honor America's military defense agreement (See Attachment B) America will fall. The critical, really critical, question is will its fall be *immediately after* it betrays Israel, or will there be a time to escape *after the treachery* of betrayal of Israel?

Upon this question will hang many lives.

As we saw in Chapter14, when God sent a message to America in response to our pressure on Israel to give up and divide its land, from George Bush (41) forward, the message (hurricane, firestorm, flood, hail, economic troubles, etc.) almost always came on *the very day*, or usually the *very next day*, after America's acts against Israel. The promise of Genesis 12:3, that God will curse those who curse Israel does not contain a timing provision, so we must arrive at a sound mind determination.

Scripture provides to us at least two clues concerning the timing of God's retribution on the Daughter of Babylon/America for allowing the slain of Israel:

TIME TO FLEE CLUE NO. 1 – A YEAR TO FLEE?

In one of Jeremiah's two Daughter of Babylon chapters, he writes:

> *"Come out of her, my people! Run for your lives! Run from the fierce anger of the LORD. "Do not lose heart or be afraid when rumors are heard in the land; one rumor comes this year, another the next, rumors of violence in the land and of ruler against ruler."* (Jeremiah 51:45 and 46)

The question that naturally arises is–do these verses state, or possibly imply, that there will be a one year period, or a portion of a year, *after* Israel is betrayed and *before* the "Great Attack on America"? Will the time to flee be as long as a year after America fails to come to Israel's military defense? That is a potential conclusion. The problem with this clue is that another clue may be seen as pointing the opposite way.

TIME TO FLEE CLUE NO. 2 – NO TIME TO FLEE AFTER BETRAYAL

There are reasons to believe, from scripture, that the *same nations* that invade Israel when she is at peace, and which invading nations the Daughter of Babylon/America does not oppose, contrary to our defense agreement, are *also* the nations that are part of the Jihadists' "Great Attack on America."

In one of Jeremiah's two Daughter of Babylon chapters (50 & 51) he specifically names the kings of the Medes as his destroying force against the Daughter of Babylon:

"Sharpen the arrows, take up the shields! The Lord has stirred up the kings of the Medes, because His purpose is to destroy Babylon." (Jeremiah 51:28)

As we previously studied, the Kings of the Medes, i.e., Iran's leaders, will *also* participate in the attacks on Israel. (Ezekiel 38):

"This is what the Sovereign LORD says: I am against you, O Gog, chief prince of Meshech and Tubal. I will turn you around, put hooks in your jaws and bring you out with your whole army.... Persia, Cush and Put will be with them, all with shields and helmets, also Gomer with all its troops, and Beth Togarmah from the far north with all its troops—the many nations with you." (Ezekiel 38:3-9).

A key nation named as a part of the invading force against Israel is *Persia,* also known as the home of the *Medes,* who lived in what is now the northwestern portion of present day *Iran,* which is now developing nuclear weapons. Thus, we see scripture from two Prophets, Ezekiel and Jeremiah, informing us that the kings of the Medes will: 1.) invade Israel and 2.) be used by God to destroy the Daughter of Babylon.

That's not all. Ezekiel, as we studied in depth in Chapter 5, identifies the predecessor nation of modern day Russia, Gog, of the land of Magog, as part of the invading force of Israel. Jeremiah, interestingly, gives us clues that the same people will be used to destroy the Daughter of Babylon/America.

"Prepare the nations for battle against her (Daughter of Babylon); summon against her these kingdoms: Ararat, Minni and Ashkenaz. (Jeremiah 51:27).

Ararat and Minni are today's Armenia, a former Republic of the Soviet Union, which borders Turkey and Iran. Ashkenaz was settled by descendants of Japheth.

Ashkenaz was Gomer's first son. Gomer's descendants dwelt on the Eurasian Steppes, including western Russia.

Gomer is listed by Ezekiel in 38:6 as one of the nations that will join Russia for the Russian-Muslim invasion of Israel, in which the Daughter of Babylon is AWOL. The Medes (Iran) and Gomer (Russia) not only *invade Israel*, they *also* are part of the annihilation attack on the Daughter of Babylon.

TIME TO FLEE CLUE NO. 3 – TWO ATTACKS

Are these verses clues, telling us that *the two attacks* are timed to occur at *about the same time*, since both involve attackers from *the same* geographic areas? Strategically, it would make sense to attack both Israel and America at the same time. Prophetic scripture spells it out in detail:

a.) The Russian-Muslim invasion of Israel commences (Joel 1 and 2 state that the ground attack into Israel takes some time);

b.) The Daughter of Babylon/America chokes, dishonors its military defense agreement and refuses to come to Israel's defense (Jeremiah 51:49), but God comes to Israel's side, destroying the invading nations' armies (Ezekiel 39:6; Joel 2:20);

c.) God honors His promise in Genesis 12:3 and curses the treacherous nation, using as his 'war club' the same nations that invaded Israel (Jeremiah 51:27-28), which, if the timing is immediately after the Daughter of Babylon/America betrays Israel, they would have had to have *previously placed weapons* in the Daughter of Babylon. God removes His hand of protection. The Daughter of Babylon is destroyed. (Revelation 18).

Ezekiel tells us that when God comes to Israel's defense He also causes great casualties among the invading forces and also back home in the invading nations. One could conclude from Ezekiel's prophecies that the destruction of Russia, Iran, etc. will be of a significant nature: *"I will send fire on Magog and on those who live in safety in the coastlands, and they will know that I am the Lord."* (Ezekiel 39:6). With that level of destruction in Russia, Iran and the other invading nations, it does not appear likely that these named nations would have the military capability, or continuing interest, in coming against the Daughter of Babylon/America *a year after* America betrays Israel.

If so, *waiting* for America to betray Israel in the Russian-Muslim invasion, and then hoping there will still be time to flee America *after* her betrayal of Israel, may very well be waiting *too late* to avoid destruction and death.

Also, waiting on the Rapture to be rescued from the coming *"Great Attack on America",* as previously noted, would be a fatal error. The Rapture does not occur until the Antichrist is in place and signs Israel's second end times peace treaty, none of which can occur while the world's only superpower, a/k/a the Daughter of Babylon, is still in power. America must be removed from the scene in order for the Antichrist to appear. Therefore, the Rapture will occur some period of time *after* the Daughter of Babylon/America has been destroyed. See Attachment C (*End Times Time Line*) for details.

The decision as to *when* to flee is one for utmost prayer, seriously seeking God's guidance.

Chapter Seventeen

WHERE WILL YOU BE?

By now you may now be thinking – why did I ever read this book? Join the club. As I was writing it over a 24 month period, I increasingly, and distressingly, agonized as I realized that America, my land of birth, the nation I love and revere, will soon be no more. The recognition that there is a spot on match between what scripture tells us will happen to our country and what radical Jihadists promise they will do to us came as a significant downer, to say the least. Further learning that what scripture tells us will happen in the end times is another spot on match (with different titles and names but the same results) with what Islam says will happen in *"The Last Day"*, also came as a wake up call. Overlay this with the widespread knowledge that radical Jihadists have acquired nuclear weapons, and one can acquire a stress headache fairly quickly.

So, how does one handle, spiritually, the knowledge that one's home nation is soon to be no more? Tough question. No easy answers. But, let's be candid – as Americans we have had it really good for a really long time. Life holds no guarantee of continuous, unending, peace and prosperity. In fact, Jesus instead promised us that in this world we will have tribulation (John 16:33).

REASONS TO CONCLUDE AMERICA IS AT ITS END

You've finished the book. By now, you've undoubtedly arrived at a conclusion as to what you believe about what you have read. Here are three powerful reasons to conclude that *America is at its End*:

a.) *America's avowed radical enemies have told us*, without any possibility to misunderstand their message-that they intend to destroy us as a nation. That, by itself, should be enough to cause prudent American Christians and Jews to give serious thought to emigrating out of harm's way.

b.) *Intelligence services of America and other nations have told us,* with some opportunity to decide if we believe their reports, that al Qaeda intends to destroy America and has purchased nuclear devices with which al Qaeda could destroy America. That, by itself, should be enough to cause prudent American Christians and Jews to give serious thought to emigrating out of harm's way.

c.) People who incessantly and fervently shout *"Death to America"*, and who have access to nuclear weapons, have to be taken seriously. That, by itself, should be enough to cause prudent American Christians and Jews to give serious thought to emigrating out of harm's way.

c.) *The Creator, Almighty God of the Universe has told us,* in many verses, that an end times nation, rich, powerful and influential, will be *destroyed* as a nation. That, by itself, *really* should be enough to cause prudent American Christians and Jews to give serious thought to emigrating out of harm's way.

Though, as stated, any one of these four reasons, by itself, is sufficient, added together they should be overwhelmingly persuasive.

Until the middle of the last century, when the Soviets acquired nuclear-armed intercontinental missiles, from its founding, America for its entire history had been safe behind its 'ocean moats' thousands of miles wide. After the War of 1812 was successfully concluded, no one in America seriously thought that the nation could be invaded and conquered by a foreign power. We were a secure and safe nation. In the Old Testament Isaiah describes that security mind set: *"You said, 'I will continue forever— the eternal queen!' But you did not consider these things or reflect on what might happen."* (Isaiah 47:7) John in the New

Testament wrote: *"In her heart she boasts, 'I sit as queen; I am not a widow, and I will never mourn.'"* (Revelation 18:7). Even after the events of 9/11, however, most Americans continued in the view that America was secure. This apathetic view can be stated: 'Oh, al Qaeda may pull off another attack, knock down another building or two, or blow up a train station as they did in London or in Spain, or bomb a crowded mall, but they can never take down the entire country, as they have threatened'. That would be Isaiah's and John's 'Queen-like, never conquered nation', thinking she will never mourn.

A major factor which helped prevent a nuclear exchange with the Soviet Union during the cold war was that the leaders of the USSR were Communists. They were atheists who had no belief in a life after death, and who had an innate desire to retain the *only lives* they ever expected to enjoy. Contrast that restraining view of the importance of preserving one's life with the Muslim teaching that those who die now in Jihad enjoy eternity in heaven with seventy two virgins. Iran's Ahmadinejad has reiterated in public speeches that he seeks a nuclear cataclysm in order to bring forth the restored Caliphate, the Mahdi, the Shiite messiah.

On January 19, 2006 Osama Bin Laden released a speech through al-Jazeera, the pan-Arab television network. In the speech he promised to some day *"announce that the US interference in the world's countries has ended forever"* and further promised that the lives of Americans will *"become miserable and things turn for the worse"*. Bin Laden said *"we will treat you in the same way"* that Bin Laden said Muslims had been treated. He said Americans *"have occupied our land, defiled our honour, violated our dignity, shed our blood, ransacked our money, demolished our houses, rendered us homeless, and tampered with our security"*. Ignoring for the moment that his charges aren't accurate, re-read the specifics of Bin Laden's threat. Osama Bin Laden, the perpetrator of 9/11, says he will shed *our* blood, destroy *our* economy, demolish *our* houses and render *us* homeless, among other things. These are Bin Laden's *promises for America.*

When did Bin Laden in his 2006 speech say these things would be done to America? *"As for the delay in carrying out similar operations in America, this was not due to failure to breach your security measures. Operations are under preparation, and you will see them on your own ground once they are finished, Allah willing."*

Emigrating from America because of enemy threats might be hard to justify, but emigrating becomes a prudent course of action when those threats of national annihilation are supported by intelligence reports demonstrating that America's enemies have the nuclear ability to destroy us, not to mention the numerous Biblical warnings we have examined in detail.

WHY DIDN'T THEY FLEE?

Remember the Jewish resident of Germany, or Poland, or Czechoslovakia in the late 1930's and early 1940's. They had numerous reliable sources, including news reports of speeches by das Fuhrer, that Jewish families were being rounded up, imprisoned, put into slave labor camps, and even killed. Some quietly moved out of harm's way. But most didn't. Millions ignored the approaching storm clouds, not willing to give up homes, jobs and surroundings to which they had grown accustomed. They died. Over sixty years later some who saw the coming danger and did escape are still alive to tell about it.

Will you, like those Jewish families who refused to escape coming certain death, ignore the danger and stay in the land you love, trading your life and well being for temporary ease and illusive safety? This question may well be the most important decision of the remainder of your life. What you decide will determine not only if you live, and how you live, but also how your family members live in the days ahead. Some members of some families may need to take the initiative to leave, to be visited in their new home by family members, who will then decide to join them. In discussing these prophetic issues during the drafting of the book, it soon became apparent that 'hunter/gatherer' males and 'nest-making' females had generally different responses. Most males said 'when do we move, where do we go?' On the other hand, most females said, 'what about the kids and the grandkids, and the house, and...'

A critical point must be emphasized: In response to *The End of America* there may be well-meaning Christians, undoubtedly some Christians in high positions, who may be expected to argue that the Daughter of Babylon prophesied in scripture is ancient Babylon or the Catholic Church, or corrupt Christianity, but not America. For all of the many reasons as set forth in this book, the Daughter of Babylon is not a pile of rubble in Iraq, and it's not a church or denomination. It never will be. Waiting for the Bible's several Daughter of Babylon verses to be fulfilled in ancient Babylon, when those verses quite clearly can *not* be made to apply to ancient Babylon, or waiting for a church or denomination to fulfill the scriptural prophecies, could prove to be *a fatal mistake*. In addition, the correct interpretation of God's prophetic word isn't a matter subject to a majority vote of the current religious establishment. If that were the case, the Sanhedrin's overwhelming rejection of Jesus and His appearance, in fulfillment of prophecy, would have been theologically correct, but it obviously wasn't.

Readers should study the Daughter of Babylon verses and decide for themselves, after praying and asking God for direction by the power of His Holy Spirit. One should especially be careful about deciding not to flee because somebody erroneously, demonstrably misinterprets the Daughter of Babylon prophecies. The prophecies are more than sufficiently specific enough to tell us: a.) that the prophecies just don't apply to ancient Babylon or a church; and b.) they fit perfectly the world's richest, most powerful nation. Just as those living today in the 'fig tree generation' of a reborn Israel will see the end times, we should also be repared to flee the Daughter of Babylon before it's destroyed.

WILL YOU BE ALIVE TO READ AN ARTICLE LIKE THIS?

Before you make your final decision, think about this. Below is a fictional news article that could one day appear after a nuclear attack. When articles like this appear, where would you want to be – in the United States, or alternatively, *outside* of the U.S., safely in another country, hopefully with your family and Christian or Jewish friends,?

LONDON (IRN News Network) --- *Al Qaeda today confirmed in a videotaped statement aired on al Jazzera television that it was responsible for the detonation of multiple nuclear weapons in America the day before yesterday. Though the exact number of nuclear devices was not disclosed in the statement, most British military experts now believe that the number was between 10 and 15, apparently of varying kilotonage. It is believed at least two detonation sites, Washington, D. C. and New York City, were hit by more than one detonation. The death count of the surprise attack is as yet unknown, but expected to be in the several tens of millions. If confirmed, the Jihadist attack on the world's leading military power would easily be the largest loss of life in one day in history. The al Qaeda spokesman claimed in the broadcast statement that "America, as we warned in 2006, is destroyed, and will never again persecute Muslims".*

British military sources said that it was still too early to determine the cities hit by the nuclear weapons detonated in what appears to have been a coordinated attack, with the weapons exploding within seconds of each other. There has been no immediate armed response from what remained of the American military, possibly complicated by the inability to target the location of al Qaeda operatives. The electromagnetic effect of the nuclear explosions knocked out most communication with America, the effect of which is continuing as this edition went to press. For those areas of the States in which communication is still possible, a disturbing picture has

306

quickly emerged of highways clogged with Americans seeking to flee from areas detonated under obviously apparent mushroom clouds. It was reported that medical facilities near blast sites were quickly overrun by blast and radiation burn victims.

No official statement has yet been released by the U.S. government, most of the officials of which appeared not to have survived the two known nuclear devices which destroyed Washington, D.C., the seat of the American government. It is anticipated that a statement will soon be made from a U.S. official who did survive the attacks. Some isolated media reports received here have said that most surviving petrol outlets have been drained of their supplies and that food markets' shelves were quickly emptied. With winter approaching, some unnamed sources in Her Majesty's government suggested that significant numbers of Americans may die in the next few months from the radiation effects from nuclear weapons, and also as a result of lack of food resulting from a paucity of petrol and any meaningful way of paying food suppliers. The sources also cited early reports of what may be widespread violence by those seeking to obtain remaining food supplies and petrol.

Her Majesty Queen Elizabeth II, who had earlier expressed her shock and dismay at the news from America, is expected to make a televised statement by week's end. Her spokesman, on background, indicated that Her Majesty will respond to published statements by Jihadists that Britain, and other European nations, would suffer a similar fate as America if the star and crescent aren't flying over government offices by year's end. Her Majesty's troops, as was earlier reported, are on full alert, and a full shut down of British ports has been ordered, on a temporary basis. The House of Commons convened in executive session late today. No reports have thus far emerged as to actions taken, nor statements made, in the closed door meeting. Some M.P.s called publically today for Her Majesty's government to immediately vacate

London and its environs. No decision has been made on their suggestions, according to government spokespersons, who asked not to be identified.

Reginald Sloane, press spokesperson for the Archbishop of Canterbury, suggested to reporters in a hastily called news conference that the Archbishop would have no problem with a Muslim "presence" at No.10 Downing Street, even if that eventually meant a PM of Islamic beliefs. Sloane dismissed as "rubbish" claims by columnists and others that the attacks on America had been prophesied in certain Biblical verses. Reports had circulated for some time before the attacks that many hundreds of thousands, possibly millions, of American Christians, and American Jews, had emigrated from the U.S., apparently relying on what they claimed were scriptural warnings about the future destruction in the "end times" of a rich and powerful nation. Leaders of the emigration had also expressed concern about America's refusal to support Israel when it was attacked by a coalition of nations led by Russia and Iran. Readers may consult news archives for more historical details on the outcome of the invasion of Israel.

Leaders of leading British charitable organizations who were contacted today expressed their sorrow at the attacks, and indicated that they are beginning to collect medical supplies and food for transport to America, if suitable transportation can be arranged. Numerous international corporations, who have now lost most if not all of the ability to sell goods to the world's leading consumer nation, expressed outrage and shock at the attacks on America. Some privately questioned their future economic viability, given the economic loss of their largest trading partner. One CEO, who refused to be identified for this article, suggested that the nations of the world reform the United Nations, whose headquarters and most of its staff were destroyed with the nuclear destruction of New York City, in Geneva, Switzerland, in order to deal with what he privately called 'this incredible Islamic violence *problem, before we're all blown up'. No United Nations official was available for a comment on his suggestion.*

TIME FOR PRAYER

How does one think and pray about all this? *God loves us,* and that's why He has given us these Daughter of Babylon warnings to 'flee', because remaining will lead to death, misery and destruction. Therefore, instead of weeping over the necessity of moving to another country – and all that will entail – we should think instead of praising our loving Father for allowing us to know what is approaching our falling nation, to see the approaching evil and flee from it (Proverbs 22:3). As difficult as moving will be, with uprooting family and goods and moving from homes and jobs long distances to foreign lands, consider the alternatives of radiation sickness and death, lack of food, lack of healthcare, no ability to earn income, and no civil government to protect people from those who seek to rob, rape and pillage. Praise the Lord that *He loves us enough* to warn us before it happens and has given us the chance to flee. Where will you be when The Day comes to pass?

If you are convinced that wisdom dictates that you should flee from evil, make your plans and emigrate to safety, trusting God throughout, and thanking Him that He warned you in advance of His judgment on America, that He warned you of *The End of America.*

> *"I am with you always,*
> *even to the end of the age..."*
> (Matthew 28:20)

Additional Resources

WHAT'S HAPPENING? For current Twitters and posted up-to-date news developing since publication of *The End of America,* go to:

www.endofamericabook.com

The website carries the latest news on the efforts of the world to force Israel to divide the land and to accept a peace treaty (its first end times peace treaty).

AMERICAN EXODUS – For helpful current information on countries friendly to immigrating Americans, how to move, what to take, how to ship, how to transfer assets, etc. visit:

www.americanexodus.org

The website will have information on the sequel to *The End of America,* a how to manual entitled *Fleeing America,* now being drafted and scheduled for publication in 2010.

DIGGING DEEPER – To learn more and to dig deeper into issues discussed in this book, it is suggested that these books would be most helpful:

- Richardson, Joel, *AntiChrist – Islam's Awaited Messiah* (Pleasant Word, Enumclaw, Washington, 2006)
- Koenig, William R., *Eye to Eye – Facing the Consequences of Dividing Israel,* (About Him, Alexandria, Virginia, 2007)
- Williams, Paul L., *The Day of Islam: The Annihilation of America and the Western World,* (Prometheus Books, Amherst, New York, 2007)

- Steyn, Mark, *America Alone: The End of the World as we Know It*, (Regnery Publishing, Inc., Washington, DC, 2006)
- Jeremiah, David, *What in the World is Going On? : 10 Prophetic Clues you Cannot Afford to Ignore,* (Thomas Nelson, Nashville, Tennessee, 2008)
- Gabriel, Brigitte, *Because They Hate,* (St. Martin's Press, New York, New York, 2006)
- Sumrall, Lester Frank, *Jerusalem, Where Empires Die,* (Sumrall Publishing, South Bend, Indiana, 1979)

WEBSITE ASSETS – Readers will find the following on the book website (www.endofamericabook.com):

Prophecy 101 – A brief survey of the analysis of prophecy over time by various Biblical scholars.

What Scripture Says About America (Hebrew and Greek Annotation of Selected Daughter of Babylon Verses) – A look at the original Hebrew and Greek words used in certain key prophetic verses and how they were interpreted in parallel verses of scripture.

Forum – For on line postings of opinion on issues raised in the book, The American Exodus and current events.

WHERE TO GO? To research specific nations in which interested visit www.internationalliving.com which has a bookstore offering resource materials for specific countries, and also a daily e-letter describing various aspects of living abroad.

By Googling individual nations a researcher can find a wealth of material specific to that nation, most available in English.

CONSULT – Consult your attorney and accountant for guidance regarding the transfer of assets, emigration taxes and regulations and overseas immigration rules, regulations and related matters.

Attachment A

THE NUCLEAR FATWA

As Issued by Wahabbi Sheikh Nasir Bin Hamid Al-Fahd and signed by other Saudi Clerics

Excerpts from:
A Treatise on the legal Status of Using Weapons of Mass Destruction Against Infidels
By Nasir Bin Hamd Al-Fahd
Rabi'I 1424 (May 2003)

(Posted by the Global Islamic Media Center)

Peace be with you and God's mercy and blessings!

Everyone knows what has been published in the media about al Qaeda's intention to strike America with weapons of mass destruction. Perhaps the so-called weapons of mass destruction are calamities of modern times. We have found no contemporary who has spoken about them.

What then is the legal ruling on their use by Muslims engaged in jihad? If one upholds the permissibility, are they permissible unconditionally? Or are they permissible for compelling necessity, for example, if the enemy's evil can be repelled only by their means? Are such weapons antithetical to humanity's purpose of making the earth prosper? Do such weapons fall under God's pronouncement: "And when he turns his back, he hastens about the earth to do corruptions there and to destroy the tillage and the stock: (Koran2:205). Or is the verse wrongly brought to bear upon the action, like the verses that occur condemning killing and the like?

ANSWER

The question that you have raised, noble brother, is one that deserves a full treatise that gathers up scholarly arguments and pronouncements; a treatise in which one records positions about questions such as the abode of war, ways of repelling assailants, the jihad of defense, the meaning in law of "destroying the tillage and the stock," and other matters. Perhaps, God willing, I can gather together what is at hand.

Know, generous brother, that the phrase "weapons of mass destruction" is inexact. By it they mean nuclear, chemical or biological weapons, and no others. If anyone should use any of these weapons and kill a thousand people, they would launch accusations and media wars against him, saying that he had used "internationally banned weapons." If he had used high explosive bombs weighing seven tons apiece and killed three thousand or more because of them, he would have used internationally permitted weapons.

Surely, the effect of several kilograms of TNT can be considered mass destruction if you compare it to the effect of a catapult stone of old. An RPG [rocket-propelled grenade] or mortar projectile can be considered mass destruction if you compare it to the shooting of arrows of old. Certainly, the infidels of our time have made these so-called weapons of mass destruction (deterrence weapons) only to frighten others. America's threat to Iraq to use these weapons should Iraq attack Israel is not remote from us. What, then, allows them to America and the infidels and forbids them to Muslims? If a Muslim group should assault life or honor and could be repelled only by killing all its members, it would be permissible to kill them, as scholars have mentioned in chapters on repelling an assailant. How much more permissible is it when it comes to an infidel assailing the faith, life, honor, the intellect, and the homeland!

If the infidels can be repelled from the Muslims only by using such weapons, their use is permissible, even if you kill them without exception and destroy their pillage and stock. All this has its foundation in the Prophet's biography, the Prophet's sayings about jihad, and the pronouncements of scholars, may God have mercy on them.

FIRST PRELIMINARY

That Proscription Belongs to God Almighty, and to None Other Than He, Such as Humans

God has said: "And do not say, as to what your tongues falsely describe, 'This is lawful, and this is forbidden,' so that you may forge against God falsehood; surely those who forge against God falsehood shall not prosper" (Koran 16:116)

I hold that things in the infidels' laws today belong in the same category. For example, they call something "internationally banned," "contrary to legitimate international authority," "forbidden by international law," "in violation of the Charter of Human Rights," or "in violation of the Geneva Convention," and so forth. The subject of this treatise belongs to the same category, insofar as they use the term "internationally banned weapons."

All these terms have no standing in Islamic law, because God Almighty has reserved judgment and legislation to Himself. As He has said: "Judgment belongs only to God: He has commanded that you shall not serve any but Him" (Koran 12:40). God has said: "Or have they associates who have laid down for them as religion that for which God gave not leave?" (Koran 42:21). And God has said: "Verily, His are the creation and the command" (Koran 7:54).

This is a matter so obvious to Muslims that it needs no demonstration.

This having been established, you will realize that their words "internationally banned weapons" have no value. In judging these weapons, one looks only to the Koran, the Sunnah, and the statements of Muslim scholars...Those who speak so pretentiously about combating the spread of weapons of mass destruction, America and Britain, for example, were the first to have used these weapons: Britain used chemical weapons against the Iraqis in World War I: America used nuclear weapons against Japan in World War II; and their arsenals- and those of the Jews-are full of such weapons!

SECOND PRELIMINARY

The Basic Rule in Killing Is to Do It in a Good Manner

An authentic tradition in the *Sahih* from Shaddad ibn Aws, a companion of the Prophet, says: "God has enjoined benevolence on everything. If you kill, kill in a good manner. If you slaughter animals, slaughter in a good manner; let the slaughterer sharpen his blade and put his victim at ease."

Al-Nawawi said in his commentary on the *Sahih* of Muslim (13:107): "The Prophet's words, "Kill in a good manner," include every animal slaughtered, every killing in retaliation or execution, and similar things. This hadith is one that sums up the foundations of Islam."

Ibn Rajab said in *Jami' al 'Ulum wa-al-Hikam*, p. 152: "Doing good with regard to such humans and animals as may lawfully be killed is to take the life as swiftly, easily, and desirably as possible without inflicting excessive pain. The easiest way to kill a human being is by striking the neck. God has said, referring to unbelievers, "When you meet the unbelievers, smite their necks" (Koran 47:4). And He has said: "I shall cast into the unbelievers' heart terror; so smite above the necks, and smite every finger of them" (Koran 8:12).

The traditions concerning this are many. All indicate that the basic rule is to kill in a good manner any such as may lawfully be killed and not to be excessive. However this basic rule has exceptions...

ARGUMENTS FOR THE PERMISSIBILITY OF USING WEAPONS OF MASS DESTRUCTION

I mentioned in the previous section that the rule is to kill in a good manner, that killing infidels falls under this rule, but that this can take place only when one has the ability to do so. The infidels might be in such a position that they cannot be resisted or repelled from Islamic territory and Muslims are spared their violence unless they are bombed with what are called weapons of mass destruction, as people with experience in jihad affirm. If people of authority engaged in jihad determine that the evil of the infidels can be repelled only by their means, they may be used. The weapons of mass destruction will kill any of the infidels on whom they fall, regardless of whether they are fighters, women or children. They will destroy and burn the land. The arguments for permissibility of this in this case are many. They fall into two divisions.

First Division: Arguments relating to a particular time period and a particular enemy. For example, with regard to America at this time, the matter of striking her with these weapons is permissible without mentioning the arguments of the second section (arguments of general legitimacy). This is because God as said: "Whoso commits aggression against you, do you commit aggression against him like as he has committed against you." (Koran 2:194). And God also said: "And the recompense of evil is evil the like of it" (Koran 42:40). Anyone who considers America's aggression against Muslims and their lands during the past decades will conclude that striking her is permissible merely on the basis of the rule of treating as one has been treated. No other arguments need be mentioned. Some brothers have totaled the number of Muslims killed directly or indirectly by their weapons and come up with a figure of merely ten million. As for the lands that their bombs, explosives, and missiles have burned only God can compute them. The most recent events we have witnessed are those in Afghanistan and Iraq, and this is in addition to the uprooting that their wars have caused for many Muslims. If a bomb that killed ten million of them and burned as much of their land as they have burned Muslims' land were dropped on them, it would be permissible, with no need to mention any other argument. We might need other arguments if we wanted to annihilate more than this number of them!

Second Division: General arguments for the legitimacy of this action universally if required by jihad in the way of God. These are texts that indicate the permissibility of using such weapons if those engaged in jihad decide that there is benefit in using them. The arguments for this are many. I shall mention three of them.

Al-Bayhaqi devoted a chapter of Al-Sunan al-Kubra (9:78) to al Sa'b's hadith, entitling it: "On Unintentionally Killing Women and Children in a Night Raid or Attack, Hadiths Transmitted Permitting Night Attacks." He cites that this hadith and then quotes al-Shafi, who said: "In our view, and God alone knows best, the meaning of the prohibition on killing women and children is on intentionally seeking to kill them when they can be recognized and distinguished from those who have been ordered to be killed. The meaning of the Prophet's words, 'They are of them' is that they unite two traits: they do not have the legal factor of faith, which spares one's blood, nor do they live in a abode of faith, which prevents an attack on that abode."

The Messenger of God commanded an attack on the enemy. In many traditions he attacked others-these we have mentioned in the chapter on prayer before fighting. He was not prevented from this by what we know, namely, that he knew that children and women would not be safe from harm. He allowed the attack because the intent on the attackers was not to harm them. This agrees with my interpretation of the hadith of al Sa'b. Thus, he has enjoined us to fight the enemy, but he has forbidden us to kill their women and children. It is a sin for us to intend to do what he has forbidden us to do, but it is permitted for us to intend to do what has been permitted for us, even if it involves harming others whom we have been forbidden to harm and for whom we are not responsible." Therefore, the situation in this regard is that if those engaged in jihad establish that the evil of the infidels can be repelled only by attacking them at night with weapons of mass destruction, they may be used even if they annihilate all the infidels.

Second Argument

The Permissibility of Burning the Enemy's Lands

The great mass of scholars held the view that burning and devastating are permissible in enemy territory. Ibn 'Umar's hadith proves that Muslims may employ any stratagems that will sap their polytheist enemy's strength, weaken their cunning, and facilitate victory over them. They may cut down their crops, divert their water, and besiege them. Those who permitted this were the Kufans, Malik, al-Shafi'I Ahmed [ibn Hanbal], Ishaq, al-Thawri, and Ibn al-Qasim. The Kufans said that their trees could be cut down, their land devastated, and their cattle slaughtered or hamstrung if they could not be dislodged. This hadith is clear in its indication that setting fire to enemy territory is permissible if the fighting requires it.

Third Argument

The Permissibility of Striking the Enemy with Weapons that Cause Mass Destruction

Scholars have agreed that it is permissible to bombard the enemy with catapult and similar things. As everyone knows, a catapult stone does not distinguish between women, children, and others; it destroys anything that it hits, buildings or otherwise. This proves that the principle of destroying the infidels' lands and killing them if the jihad requires it and those in authority over the jihad decide so is legitimate; for the Muslims bombarded these countries with catapults until they were conquered. No one reports that they ceased for fear of annihilating their infidels or for fear of destroying their territory. God alone knows best.

320

ATTACHMENT B

Memorandum of Agreement between the Governments of the United States of America and the State of Israel
(March 26, 1979)

Recognizing the significance of the conclusion of the Treaty of Peace between Israel and Egypt and considering the importance of full implementation of the Treaty of Peace to Israel's security interests and the contribution of the conclusion of the Treaty of Peace to the security and development of Israel as well as its significance to peace and stability in the region and to the maintenance of international peace and security; and Recognizing that the withdrawal from Sinai imposes additional heavy security, military and economic burdens on Israel;

The Governments of the United States and the State of Israel, subject to their constitutional processes and applicable law, confirm as follows:

1. In the light of the role of the United States in achieving the Treaty of Peace and the parties' desire that the United States continue its supportive efforts, the United States will take appropriate measures to promote full observance of the Treaty of peace.
2. Should it be demonstrated to the satisfaction of the United States that there has been a violation or threat of violation of the Treaty of Peace, enhance friendly and peaceful relations between the parties and promote peace in the region, and will take such remedial measures as it deems appropriate, which may include diplomatic, economic and military measures as described below.
3. The United States will provide support it deems appropriate for proper actions taken by Israel in response to such demonstrated violations of the Treaty of Peace. In particular, if a violation of the Treaty of Peace is deemed to threaten the security of Israel, including, inter alia, a blockade of Israel's use of international waterways, a violation of the provisions of the Treaty of Peace

concerning limitation of forces or an armed attack against Israel, the United States will be prepared to consider, on an urgent basis, such measures as the strengthening of the United States presence in the area, the providing of emergency supplies to Israel, and the exercise of maritime rights in order to put an end to the violation.

4. The United States will support the parties' rights to navigation and overflight for access to either country through and over the Strait of Tiran and the Gulf of Aqaba pursuant to the Treaty of Peace.

5. The United States will oppose and, if necessary, vote against any action or resolution in the United Nations which in its judgments adversely affects the Treaty of Peace.

6. Subject to Congressional authorization and appropriation, the United States will endeavor to take into account and will endeavor to be responsive to military and economic assistance requirements of Israel.

7. The United States will continue to impose restrictions on weapons supplied by it to any country which prohibit their unauthorized transfer to any third party. The United States will not supply or authorize transfer of such weapons for use in an armed attack against Israel, and will take steps to prevent such unauthorized transfer.

8. Existing agreements and assurances between the United States and Israel are not terminated or altered by the conclusion of the Treaty of Peace, except for those contained in Articles 5, 6, 7, 8, 11, 12, 15 and 16 of Memorandum of Agreement between the Government of Israel and the Government of the United States (United States-Israeli Assurances) of September 1, 1975.

9. This Memorandum of Agreement sets forth the full understandings of the United States and Israel with regard to the subject matters covered between them hereby, and shall be implemented in accordance with its terms.

SIGNED on MARCH 26, 1979 by JIMMY CARTER, PRESIDENT OF THE UNITED STATES OF AMERICA and MENACHEM BEGIN, PRIME MINISTER OF ISRAEL

ATTACHMENT C

END TIMES
TIME LINE

- **MAY 14, 1948 – ISRAEL REBORN – THE FIG TREE BUDS** (Matthew 24:32-34)

- **AMERICA *BLESSES* ISRAEL -1948 - 1989 (PRESIDENTS TRUMAN through REAGAN)** (Genesis 12:3)

- **AMERICA *PRESSURES* ISRAEL TO GIVE UP ITS LAND CONTRARY TO SCRIPTURE** (Ezekiel 48:14 and Joel 3:2) **1989 TO CURRENT DATE (PRESIDENT BUSH [41] through PRESIDENT OBAMA)**

- **ISRAEL AGREES TO 1ST END TIMES PEACE TREATY – ISRAEL AT PEACE** (Ezekiel 38:10-14)

- **RUSSIA, IRAN, LIBYA, ET AL. INVADE ISRAEL – ISRAEL AT WAR** (Ezekiel 37-39)

- **DAUGHTER OF BABYLON/AMERICA BETRAY ISRAEL – FAILS TO HONOR MILITARY DEFENSE AGREEMENT** (Jeremiah 51:35 and Lamentations 4:17)

- **GOD INTERVENES TO SAVE ISRAEL – SENDS DESTRUCTION ON INVADING ARMIES AND NATIONS** (Ezekiel 39:6)

- ***DAUGHTER OF BABYLON/AMERICA DESTROYED*** (Jeremiah 51:49; Revelation 18)

323

- **JIHADISTS THREATEN OTHER NATIONS WITH SAME DESTRUCTION IN EFFORT TO CONQUER THE WORLD FOR ALLAH**

- **ISRAEL BUILDS TEMPLE** (Ezekiel 40-44)

- **MUSLIM LEADER EMERGES AS LEADER OF A EUROPEAN NATION, OVER THREE NATIONS, THEN OVER TEN NATIONS** (Daniel 2; Revelation 12 and 17)

- **MUSLIM RULER OF EUROPE/REVIVED ROMAN EMPIRE ENTERS 2ND END TIMES PEACE TREATY WITH ISRAEL - SEVEN YEARS OF TRIBULATION BEGINS** (Matthew 24:27-31)

- (*Pre-trib Rapture*) (John 14:3; I Corin. 15:51,52) *(Scripture presents one Rapture. Scholars differ as to its pre, mid or post-Tribulation timing.)*

- **MUSLIM LEADER OF EUROPE EXTENDS REACH OVER THE WORLD – DEMANDS WORSHIP AND CONVERSION** (Revelation 13:16; 14:9,11)

- **MUSLIM LEADER OF EUROPE BREAKS PEACE TREATY WITH ISRAEL – ENTERS TEMPLE STOPS DAILY SACRIFICE– GREAT TRIBULATION OF 3 ½ YEARS BEGINS** (*Mid-trib Rapture*) (Daniel 9:27, 12:11; Mark 13:14; Matthew 24:15)

- (*Post trib – pre-wrath Rapture*) (I Thessalonians 4:13-17)

- **GOD POURS OUT HIS WRATH ON THE WORLD** (Revelation 19:21)

- **JESUS RETURNS FOR THE ELECT OR NO FLESH WOULD BE SAVED** (Matthew 24:22) (*"If those days had not been cut short, no one would survive, but for the sake of the elect those days will be shortened."*)   (Matthew 24:22)

- **ANTICHRIST AND FALSE PROPHET IMPRISONED FOR 1,000 YEARS** (Revelation 19:20)

BIBLIOGRAPHY

- *America in Prophecy*, (Inspiration Books East, Inc., Jemison, Alabama, 1988)

- Bawer, Bruce, *While Europe Slept: How Radical Islam is Destroying the West from Within,* (Broadway Books, New York, 2006)

- Ben-Mardechai, Avi, *Signs in the Heavens,* Millennium 7000 Communications International, 1995)

- Blum, William, *Rogue State & Guide to the World's Only Superpower,* (Common Courage Press, Monroe, Maine, 2005)

- Bostom, Andrew G., *The Legacy of Jihad: Islamic Holy War and the Fate of Non-Muslims*, (Prometheus Books, Amherst, New York, 2005)

- Boyer, Paul S., *When Time Shall Be no More: Prophecy Belief in Modern American Culture*, (Harvard College, 1992)

- Carter, Jimmy, *We Can Have Peace in the Holy Land: A Plan that will Work*, (Simon & Schuster, New York, New York, 2009)

- Criswell, David, *She Who Restores the Roman Empire*, (Writers Club Press, 2002)

- D'Souza, Dinesh, *What's So Great about Christianity*, (Tyndale House Publishers, Inc., Wheaton, Illinois, 2008)

- Doyle, Tom, *Two Nations under God*, (B&H Publishing Group, Nashville, Tennessee, 2004)

- Ehrman, Mark, *Getting Out - Your Guide to Leaving America* (Process Media, Los Angeles, California, 2006)

- Evans, Michael D. and Jerome R. Corsi, *Showdown with Nuclear Iran: Radical Islam's Messianic Mission to Destroy Israel and Cripple the United States,* (Nelson Current, Nashville, Tennessee, 2006)

- Evans, Mike, *The Return,* (Thomas Nelson, Inc., Nashville, Tennessee, 1986)

- Foxe, John, *New Foxe's Book of Martyrs 2001*, (Bridge-Logos Publishers, Gainesville, Florida, 2001)

- Gabriel, Brigitte, *Because They Hate,* (St. Martin's Press, New York, New York, 2006)

- Gabriel, Mark A., *Islam and the Jews, The Unfinished Battle* (Lake Mary, Florida, Charisma House, 2003)

- Gabriel, Mark A., *Islam and Terrorism*, Strang Communications/Charisma house, Lake Mary, Florida, 2002)

- Gabriel, Mark A., PhD, *Jesus and Muhammad*, (Strang Communications/Charisma House, Lake Mary, Florida, 2004)

- George, Barney, *All Nations Against Jerusalem,* (Christ for the World, Orlando, Florida 32802)

- Grant, George, *The Blood of the Moon*, (Wolgemuth & Hyatt, Brentwood, Tennessee, 1991)

- Henry, Matthew, *Matthew Henry Complete Commentary on the Whole Bible*, (Hendrickson, 1991)

- Hersey, John, *Hiroshima*, (A.A. Knopf, New York, 1985)

- Hislop, Rev. Alexander, *The Two Babylons,* (Loizeaux Brothers, Neptune, New Jersey

- Hitchcock, Mark, *Is America in Bible Prophecy?* (Multnomah Publishers, Inc., Sisters, Oregon, 2002)

- Hitchcock, Mark, *The Coming Islamic Invasion of Israel,* (Multnomah Publishers, Inc., Sisters, Oregon, 2002)

- *Israel - America's Key to Survival,* Tyndale House Publishers, Wheaton, Illinois, 1983)

- Jeremiah, David, *What in the World is Going On? : 10 Prophetic Clues you Cannot Afford to Ignore,* (Thomas Nelson, Nashville, Tennessee, 2008)

- Koenig, William R., *Eye to Eye – Facing the Consequences of Dividing Israel,* (About Him, Alexandria, Virginia, 2007)

- Lightle, Steve, *Exodus II - Let My People Go!* (Hunter Books, Kingwood, Texas 1983)

- Lindsay, Hal, *The Late Great Planet Earth*, (Zondervan, Grand Rapids, Michigan, 1970)

- Logsdon, Dr. S. Franklin, *Is the U.S.A. in Prophecy?* (Zondervan Publishing House, Grand Rapids, Michigan, 1968, 1974)

- McKeever, James M., *Christians Will go Through the Tribulation and How to Prepare for it,* (Alpha Omega Publishing Company, Medford, Oregon, 1978)

- McTernan, John, *God's Final Warning to America*, (Hearthstone Publishing, Oklahoma City, OK, 2000)

- Phillips, Melanie, *Londonistan*, (Encounter Books, New York, New York, 2006)

- Richardson, Joel, *AntiChrist - Islam's Awaited Messiah* (Pleasant Word, Enumclaw, Washington, 2006)

- Rosenthal, Marvin J., *The Prewrath Rapture of the Church* (Thomas Nelson, Inc., Nashville, Tennessee, 1990)

- Showers, Dr. Ronald, *What on Earth is God Doing?* (Loizeaux Brothers, Inc., Neptune, New Jersey, 1973)

- Steyn, Mark, *America Alone: The End of the World as we Know It*, (Regnery Publishing, Inc., Washington, DC, 2006)

- Sumrall, Lester F., *Jerusalem, Where Empires Die*, (Sumrall Publishing, South Bend, Indiana, 1979)

- *The Nations in Prophecy*, (Zondervan Publishing House, Grand Rapids, Michigan, 1967)

- Weber, Timothy P., *The Future Explored*, (Victor Books, Wheaton, Illinois)

- Williams, Paul L., *The Day of Islam: The Annihilation of America and the Western World*, (Prometheus Books, Amherst, New York, 2007)

- Wildmon, Donald, *Speechless: Silencing the Christians*, (Richard Vigilante Books, 2009)

- Zakaria, Fareed, *The post-American world,* (W.W. Norton & Company, Inc., New York, New York, 2008)

NOVELS
(Listed for readers interested in fictional treatment of nuclear destruction.)

- Allen, Steve, *The Shell Game,* (Sweetwater Books-an imprint of Cedar Fort, Inc., Springville, Utah, 2007)

- Brin, David, *The Postman,* (Bantam Books, New York, New York, 1985)

- Forstchen, William R., *One Second After,* (A Forge Book published by Tom Doherty Associates, LLC, New York, New York, 2009)

-
- Frank, Pat, *Alas, Babylon,* (Harper Collins Publishers Inc., New York, New York, 1959)

- Strieber, Whitley, *Critical Mass,* (Forge Book, New York, New York, 2009)

INDEX

ABOUT THE AUTHOR

JOHN PRICE is an Indianapolis Attorney and Author. He has practiced law since 1971, specializing in corporate, banking, educational and Constitutional law. In 1993, he founded a public interest law center assisting home educators, and representing persons on First Amendment, right to life and religious rights issues. Constitutional law cases have included defense of school prayer and Gideon Bible distribution, challenges to public school surveys of students' religious and personal beliefs and the use of taxpayer funds to sponsor attacks on religion. He has represented Christian teachers and others demoted or fired because of their faith.

Price served as Deputy State Treasurer of the State of Indiana and executive Secretary of the Indiana Republican State Committee. In 1998 he narrowly missed the Republican nomination for the United States Senate, by about one vote per precinct. He founded and served as Chairman of the Board of a Bank in his hometown. He is a 1963 graduate of Wabash College and 1968 graduate of Indiana University-Indianapolis School of Law. John and his wife of 48 years are blessed with four children and nine grandchildren.

John has taught two business persons Bible Studies, one in downtown Indianapolis for 25 years. He authored *"America at the Crossroads: Repentance or Repression"* (Christian House – 1976) and *"America at the Crossroads: Can America Escape National Decline, Economic Collapse and Devastating Conflict?"* (Tyndale House,1979, three printings). He was a Contributing Author to *"The Rebirth of America"* (S. DeMoss Foundation, 1986, two million in circulation).

The author may be contacted at:
john@endofamericabook.com

ACKNOWLEDGEMENTS

The many persons who were helpful, even instrumental, in bringing this book to publication, are not listed by their names, for somewhat obvious reasons. They, and the Lord, know who they are. The only person listed, Jack Brown, author of the Foreword, is 90 years of age, and not at all concerned about his safety. God's blessings upon those who labored in editing, designing, critiquing and praying. His blessing and guidance also upon those who read and heed the words herein.

TO PURCHASE 'THE END OF AMERICA'

Visit www.endofamericabook.com with links to:

WWW.AMAZON.COM
WWW.BORDERS.COM
WWW.BARNESANDNOBLE.COM
WWW.BOOKSAMILLION.COM

Or order directly from these book vendors.

Thank you for your reading patronage.

LaVergne, TN USA
11 March 2010
175637LV00003B/3/P